Uncertain Belief

Uncertain Belief

Is it Rational to be a Christian?

DAVID J. BARTHOLOMEW

CLARENDON PRESS · OXFORD

OXFORD
UNIVERSITY PRESS

Great Clarendon Street, Oxford OX2 6DP

Oxford University Press is a department of the University of Oxford.
It furthers the University's objective of excellence in research, scholarship,
and education by publishing worldwide in

Oxford New York

Athens Auckland Bangkok Bogotá Buenos Aires Calcutta
Cape Town Chennai Dar es Salaam Delhi Florence Hong Kong Istanbul
Karachi Kuala Lumpur Madrid Melbourne Mexico City Mumbai
Nairobi Paris São Paulo Singapore Taipei Tokyo Toronto Warsaw

with associated companies in Berlin Ibadan

Oxford is a registered trade mark of Oxford University Press
in the UK and in certain other countries

Published in the United States
by Oxford University Press Inc., New York

British Library Cataloguing in Publication Data

Data available

Library of Congress Cataloging in Publication Data
Bartholomew, David J.
Uncertain belief : is it rational to be a Christian? / David J.
Bartholomew.
p. cm.
Includes bibliographical references and index.
1. Apologetics. 2. God—Proof. 3. Probabilities.
4. Uncertainty. 5. Faith and reason—Christianity. I. Title.
BT1102.B315 1996
239—dc20 95-24826
ISBN 0-19-826378-3 (hbk)
ISBN 0-19-827014-3 (pbk)

1 3 5 7 9 10 8 6 4 2

Printed in Great Britain
on acid-free paper by
Biddles Ltd.,
Guildford and King's Lynn

Preface

The contemporary spectacle of clashing fundamentalisms, whether of politics or religion, is not an edifying sight. This state of affairs is especially to be regretted when it relates to the ultimate religious questions of the origin and purpose of human existence. The dilemma which many face is that though the evidence for belief often seems ambiguous and uncertain, the consequences are so profound as to demand a decision. It is therefore of more than passing interest to know how well-founded Christian belief, say, really is. If certainty proves to be unattainable we have to deal in uncertainties and to decide whether the evidence is strong enough to justify the commitment which belief requires.

The question of the reasonableness of Christian belief has been tackled many times before by theologians and philosophers, including some with expertise in probability. So far as I am aware no contribution has come from statisticians who are professionals in the science of uncertainty on which the matter crucially depends. Probability, the language of uncertainty, has its own logic which, if ignored, easily leads to the exaggerated claims on which fundamentalisms feed. This is equally true whether we are dealing with the data of science or the subjective assessment of the qualitative evidence which historical and literary sources provide.

This book is written out of the conviction that the investigation of the perennial questions of the nature of human existence would greatly benefit by being more widely informed by the logic of uncertainty. As we shall see, this makes things harder rather than easier: but that should not deter us. It is possible to approach questions such as God's existence or the occurrence of miracles in a rational way using the same tools as serve in other areas of human enquiry. This is not to exclude other avenues to truth nor to deny the validity of convictions arrived at more intuitively. It is to claim, however, that beliefs which cannot survive rational scrutiny in reasonably good order should be treated with extreme caution.

The book falls into three parts. In the first chapter the all-pervasive nature of uncertainty and ways of coping with it are described. The main contention is that probability theory provides the appropriate framework for the discussion. The basic ideas are explained in a non-technical way in Chapter 2. Chapter 3 deals with the widely held view that the main religious tenets have been disproved by science and, in particular, by its understanding of the human self. Until this credibility gap has been bridged the main programme cannot proceed.

Having defined the problem and provided the tools we turn in Part II to four controversial topics which bear on the central question of whether there is a reality beyond the physical world. These are miracles, the paranormal, the existence of God, and the Bible as inspired revelation. All are beset by uncertainties and we shall aim to see where the principles set out in Chapter 2 lead us.

In Part III we point out that Christianity calls for commitment, and this shifts the centre of attention from belief to behaviour. Rational decision-making in the face of uncertainty has its own logic and this is the subject of Chapter 8. In the final chapter we draw the threads together and assess how far the initial objectives have been achieved. The choice, rationally speaking, is between an uncommitted agnosticism and commitment without absolute certainty. Uncertain belief is defensible in a way that certain belief never can be.

It is inevitable in a study which ranges over so many fields that there will be omissions and misunderstandings especially in relation to philosophical and biblical matters on which I claim no professional expertise. They would certainly have been more serious but for the friendly help of many who have asked awkward questions at talks I have given over the last ten years or so. I can only ask for the same tolerance that I have tried to show in dealing with the use of probability by writers in disciplines other than my own!

My chief thanks must go to my wife, Marian, whose support and assistance in this enterprise has been, as always, indispensable.

Biblical quotations are from the Revised English Bible.

Contents

If a man will begin with certainties, he shall end in doubts; but if he will be content to begin with doubts he shall end in certainties.

Francis Bacon

No man can be assured that all his opinions taken together are true. Nay every thinking man is assured that they are not . . . He knows, in the general, that he himself is mistaken; although in what particulars he mistakes, he does not, perhaps he cannot know.

John Wesley

We must come to terms with the fact that we live in a world in which almost everything which is very important is left essentially unexplained.

Sir Karl Popper

For we must never never doubt
what nobody is sure about.

Hilaire Belloc

Part I

I

Certainty and Uncertainty

Any religious belief worthy of the name is based on the idea that there is more to the world than can be apprehended by the senses. The task of natural theology has been to explain how such a belief can be justified from what we know about the natural world. The days are long past when the traditional 'proofs' of the existence and nature of God commanded the assent of thinking people. It is not simply that the logic of such proofs was at fault but that their presuppositions about the nature of the world have been undermined. The universe as science reveals it is now known to be a much more complicated place in which chance and necessity combine to produce a rich tapestry of phenomena in which it seems less easy to discern the hand of God.

All of this means that beliefs about a world beyond this have to be expressed in terms of probabilities. The evidence must be weighed as carefully as possible but, in the end, we have to accept that certainty will elude us. The language of theology has always acknowledged the uncertainties surrounding its material, though not, perhaps, as often or as fundamentally as the circumstances demand. In recent years there has been greater explicit recognition of the need to reckon with uncertainty and to temper one's conclusions accordingly. If we look no deeper than the titles, *The Probability Of God* (Montefiore, 1985), *Probability and Theistic Explanation* (Prevost, 1990) and *Reasonable Uncertainty* (Priestland, 1982) bear witness to the growing interest. Although the language of probability is increasingly used in many fields of religious enquiry it is often deployed with

scant regard for its underlying logic. There is a logic of
uncertainty which is no less demanding than its more familiar cousin. Reasoning about uncertainty is not the same as
uncertain reasoning! It is the purpose of this book to deal
with the questions which such assertions immediately bring
to mind. Can claims made about God's extremely high (or
low!) probability be justified? How do we actually 'weigh the
probabilities'? Is not belief too personal a matter to be sub-
jected to any calculus? Is anything approaching certainty, one
way or the other, ever likely to be achievable? Is certainty
necessary before we can make a commitment? And so on.
But first we must retrace our steps, set the scene, and prepare
the ground.

THE EROSION OF CERTAINTY

The confidence of early writers on science and religion in the
seventeenth and eighteenth centuries is almost breathtaking.
William Derham surveyed the heavens from his Essex parish
and saw unmistakable evidence of a master plan. Isaac
Newton's grand mechanical account of the way the universe
works left little room for doubt that a rational mind lay at the
heart of things. John Ray, also an Essex man, described the
world of animals and plants and saw there the unmistakable
signs of plan and purpose. For the theologians, William
Paley, in more measured terms, encapsulated it all in his par-
able of the divine watchmaker. We now feel less sure. The
certainties have become uncertainties as, one by one, the
seemingly necessary links between pattern and purpose have
been broken. Chaos, we now know, gives rise to order without the interposition of the divine hand. The interplay of
chance and necessity appear to be sufficient to account for
the enormous variety and complexity of the living world.
The combined efforts of astronomers, physicists, and biolo-
gists have produced an immensely impressive picture of a
self-regulating cosmos containing sufficient inbuilt variety

and flexibility to support a rich variety of life. The earlier confidence has so far evaporated that Richard Dawkins can claim that Paley's 'divine watchmaker' has been replaced by the 'blind watchmaker' (Dawkins, 1986).

It is not an edifying sight to watch beleaguered theologians throwing out the ballast of belief in a desperate attempt to keep the ship afloat. Rather than cling to the few shrinking gaps in the web of knowledge which still seem to call for something beyond science many thoughtful Christians have retreated into a subjectivism in which their faith is unthreatened by knowledge of the real world. Others have concluded that honesty demands the abandonment of a belief system now seen to be incredible. Their position finds strong support in the trenchant writings of those such as Stenger (1990) who insist that there are no scientific grounds whatever for believing that there is anything in the universe beyond observable matter and energy.

There are other areas where the certainties of belief have been similarly eroded. The simple view of the Bible as the inerrant word of God dictated to the writers has crumbled in the face of historical and textual analysis. A 'scientific' approach which makes no assumptions about the special status of the documents finds much in common with other ancient texts. The mere assertion that something is to be accepted because 'the Bible says so' now cuts very little ice among the uncommitted. Finally, the seeming bedrock of personal religious experiences has been brought into question by the insights of psychology which suggest that one need not look beyond the subconscious mind for their source.

Looking below the surface we can detect two almost contradictory tendencies in the contemporary scene. On the one hand the theological writings of reputable scientists such as Arthur Peacocke, John Polkinghorne, and others have shown that a deep religious belief can be combined with complete scientific integrity and this has gone far to demolish many of the supposed barriers which science erects for believers. Scientifically informed bishops such as John Habgood and Hugh Montefiore have, from the other side, made common cause with scientists. Paul Davies, writing without any Christian presuppositions, can speak of the scientific quest revealing the mind of God (Davies, 1983). The result has been a willingness on the part of many uncommitted scientists to take religion seriously even if their agnosticism is not overcome. Indeed a selective view of the scene could be held to support the proposition that we are now seeing a recovery of confidence if not of certainty.

But alongside this *rapprochement* there has emerged, especially in the last few years, a revival of aggressive scientific atheism from the biological quarter which has attracted media attention to a degree rarely accorded to such fundamental matters. Richard Dawkins, for example, like a latter-day Thomas Paine, has repeatedly entered the lists on behalf of a science-based rationalism on occasions ranging from Christmas lectures for children at the Royal Institution in London to a public debate with the Archbishop of York in Edinburgh. Stephen Jay Gould, the Harvard palaeontologist, has weighed in with an attempt to demolish the traditional evolutionary account of how we came to be here and to evacuate it of any notion of it being an expression of divine purpose. Others, to whom we shall shortly come, have not hesitated to show how their branch of science has rendered traditional belief untenable. It almost seems as if the mantle of certainty has been taken over by unbelief.

We now have the spectacle of those professing adherence to scientific canons of evidence coming to diametrically opposed conclusions on much the same evidence. Dawkins, for example, was widely quoted as saying, 'We cannot prove that there is no God but we can safely conclude that he is very, very improbable indeed.'[1] Montefiore's conclusion at the end of his survey of evolutionary biology was that 'on the evidence atheism is wildly improbable' (Montefiore, 1985: 173).

[1] As reported in the *Independent*, 20 Apr. 1992.

What is the lay person to make of such different conclusion from the same data? At this stage it serves to underline one very important point which this book seeks to address; namely, it is not so much the facts which are in dispute but the interpretation to be put upon them. It is a cardinal principle of scientific, indeed all rational, thinking that given the same data all reasonable people should come to the same conclusion. If this does not happen, as in this case, it behoves us to look at the steps in the argument more closely. The trouble here and in almost all other hotly disputed areas is that the evidence is incomplete and hence the conclusions have to be hedged about with uncertainty. There is no problem with such clear-cut propositions as that the sum of the angles of a triangle is two right angles. Once the logic of reasoning is understood all reasonable people accept the conclusion—indeed acceptance might well be held to characterize what we mean by saying that a person is reasonable. But if we enquire about the reality, time-scale and extent of global warming, for example, the position is very different. The data are fragmentary and the logic of uncertain inference is less well understood and, in any case, difficult to apply with any semblance of rigour. The temptation to profess a confidence well beyond what the evidence will bear is almost irresistible and afflicts believer and unbeliever alike.

It is thus vital that the voices of those who are the experts in making inferences on uncertain evidence should be heard above the clamour of those who seek for simple certainties. The intervention of a statistician therefore needs no apology.

Like all attempts to summarize the state of the public mind this account is, of course, a gross over-simplification. Many, in the physical sciences especially, would strike a more optimistic note. Indeed, the simple certainties of atheism are no less vulnerable to rational assault than are those of belief. Notwithstanding the voices of opposition, I believe that such a renaissance is taking place but that it will not lead to a recovery of the old certainties based, as they were, on a very incomplete understanding of how the world works. In one respect, however, a return to former things is an essential pre-requisite of a new natural theology. Many of the pioneers were both scientists and theologians. At a time when it was relatively easy for a wide sweep of knowledge to be encompassed by a single human mind it was possible for the great scientists of the day to be at ease in both worlds. Isaac Barrow, who gave up the Lucasian chair in mathematics at Cambridge so that Isaac Newton might have it, was no mean mathematician, but he also left two substantial volumes containing his collected religious writings. In Newton's own case, one might well feel that his scientific writings have stood the test of time better than his theology.

THE SCIENTIFIC APPROACH

However we assess the current state of play it is beyond argument that it is the scientific approach to the acquisition of knowledge which has undermined the traditional certainties. To the common way of thinking it has replaced the old certainties by new ones based on hard facts. Naïve though this view may be it directs our attention to some fundamental questions which arise when we enquire whether any of the lost ground can be recovered. For example, is the scientific method itself capable of establishing results which are favourable to the claims of theology? Or, is scientific method the only valid way of obtaining knowledge about reality? These are matters which we shall have to consider but first we must say something about what the scientific method is. We first distinguish between 'science' as the body of knowledge and the 'method' or 'approach' by which that knowledge is obtained. It is the method that we shall be concerned with here though it should be noticed in passing that scientists themselves often seem unconcerned about such matters and simply get on with the job.

Reasoning about the world and what may lie beyond it starts with data derived from that world. Scientific method is a set of ideas and principles about how to collect data and draw valid inferences from them whatever their subject happens to be. The disciplined use of that method is one of the great achievements of civilization which in no small measure is also a product of it. If we are to make any progress through the mists of uncertainty to a well-founded knowledge on which rational decisions can be based we must have due regard to the logic of scientific investigation. We shall aim to observe, so far as they are relevant, the standards of evidence demanded by scientific method. There must be no special pleading. The philosophers of science are not of one mind about what the scientific method is so it is therefore appropriate to identify the kind of approaches which are open to us.

According to Sir Karl Popper, science proceeds by conjectures and refutations. One sets up a hypothesis and then attempts are made to falsify it. Indeed, according to Popper, what distinguishes a scientific from a metaphysical hypothesis is that the former can, in principle at least, be falsified. A well-corroborated hypothesis is, therefore, one which has withstood many attempts at falsification.

Others, however, see science as a process by which our beliefs are changed by evidence and hypotheses are verified to a degree expressed by probabilities. In practice, of course, falsification is a valuable way of sifting truth and error. Aspects of the religious world-view have in fact been falsified many times in the past as when, for example, fossil evidence showed that the earth was much more than a few thousand years old. But the inductive approach in which our uncertainties are quantified often seems closer to what is required in establishing the credibility of religious claims. The thing which is common to both approaches is that what can be known is contained in the raw data available through the senses. The problem is how to extract that information, to summarize and structure it so that it presents to us a coherent picture of the world 'out there'.

Philosophers quite properly concern themselves with the

question of what science actually tells us about the reality of that world. Naïve realism, critical realism, idealism, instrumentalism, and positivism are all possible positions on which the interested reader will find Barbour (1966) a useful starting point. However, the potential conflict with religion is greatest among those who see science as telling something, albeit incomplete, about what really exists. Most of those who are unacquainted with philosophy take some kind of realist position for granted as do most scientists themselves. We shall adopt the same attitude though much of what we have to say does not depend on this.

Our next question is whether scientific method has any use in exploring the world of belief in something beyond the senses. It may seem paradoxical that we should propose to search for something beyond science using the method of science itself. We are indeed arguing that if religion is to be credible there must be territory into which science, even in principle, cannot go. If that is the case how can we possibly use it to map out for us a territory from which it is excluded? The answer depends upon how we regard the relationship between the natural and what lies beyond. If they were totally different realms it would be impossible to bridge the gap. If, on the other hand, they are interdependent parts of a single whole then we might expect there to be detectable interactions between them. This would imply that there are some natural phenomena within the territory of science which can only be fully explained by reference to something beyond its borders. We take the latter view which will be justified or not by the results which it yields. (It is important to emphasize, in view of remarks sometimes made to the contrary, that this way of proceeding cannot possibly undermine traditional science. It does nothing to change existing data to which any enlarged frame of reference must do full justice.)

We therefore now have to look in more detail at how we might legitimately infer the existence of something beyond science by the exercise of scientific method. To get some idea of what might be possible we note that there are two features of scientific method which bear upon our belief in the truth of its results. The first is correspondence with observation especially in respect of the power which it gives us to predict accurately. By this means we can test the validity of our inferences by experiment. In this way we have built up an impressive picture of the world which enables us to exert considerable control over it. In practice, of course, things are not quite as simple as that. The 'facts' may be somewhat ambiguous or even wrong. Our logic in fitting the one to the other may be at fault, so in practice we shall have to adopt a somewhat looser definition by asking that there be a close correspondence between the hypothesis and the facts of the case.

A second feature which increases in importance as our theories become more comprehensive is that of internal consistency or coherence. If a theory contains mutually contradictory elements, parts of it cannot be true. There is rather more to coherence than the mere absence of logical flaws. Successful theories often have about them an elegance and economy which gives them a compelling sense of 'rightness' which leads scientists to believe that they must be true before the evidence is fully available or, sometimes, in the face of evidence to the contrary. Mendel's experimental evidence for the laws which bear his name was apparently very shaky but the theory had that quality which strongly suggested its truth.

As we reach the boundary of the realm where the writ of science does not run, experimental verification or falsification is no longer possible but we can still reasonably require that our account should be self-consistent. A minimum criterion for any rational explanation is therefore that of consistency: if it also bears the other marks of a good scientific theory its credibility will be further enhanced.

The model of natural science has to be used with great care since coherence and truth are not so closely linked elsewhere. If we move no further than the social sciences the risks become apparent. The chief difference is that experimental verification, or falsification, is rarely possible. One can observe real social processes and construct models which purport to explain what is observed. Such a model can be used to predict aspects of the future of the process but its value will be limited by the fact that we have no control over the environment. We cannot hold other things constant. Our predictions may fail not because the model is wrong but because uncontrolled factors have changed. Again, when observing a process through time we may find we have too little data to verify some hypothesis. The natural scientist's remedy in such circumstances is to go back into the laboratory and repeat the experiment but there is no way the social scientist can turn the clock back and replicate the material. It can well turn out that any number of coherent hypotheses can be formulated several of which fit the data but we have no means of deciding whether any of them is 'true' in any sense. One of the few attempts to provide an all-embracing account of human activity was by Zipf (1949) who proposed a *principle of least effort* which sought to explain aggregate human behaviour. His basic idea was that people will always behave in a way which demands the least effort—mental, physical, or whatever—and he then set out to show how this could account for a great variety of social 'laws' of which the size distribution of towns is but one example. However, in this last case there are other quite different models which predict exactly the same form of distribution.[2] The kind of phenomena with which we shall be concerned are often much more akin to those dealt with by social scientists than their experimentally based colleagues. There are inherent limits on what is knowable imposed by the restricted range of data which is available to us. It is this fact which brings uncertainty into the picture. The idea that science deals in certainties derives especially from the physical sciences but even there it is subject to important qualifications. When we

[2] A point of entry to the literature in this area will be found in Bartholomew (1982: 211).

turn to phenomena which are of interest to the believer the data are scarce and, often, ambiguous. The proper handling of uncertainty then becomes of paramount importance.

So far I have avoided describing the two aspects of reality with which we are concerned as the natural and the super-natural. Indeed it is difficult to find terms in this area which do not carry undesirable connotations and these two are no exception. It often used to be argued in the secularizing 1960s and 1970s that the term 'supernatural' was unnecessary. If the unseen (supposing it to exist) was, equally with the nat-ural, the creation of the one God then there was no essential difference between them. The supernatural was simply that part of the natural which was unknown to us. All of that may be true but if there is a useful distinction to be made, not so much between the known and the unknown as between the knowable and the unknowable, then there is no virtue in abandoning a term which makes for clarity in the argument. We shall use it here to refer to that part of reality which lies, in principle, beyond the reach of science. To draw a distinc-tion between the spiritual and material worlds would serve much the same purpose but I prefer to use the natural/super-natural dichotomy. The question is: how can we find out about the supernatural?

One common way of side-stepping the question is to deny its presuppositions. One could argue, as many do, that the worlds of belief and reason represent different categories of thought and that it is a mistake to mix the two kinds of discourse. Even those who view things in a more matter-of-fact way are prone to separate them by saying that science is concerned with the 'how' and religion with the 'why'. However, this is not the way that things appear to most ordi-nary people who, rightly or wrongly, have the idea that the Bible says something about how the world is ordered and, for the most part, that what it says is now known to be wrong. The question of what is to be regarded as factually true is somewhat fluid but that does not essentially change the position. At one time Darwinian evolution seemed to be in direct contradiction to the biblical account of the origin of species and, for some, this issue became crucial for the credibility of Christianity. Now that the literal interpretation of the Genesis story is, for other reasons, no longer seen by most as a necessary or desirable element of Christian belief the point of conflict has moved elsewhere. Nowadays, for example, things such as the virgin birth, bodily resurrection, or God's providential action are the parts of Christian belief which do not fit easily with the scientific account of how things really are. Retreat from the confrontation is simply not possible for a religion such as Christianity which has so much to say about the physical world. The question has to be faced.

REVELATION

There is, of course, an alternative and much more direct way in which one might expect to come to know of realities which cannot be reached by human enquiry. This is by the traditional route of revelation unencumbered by uncertainty. Science, the argument goes, is concerned with what we can find out about the nature of things by our own unaided efforts and here uncertainty is inevitable. But we can only know of the existence of something which lies beyond our powers of discovery if someone tells us, or to put it more formally, if there is some self-authenticating disclosure through the medium of the natural world which we can apprehend with our senses and recognize for what it is.

If such revelation does take place there are two ways in which it might happen. It might be an entirely private affair involving single individuals. If there is a supernatural realm and if people share, in part at least, in its nature there is no obvious reason why this should not happen; mystics and others claim that this is precisely what does sometimes occur. Those who have had such experiences often have an unshakeable confidence in the reality of their encounter with the ultimate. This, however, is a private matter which is not open to scientific examination. We do not reject it for that reason but rather because we wish to see how far we can go without it. In any case it would be surprising, supposing the existence of the supernatural, if it were not also detectable in some more public manner. We shall therefore be concerned with publicly observable events which are not explicable or even fully describable within the framework of science. Genuine miracles would come into this category as would mystical or conversion experiences leading to radical changes in behaviour. They have to be verifiable happenings which are intelligible only by an appeal to something outside the system.

For Christians the Bible contains accounts of happenings which, it asserts, did originate beyond the physical world. But the events are not themselves directly accessible to us having been mediated to us through material things. In tracing our way back to the boundary of the natural and supernatural the only landmarks and tools we possess are those devised for the natural world. They will take us to the boundary but how shall we know that we have arrived and how can the reality of what lies beyond be tested? Even, therefore, if there is a public revelation it can only be apprehended through the senses and thus falls into the category of the cross-border activity which we have argued is necessary to render belief credible.

Revelation must be, in my view, an essential element in any account of supernatural religion but claims to be in possession of such a revelation must be approached with great care. Even in the mainstream of Christian tradition the sheer bulk of the material makes it very hard to provide a coherent picture of what is held to be revealed. This very often leads to some favoured pieces of evidence being given a special status—they become determinative and other elements which obstinately refuse to fit the pattern are quietly ignored. Natural science has not been immune from this tendency as the history of the Ptolemaic theory of planetary motion shows. In the 'softer' sciences and beyond the practice is commonplace. People fasten on to a key to truth against which all evidence has to be measured. The idea of a key to understanding is deeply ingrained and motivates many in the search for the touchstone of truth. The feeling is that if only we can find the secret of the universe everything will fall into place and from there on the search for knowledge will be little more than a tidying-up operation. The possessors of what we might call 'the definitive insight' commonly show great impatience with those who have not grasped the essential simplicity of it all. Indeed, one of the more impressive features of the many competing cults, ideologies, and philosophies is the way that virtually everything that happens can be fitted into their world-view. It is reminiscent of G. K. Chesterton's Turk in *The Flying Inn* (Chesterton, 1958: 9 ff.). Holding forth on the sea front to an audience of one he advocates the view that English inns were not 'poo-oot up in the beginning to sell ze alcoholic Christian drink. They were put up to sell ze non-alcoholic Islamic drink'. This seemingly unlikely hypothesis finds support, he claims, in the fact that the names are Eastern, at least to the eyes of the true believer. Thus 'The Bull' is really the Bul-Bul; 'The Saracen's Head', the Saracen is Ahead; 'The Green Dragon', the Agreeing Dragoman, and Amir Ben Bhoze, he argues, has been corrupted to the 'Admiral Benbow'. The 'Elephant and Castle' and 'The Old Ship' receive similar ingenious treatment and a wealth of supporting evidence from other sources is plausibly brought to bear to the same end.

How accurately the caricature reflects reality is tellingly portrayed by Sir Karl Popper speaking of his student days in Vienna. Psychoanalysis, logical positivism, and Marxism all seemed to partake of that compelling plausibility. He writes (in Popper, 1969: 34 f.):

These theories appeared to be able to explain practically everything that happened within the fields to which they referred. The study of any of them had the effect of an intellectual conversion or revelation; of opening your eyes to a new truth hidden from those not yet initiated. Once your eyes were opened, you saw confirming instances everywhere: the world was full of *verifications* of the theory. Whatever happened always confirmed it. Thus its truth appeared manifest; and unbelievers were, clearly, people who did not want to see the truth; either because it was against their class interest, or because their repressions were still 'unanalyzed' and crying aloud for treatment.

He would have noticed exactly the same attitude of mind had his lot fallen in with many varieties of Christian believers for they, like the psychoanalyst, can appeal to something hidden from sight and consciousness which can be invoked to explain virtually anything. An incident reported in the BBC Sunday programme (10 January 1988) illustrates the point. The missionary ship Logos had been shipwrecked off South America. Those on board had prayed that it would be saved because they believed what it was doing was God's will. When the ship was lost they were dismayed but were cheered up when they recognized that God must have something better in store (a new ship) because 'he co-operates for good with those who love God . . .' (Romans 8: 28).

Under pressure of the facts the original pure Freudian or Marxist faith, for example, may become fragmented but the resulting sects are likely to retain their confidence that they alone have the key and hold to it with even greater fervour. This is not so very different, of course, from the way that scientists behave. The reductionist tendency of the natural sciences leads to the search for an ever more economical description of nature in terms of the smallest possible number of elementary particles and forces. The idea is that once the basic essentials are laid bare everything that happens will be seen as the natural outworking of the fundamental principles.

In religion things are a little different because there are reasons for believing that there ought to be a key to the truth on which belief can be surely founded. There, the argument is often expressed on the following lines. If God really exists and if it is part of his plan that human creatures shall come to know what that plan is and how to avail themselves of what it offers then it is inconceivable that the same God would have failed to provide a key. The only question then to be

settled is which of the keys on offer actually unlocks the door
of salvation. If this argument is correct the instructions are to
be found somewhere—but where? To some the question
will be, which of the Christian churches speaks with the true
voice of God? Which church's teaching is guaranteed to be
true? In ages when people thought that their eternal destiny
depended on finding the right answers to such questions they
had to be wrestled with in fear and trembling. Some will still
see it in that extreme way but for many more the assurance
of being in the right fold nevertheless still seems to be the
surest, if not the only way to the truth. On the other wing of
the church it is equally clear that the key to understanding has
been written down and is to be found in the collection of
books which make up the Bible. But even among those who
are agreed that the search for truth ends between the covers
of the Christian Scriptures there is a diversity of belief about
what that truth actually is. For a clear perception of what
God is saying in these writings one needs a further definitive
insight into what their central message is. In many cases this
takes the form of identifying certain key texts or doctrines in
the light of which the rest of the Bible must be interpreted.
Once this has been done the adherents of a particular view
seem genuinely unable to understand how anyone with their
eyes open could fail to see what is so obvious to them. A
publication sent to the author bearing no sign of its origin
other than that it was from a 'servant of the Lord' sweeps
aside the sacraments (*sic*) saying 'The theologians cannot and
will not understand that the christians *broke bread in their
houses* and not in the Temple (Acts 2: 45) and the reply that
Jesus gave to the high priests and senators (Matthew 21: 25)
was, simply, that *the baptism of John is not a thing of God but of
men.*' It should come as no surprise to the reader that the same
principles of exegesis lead, inexorably, to the conclusion that
'the great Babylon, mother of prostitutes and of the abomi-
nations of the earth, is not Rome, but Brussels'. But though
we may smile at such eccentricity the idea that there is a
definitive insight to be had is one shared by many more

sophisticated interpreters of Scripture. These examples all illustrate our very natural tendency to cling on to our certainties at almost any cost.

PROBABILITY AND BELIEF

If there is no certain source of public, revealed knowledge about the supernatural and no magic key to unlock the truth then we must perforce talk in terms of probability. For most of us this goes against the grain; we like to be certain about things and feel uncomfortable about uncertainty. Our education and culture fail to equip us to cope with uncertainty. Yet we live in an uncertain world in which we often have to act without certain knowledge of the consequences. So whether we like it or not our logic has to be the logic of uncertainty— and this applies to unbelievers no less than believers.

Probability is not only the guide of life as Bishop Butler said (though he was not the first)[3] but the necessary accompaniment of statements of belief. We must accept that there is, and can be, no watertight deductive proof that God exists or, more generally, that there is any reality beyond the world of the senses. This is now virtually common ground among apologists and there is no point in rehearsing the arguments again. A recent and detailed case to this effect has been made by Stannard (1989) who is equally firm on the complementary proposition that there is no disproof either. This second aspect is not something which we shall take for granted because, as we have noted, there are reputable scientists who have claimed that current knowledge does rule out the religious view, or, at the very least destroys some vital element. Monod (1972) was one such and we shall meet similar claims by Minsky among others in Chapter 3. Perhaps none of them would go so far as to say that they had a disproof in the formal sense but the distinction is so fine as not to be worth pressing.

[3] I. J. Good attributes it to Cicero (*De Natura*).

It should be remembered, in passing, that the ontological argument provides another approach to the question of God's existence which is different from what we have called a deductive proof. It involves the claim that God's existence is somehow implicit in the very notion itself. Although the argument enjoys periodical revivals its failure to carry the day undermines its claim to be a 'proof'.

We are not proposing anything so absurd as the mental punctuation of the creeds by declarations that we believe in God the Father with probability 0.95, say, and the life everlasting with probability 0.5, though a survey conducted along these lines among churchgoers might be very illuminating! The position is that we have a large number of strands of evidence to evaluate and what we need is some means of knowing what they all add up to. We need to know whether the uncertainties can be made precise and, if so, how their cumulative effect can be gauged.

There is an analogy here with built-in redundancy whereby a reliable piece of equipment can be built from unreliable components. If they are appropriately linked together the system will be able to continue operating even if some items fail and the whole system will have much greater reliability than any item taken on its own. A rather more vivid picture of what we are driving at is provided by the problem which the early railway engineers faced when attempting to take the Liverpool and Manchester Railway across Chat Moss. They did not follow the practice of driving in piles until solid rock was reached, for they could find none. Instead they floated the line across on hurdles interwoven with heather. By distributing the weight over a large area they were able to obtain a secure foundation. In the same manner the intellectual foundation of belief is not the solid rock of incontrovertible evidence but a rather fragile collection of bits and pieces which must derive their strength from mutual reinforcement.

The way in which we have to approach these questions is the same as that which we adopt for almost all other matters about which we have to make up our minds. We proceed inductively accumulating evidence, assessing its value in relation to the various hypotheses which occur to us and then form a judgement as to which is the best supported. Most of the time we do this informally and without much regard for the logical coherence of what we are doing. As we shall see later, intuition and 'common sense' can sometimes be poor guides when handling uncertainties and then we must turn to the professionals—in the shape of philosophers and statisticians—to keep the argument on the rails. So far as the principles are concerned there is little problem but, even though translating them into practice is extraordinarily difficult, the attempt must be made.

We should disabuse the reader of any expectation which these remarks may create that the rest of the book is to be a formal exercise in inductive logic in which the whole collection of human knowledge is ransacked for mites of evidence which can be processed to yield a final probability for a supernatural interpretation of the universe. The raw material is too ill-prepared and incomplete for that. We shall, however, consider in turn a number of topics which bear directly on the plausibility of the supernatural and which have also been the subject of hot dispute. These will include, among other things, the Bible on which we have already commented, miracles including the virgin birth and resurrection, and the paranormal. We shall examine the evidence taking care especially of the uncertainties involved and how they have traditionally been handled. In this way the strength of the evidence will be tested and we shall aim to assess the progress made towards the final goal which is to gauge the strength of the intellectual case for believing that 'this is not all there is'.

It should be noted that the notion of probability enters in a second way. This is through the element of randomness which pervades so much of the world around us. Modern biology accords an important place to chance in the processes of evolution; accident and coincidence seem to play a significant role in the progress of human affairs; the processes of the human brain, and hence our very thinking about these things, appear to involve an element of randomness. All of these things have profound implications for the subject-matter of theology which characteristically speaks of a purposeful Creator presiding over an orderly world of responsible human creatures. In addition to placing serious question marks against certain beliefs this randomness in the data of experience injects a further degree of uncertainty into the inferences which we are able to draw from them.

Our treatment of these matters will follow a somewhat different path from our predecessors by giving greater emphasis to empirical questions. We shall not attempt to assess all the evidence which might be mustered in support of supernaturalism. Instead we shall select a number of topics where the nature of the evidence lends itself to a degree of quantification. These focus on what can be legitimately inferred from the facts of experience about the existence of a non-material dimension to reality without which theology has nothing to bite on. To some extent we shall be able to assess the strength of available evidence but, and of equal importance, we shall aim to clarify the question of what counts as evidence and the methods by which it should be handled. In no sense do we intend to imply that only matters which lend themselves to a degree of quantification are to be taken seriously—far from it. Rather we intend to redress the balance in the debate somewhat and to give easier access to those who feel at home with an approach more in tune with contemporary scientific culture.

WHAT FOLLOWS?

Chapter 2 is concerned with methodology, that is, with the ways and means of making inferences in the face of uncertainty. It is written in a non-technical way and, though it might not satisfy the experts, it will have served its purpose if it gives some insight into the discipline of thought imposed

on those who seek to reason about uncertainty. Readers
already familiar with probability could proceed immediately
to Chapter 3. Those who find even this modest level of tech-
nicality beyond them will still find much to interest them in
the body of the book. However, their role will be that of
spectator; playing the game is for those who have mastered
the rules. Chapter 3 tackles two issues which threaten to
derail the project at the outset. One is the contention that
religious claims have been comprehensively falsified by the
scientific view of reality which shows the supernatural
hypothesis to be unsustainable and unnecessary. Without a
toe-hold of prior credibility any programme of weighing the
accumulated evidence cannot even take its first step. The second issue is concerned with the mental apparatus with which
we do our thinking. If, as some claim, the operation of our
brains involves random processes it is difficult to see what
meaning their outputs might have. Probability enters here in
a different guise; not as a way of quantifying our incomplete
knowledge but as a description of the irreducible indeter-
minism of the world—including ourselves. Even if this
hurdle can be cleared it is difficult to see how the self could
have the autonomy required by the religious view.

With these problems behind us we move on in Part II to
examine four topics all of which have generated a good deal
of controversy; miracles, the paranormal, God's existence,
and the Bible. These are not equally central to the believer's
case but all bear upon it at different points. We shall attempt
to apply the methodology of Chapter 2 and some of the principles of Chapter 3 to each in turn and see how far we can go
to adjudicate among the contending factions.

In Part III our aim is twofold. First, and arising out of the
principal conclusion of Part II, we introduce the need to
weigh not only probabilities but also the consequences of
making choices in the light of those probabilities. This
involves some further technical material which is necessary
in order to position ourselves to bring the threads of the
argument together in the final chapter.

2

The Logic of Uncertainty

Most statisticians have found themselves at one time or another asked to say what is the probability of some everyday event—often of some rather surprising coincidence. For example, of bumping into a long-lost acquaintance twice in the same week. The question is often put in a way which suggests that to each and every such event there is a numerical probability which the expert ought to be able to calculate. In some cases, of course, like the birthday problem we shall meet below, it is possible to provide what is asked for. More commonly the matter is not so simple and the question may, even, be meaningless. We need first to look at how probabilities might be measured and manipulated. Only then can we begin to see whether they have any role to play in reasoning about uncertainty in the search for the supernatural.

Textbook discussions of the matter often begin with examples of tossing coins and drawing cards from packs. Few people are disposed to doubt that 0.5 is a reasonable measure of the probability that a tossed coin will fall tails. Often this will be based on a strong intuitive feeling that there is nothing to favour either face so each has an 'equal chance'. Alternatively an empirical justification might be based on experiment. Because in a large number of tosses the two faces turn up roughly the same number of times, the proportion of tails seems a sensible measure of the probability. These two approaches are quite distinct. One rests on a perceived symmetry of the coin and can be arrived at without actually tossing the coin at all. The other, based on relative frequencies, can only be inferred after a large number of tosses. Fortunately the two approaches agree and there are good reasons why they should. The symmetry idea has little application outside the realm of cards, dice and coins and so is of little use for our purposes. The idea of relative frequency is more widely applicable and forms the basis of much modern statistical theory. However, neither approach is of very much help in matters of religious belief. Whether or not some alleged miraculous event, for example, occurred in the past is obviously not an event whose probability can be estimated by repeated trials. We have therefore to consider whether it is possible to use probabilities in non-repeatable situations. Gamblers have no doubt about it. They are prepared to lay odds on all manner of non-repeatable events, even the appointment of archbishops, and to back their judgement by staking money on them. Odds are probabilities in another guise and the fact that bookmakers continue to flourish strongly suggests that they must know something about the calculus of uncertainties.

There are many ways of approaching probability as a degree of belief—which is what the gambler is expressing in the odds just mentioned. Some would argue that a degree of belief is an objective thing which expresses the relationship between the evidence for a proposition and its truth. Others treat the matter purely subjectively and regard probability as a personal matter. In that case there is no such thing as a 'correct' probability, the question of correctness only arises when we come to combine probabilities. Of course, even then, as evidence accumulates, two people's probabilities ought to converge however diverse their starting points might have been.

There is no logical reason why an extreme subjectivist should agree with us that the coin has an equal chance of falling heads or tails but there may be a penalty for believing otherwise. An idiosyncratic life insurer who made impeccable probability calculations would soon go out of business if his probabilities did not correspond with actual frequencies of death at various ages. But what if there is no long run, such as there is in insurance, against which the appropriateness of a probability can be tested? There is another kind of long run to which we can appeal even if all the events we consider are unique. Suppose that we make a large number of probability judgements and consider that subset of judgements for which we arrive at a figure of 0.4 for the probability. We say that our judgements are well calibrated if on 40 per cent of the occasions where we claim that the probability is 0.4 the judgement turns out to be correct. If, on the other hand, the success on such occasions turned out to be 80 per cent our critics might well feel justified in thinking that our judgements were unduly pessimistic. Most people do not make well-calibrated judgements but, in appropriate contexts, they can be trained to do better.

Another way of arriving at numerical probabilities is by considering hypothetical bets. Suppose you are presented with a choice between accepting a gift of £100 or being offered a chance in a lottery of winning £1,000. Your choice (assuming you have no moral scruples about gambling) reveals something about your views on how likely a win is. If you accept the gift you are implicitly saying that you rate the chance of winning fairly low. For if you thought it was very high, say 0.99, you surely ought to opt for the lottery. By presenting you with a variety of alternative bets and observing your choices I can get an increasingly clear idea of how you rate the chance of winning in the lottery. These ideas can be made the basis of a coherent theory of personal probability though there is rather more to it than is apparent from this brief discussion. In particular, the argument has to be conducted in terms of utility rather than money. If we were offered a choice between the certainty of £1 million or an even chance of £3 million most of us would opt for the certainty even though our 'expectation' is greater in the second case. This reflects the fact that £3 million does not have three times the utility for us of £1 million. In technical language the utility of money is not linear.

There is an important distinction to be made which has only been hinted at so far. Probabilities may refer to *events*, such as who will win a football match or whether it will rain tomorrow. They may also refer to *propositions* or *hypotheses* about the state of the world; for example, whether telepathic communication is possible or whether God exists. These are things which are either true or false and are certainly not the kind of thing which could be investigated by repeated trials of any kind. A probability of such a proposition is a measure of how strongly we believe in it. It is this sort of probability with which we shall be primarily concerned and much confusion has arisen over the theological implications of probability calculations by failure to make this distinction.

A final point to make about probabilities is that they are almost always conditional. Their value depends on what we choose to regard as 'given'. Often there is no need to be explicit about the conditions in question because they are clearly understood but their existence must not be forgotten. Probabilities may depend very strongly on the conditioning as is clear if we consider something like a miracle. Our judgement of the probability of a miracle depends very much on what kind of place we assume the world to be. If the world is presided over by a beneficent and powerful God (the conditioning event) a miracle may be quite likely; otherwise it may be virtually impossible. An important conditioning event concerns the data that we have available on which to base our probability judgement. The more evidence we have the less uncertain would we expect to be about the truth of the proposition under consideration. A doctor faced with a puzzling case may order a series of tests to help in deciding whether the patient has X. If the tests are genuinely able to discriminate the diagnosis should become progressively clearer as the results come in. As the data accumulate the probability of X will then change as it moves towards zero or one. One of the claims we shall meet later is that it is just such an accumulation of pieces of evidence which makes it almost certain that God exists. Since so much is at stake it is clearly rather important to know just how the calculation should be made.

COMBINING PROBABILITIES

The calculation of probabilities is greatly facilitated by the fact that many of the events or hypotheses in which we are interested can be broken down into simpler elements whose probabilities are more easily judged. For example, a car will only start if there is petrol in the tank, charge in the battery, appropriate electrical connections and so on. It is often easier to make estimates of the probabilities of these constituent elements than of the overall probability that the car will start. We need to know how to combine these component probabilities to yield the overall probability and that is what probability theory does for us. It provides a set of rules governing how this should be done. These are not arbitrary but reflect the inner logic of the definition. However we arrive at the individual probabilities we must stick to the rules or we shall fall into contradiction. Once we fix the probabilities of certain events or propositions we are not free to choose others for related things without regard for what we have already done. For example, once we have committed ourselves to a value of 0.7 for the chance that an expected letter will arrive tomorrow the only possible value for the chance that it will not come is 0.3. Not all potential inconsistencies are as obvious as this and some can be counter-intuitive but there is no escape from the logic.

The theory, however, should not be seen as a prison in which we are prevented from doing what we wish. It actually liberates us from the tyranny of arbitrariness. We can use it to limit the range of things about which we have to make judgements and to focus our attention on those aspects of the problem where our judgement can be used to best effect.

In Chapter 6 we shall meet an example which illustrates

this point admirably. At the end of his guide to the debate about God Prozesky (1992) considers three hypotheses and claims to have shown that the probabilities of two of them are about equal and both are significantly greater than a third. As we shall see, this simple statement tells us quite a lot about the possible numerical values of the probabilities which may take us further than the author intended.

One important class of such problems is where the event (or proposition) in question requires the conjunction of several constituent events. For example, the completion of a complex manufacturing task on schedule may require that all the sub-tasks shall be completed. The familiar analogy is that of a chain; it will carry its load only if all the individual links hold. Probability theory tells us that the total probability in such cases is obtained by multiplying the constituent probabilities. There is a very important qualification to this rule which says that the events must be independent. The failure to take account of this is the source of many fallacious conclusions, some of which we shall have cause to notice in the course of the book. (A fascinating review of the pitfalls with many theological and related examples has been given by Kruskal (1988).) Independence means the absence of any causal link between the events in question; the outcome of one must be completely unaffected by the others. It is relatively easy to ensure this with cards and dice where, for example, by proper shuffling of the pack, after a single card has been selected we can make sure that the probability that the same card is drawn again is unaffected. But with real life examples it is not so easy to be sure. The point is nicely illustrated by a famous argument originating with A. S. Peake against the claims of the papacy.

The argument depends upon decomposing the main proposition into many components in a manner which allows a probability argument to establish the desired conclusion. In part this relates to biblical testimony. Speaking of the Roman doctrine of the infallibility of the Pope, Peake (1928) said (see Wilkinson, 1958: 154)

It is suspended by a chain of hypotheses of which very few are raised above a narrow margin of probability while several are improbable in the last degree.

If Matthew 16.18 is authentic; and if by the 'rock' Peter is intended; and if the passage implies the infallibility of Peter; and if Peter ever resided in Rome; and if residing there he was its bishop; and if he passed on his prerogative to later Bishops of Rome; and if he did not pass them on to the Bishops in other places where he resided; if indeed there was any monarchical episcopate in Rome till decades after his time; and if the explicit utterances of Jesus did not forbid such a claim; and if it was not incompatible with much in the New Testament record—then and then only could one consider Roman claims.

The implication is that since, in Peake's view, most of these propositions have very low probability the probability of their conjunction must be negligible. There is, of course, room to argue that the conjunction of all events listed is not required and that some of them are tendentious but the great merit of the argument is its structure. It shows exactly what we have to do to uphold the claim.

We have to be careful about using the multiplication rule here because the conclusion rests on the assumption that the ten components listed are independent. If Matthew 16:18 is authentic it becomes more likely, one presumes, that Peter was intended and if that were the case his infallibility would be more likely and so on. If independence cannot be assumed, there is still a multiplication rule but it is now expressed in terms of *conditional* probabilities. If the propositions can be arranged in a sequence the probability of each has to be calculated conditional on all that have gone before. If the conditioning increases the probability, as seems to be the case here, the total probability will not decline so rapidly with the number of 'ifs' as would be the case if they were genuinely independent. To establish the desired conclusion it has to be shown that the probability of each proposition in the sequence given the truth of its predecessors is relatively high. If each item had a conditional probability of 0.9 given its predecessors, the overall probability would be 0.35. To get a final probability of at least 0.5 the individual probability would have to rise to 0.933. For individual values between 0.9 and 1 the final probability increases quite rapidly; for example, it increases to 0.6 when the component probability reaches 0.95.

Whatever the weaknesses of this particular application the argument shows a clear appreciation of how the weight of a case based on uncertain evidence can be gauged by an analysis of its structure and a knowledge of how probabilities combine.

Another class of composite events involves disjunctive events. Many vital control systems in such things as aircraft have built-in redundancy to increase reliability. If several components are provided but only one is needed to operate the system it will continue to function until the last one fails. A four-engined aircraft can fly on a single engine. Other things being equal it is less likely to crash than a two-engined plane and for that reason, until recently, two-engined planes were not allowed to fly long distance over water. Simple calculations show how even a modest degree of redundancy can increase reliability (the probability of non-failure) quite dramatically. For example, if each component has a probability of failure of 0.5 in some time interval the probability of the system failing will be reduced to 0.125 if two independent back-up components are provided and to 0.001 if there are nine. Once again there is an independence assumption involved in that the failure of one component must not affect the reliability of the others. Without that, reliability may still be improved but not to the same degree.

One of the main obstacles to applying formal probability arguments to matters of belief is that the probabilities cannot easily be quantified. However, this is not necessarily such a disadvantage as one might think, especially if the aim is to see whether some composite probability is very small or large. Lack of precision in the component probabilities can be compensated by having a large number of cases. To illustrate the point let us continue with the example on reliability where we showed that the probability of failure decreased very rapidly when the number of back-up components was increased from two to nine. There the probability of an individual component failing was 0.5; let us now see what it would be if that figure were changed to 0.75 and 0.25. The corresponding failure probabilities for the complete system are now 0.06 and 0.000001 respectively. In relative terms these differ enormously but in absolute terms they are both small. If we would have been satisfied with a failure risk of 0.1 it would not have mattered what the individual probability was as long as it was not much larger than 0.75. Furthermore if we wanted the risk to be much smaller it would only be necessary to increase the number of back-up items sufficiently. This example shows one way in which it might be possible to build up a very strong case in favour of some hypothesis even though the individual strands in the argument were weak.

BAYES' RULE

One of the most important things which we sometimes need to do when conducting a probability argument is to interchange an event with a hypothesis in a conditional probability statement. To see what this means consider the following example. Let us imagine that a child is given a multiple-choice question to test geographical knowledge. Suppose that the question asks for the capital of Iceland and that five possible answers are given including the correct one. A candidate who knows the answer should get the answer right but one who does not will have to guess. In that case we might reasonably assess the probability of a correct answer as 0.2. Put more formally the probability of a correct answer *given* that the candidate is guessing is 0.2. Suppose next that we are interested in the probability where the event and hypothesis are reversed, that is, we want to know what is the probability that the candidate is guessing *given* that the answer is correct? It is certainly not 0.2, in general, though examples can be found where eminent scientists have supposed that it would be. One such is provided by Hoyle and Wickramasinghe (1981) in their book *Evolution from Space*. Having calculated the probability that the 2,000 enzymes involved in living things were assembled at random from the 20 different amino acids is $1/10^{40,000}$ they go on (p. 130) to say that any theory with a probability of being correct which is greater than this must be preferable. But in saying that they have reversed the two parts of the probability. They calculated it as the probability of getting the enzymes *given* the random theory but are interpreting it as the probability of the random hypothesis being true *given* the enzymes which is not the same thing at all. (In Bartholomew (1984: 44) I argued that the calculation was wrong in any case so it fails on two counts.)

It was in anticipation of the need for this kind of reversal that we drew the distinction between an event and a hypothesis (or proposition). It is often the case that we can estimate the probability of some event given some hypothesis whereas what we really want to know is the probability of the hypothesis given that the event has occurred. The way of moving from one to the other is provided by a celebrated theorem, or rule, due to Thomas Bayes, an eighteenth-century Presbyterian minister, after whom it is named. We shall not need a full statement of the theorem but the following version will be sufficient for our purposes. Suppose E denotes the event in question and H the hypothesis. We know Prob(E given H) and we wish to find Prob(H given E). The rule says that:

> Prob(H given E) is proportional to
> Prob(E given H) × Prob(H)

The 'proportional to' part need not trouble us as it is only a matter of scaling which will turn out to be irrelevant when we come to use the rule for inference later. The new element is Prob(H), the probability that H is true. This is called the *prior* probability because H is prior to the event occurring and its probability does not therefore depend on how the event turns out. Prob(H given E) is called the *posterior* probability because it expresses the strength of our belief when the outcome of E is known. The great difficulty about applying the theory is that it is often not at all clear what value should be given to the prior probability. In the case where H represents God's existence it is not even clear whether it can be given a meaning, as we shall see in Chapter 6. For the moment we merely state the result for further reference noting that E may be, and often is, composite and so may need to be calculated using the rules referred to earlier. In particular the question of independence will rear its head again.

PROBABILITY IN PRACTICE

All of the foregoing is concerned with how rational people *ought* to form probability judgements. We should therefore pause at this point to ask whether in fact they do behave as the theory says they should because that will help us to evaluate the worth of some of the arguments we shall meet.

There is growing experimental evidence that people are not very good either at estimating probabilities subjectively or at combining them consistently. It is well known, for example, that most people grossly overestimate the risks of flying or of nuclear accidents. This might even be held to be a good thing if it caused us to err 'on the safe side'. However, there are many circumstances in which an accurate assessment of uncertainty impinges directly on human welfare. If in legal proceedings a jury is required to judge a case 'on the balance of probabilities' the accused, not to mention society at large, has a vital interest in how that balance is struck. A patient facing a major operation needs to know as accurately as possible the chance that he or she will survive without major handicap. A director investing shareholders' money must take risks, but failure to assess those risks accurately may be very costly. In the matters of even greater ultimate importance for the individual and society with which theology is concerned one would hope that the inevitable uncertainties would be handled with no less seriousness.

A useful starting point is the non-numerical gradations of uncertainty which we make in everyday language. Although the English language is extraordinarily rich in words to express uncertainty it is ironic that their meaning turns out to be so uncertain. Moore (1977, 1983) has reported some experiments with managers and Mosteller and Youtz (1990) with medical writers. The discussion of the latter paper brought together other examples from all of which similar conclusions seem to emerge. In one experiment reported by Moore, managers were asked to rank ten expressions, such as 'quite certain', 'likely', 'possible', 'unlikely', in decreasing order of the degree of uncertainty which they expressed. Only 4 out of the 250 taking part produced exactly the same rankings and the word probable, for example, was sometimes as high as second and sometimes as low as ninth in the list. Furthermore, when a similar experiment was repeated after a month's interval, it appeared that individuals were not even consistent over time. There was rather more consistency within certain professional groupings who might have had experience of working together and so had arrived at conventions by which such terms might be interpreted. It is very doubtful whether there is such a common currency among theologians and biblical scholars who, on the whole, seem to favour the extremes of the scale.

Any attempt to translate verbal expressions into numbers is even more hazardous. When asked where they would place an outcome described as 'possible' on a numerical probability scale extending from 0 to 1, a group of managers gave answers which spanned virtually the whole interval. Thirty-seven gave figures between 0.3 and 0.8 with 0.4 to 0.6 containing 22 of those.

Mosteller and Youtz also used the method of asking subjects to relate words expressing uncertainty to values on a numerical scale. They too found that there was no unanimity in these matters but they went further by showing that some words and phrases have a greater common currency than others. 'Possible', for example, can mean almost anything with different individuals locating it at almost all points on the scale. 'Not unreasonable' does little better. On the other hand to say of something that there is an 'even chance' is to place it in most people's minds very close to the midpoint of the probability scale. Other terms like 'always', 'never', 'impossible', and 'certain' also have fairly precise meanings but being close to the extremes this is no help in the range where precision is most needed. The study goes into the effect of qualifiers ('very', 'moderately', and so on) and notes the effect of context on the meaning of words.[1] It raises the question, without undue optimism, of whether it might be possible to agree on a calibration of the meanings of certain terms which would allow a degree of effective communication. Even in the present primitive state of these studies it is abundantly clear that arguments couched in probability language must be treated with extreme caution. If the purpose of language in this context is to convey a degree of belief from one mind to another using everyday words this work shows that it is conspicuously unsuccessful.

In my own view this work points, paradoxically as it might seem, to the need to convey uncertainties as numbers.[2] However much this may seem to introduce a spurious precision into the discussion and however abhorrent it may appear to those accustomed to trade in the subtleties of language it

[1] Similar problems arise in the wording of questions in surveys. One would expect, e.g., 'very unsafe' to represent a more extreme feeling of insecurity than 'unsafe'. O'Muircheartaigh, Gaskell, and Wright (1994) have investigated the effect of 'intensifiers' such as *very*, *really*, and *extremely* and find that it is highly variable. In so far as this carries over to statements of uncertainty it would reinforce the observations made here.

[2] The same need has been found in archaeology where the problem of communicating uncertainties is also acute. In an amusing note on the matter Rahtz (1975) proposed a 10-point ('Beaufort') scale ranging from *very unlikely* (1) to *certain* (10); *likely* (5) comes in the middle and *probable* (7) rates more highly than *more than likely* (6).

is difficult to see what alternative might serve as a common currency. As we have shown above, methods are available for quantifying uncertainties. Statements of uncertainty, which abound in the literature of religious studies no less than elsewhere, are often too imprecise to be taken seriously. Given this unpromising beginning it will come as no surprise to learn that our informal reasoning about uncertainty is in no better case. Even when the issue seems fairly clearcut with some data on which to base the calculation, intuition is likely to be a poor guide. There is a well-known illustration of the point which never fails to surprise students on whom it is tried. The teacher asks the class what they think is the probability that there are at least two persons present with the same birthday. In a group of 50 or 60 most feel that such a coincidence is unlikely and they express this by quoting a very small number. In fact, the true probability is over 95 per cent and it is rare to find a class of about that size without at least one pair having the same birthday.

The bias in judgement which the birthday problem reveals arises because our own private logic of uncertainty does not match the objective logic which must be used if probability reasoning is to be consistent. In this case everything depends on assigning a probability to the chance that any randomly chosen individual was born on a given date and on the assumption that birth dates in a class are independent. The possibility of having a pair of twins present would invalidate this assumption but not by enough to matter. Given that the birth date probabilities must be something like $1/365$ the result follows.[3]

[3] The trick here is first to work out the probability that there is no coincidence. The probability of at least one coincidence is then obtained by subtracting the answer from one. The probability that the second individual has a different birthday from the first is $364/365$; that the third is different from the first two is $363/365$, and so on. The product rule then yields the probability of no coincidence by multiplying these fractions. There are many variations on this theme. For example, if a random sample of 331 unrelated people, who were born over a 50-year period, is taken there is a 95% chance that two will have been born on exactly the same day.

Even when no probability reasoning is involved judgements can be severely biased. It is common to investigate this phenomenon by asking questions to which there are two possible answers only one of which is correct and about which most people are not certain. They will have a degree of general knowledge on the basis of which they can form a judgement about which is more likely to be true. If the information which people have is well founded one would expect the majority to favour the correct answer, yet often this turns out not to be the case. For example, there are more English words with *r* as the third letter than there are words beginning with *r* but a majority of people think it is the other way round.[4] It is not unusual to find that when forced to one extreme or other of the probability scale most people go the wrong way.

Particular problems arise when trying to combine new evidence with beliefs which are already held. In Bartholomew (1984: 52 ff.) I gave an example of how the results of a medical test would alter a doctor's judgement about whether a patient was suffering from a rare disease. The calculation has to be made using Bayes' rule. If we were asked to pit our intuition against the rule, experiments tend to show that we should not fare well. This is not a matter which can be safely ignored as something which, even if it can be guaranteed to impress at parties, has no practical importance. In criminal cases at law juries have to make decisions using pieces of information gleaned from witnesses who may not be totally reliable. The difficulty of doing this accurately is nicely illustrated by the following example from Loh (1984: 534) on social research in the judicial process. It concerns a hit–and–run case in which a taxi was involved. There are two suspects, one with a blue cab and one with a green cab. Because the accident took place at night there is some doubt about the colour though the only witness says it was blue. In deciding whether the witness is telling the truth the

---

[4] This example is taken from Tversky (1974) who gives many examples of similar misjudgements.

jury have the following two pieces of information: (*a*) of the taxis in the city 85 per cent are green and the rest are blue, (*b*) vision tests carried out under the lighting conditions of the accident show that witnesses are correct about the colour 80 per cent of the time. What is the probability that a blue taxi was involved in the accident? The reader may care to make a judgement without using the rule and before looking up the answer.[5]

As we have already noted, the events or propositions on which we have to make judgements are often composite. In the birthday problem we start with the probability that each individual has a particular birth date and then, from that, build up the probability that there is at least one coincidence. The logic of uncertainty concerns how this should be done. In the case of the conjunction of independent events, for example, it tells us that we should multiply the constituent probabilities.

Psychological experiments show that we tend to overestimate the probability of such conjunctive events; in other words we tend to be more optimistic about the outcome than the evidence about the individual links justifies. This conclusion is supported by the common ill-founded optimism about the completion of any complicated task. Whether it is writing a book, decorating a room, or building a ship we seem to be incurably optimistic about the chances of meeting our deadlines. In the disjunctive case it turns out that we tend to be unduly pessimistic in our informal assessment.

Part of the trouble which people have in correctly judging the probability of a conjunction may be not so much that they do not know the rules of probability as that they do not think they are appropriate in this field. Again we may turn to the law to provide an illustration. Cohen (1977) has argued, in fact, that traditional probability reasoning is inappropriate

---

[5] The probability is $(0.15)(0.8)/\{(0.15)(0.8) + (0.85)(0.2) = 0.41$. Experiments indicate that most people think it should be around 0.8. This example is quoted in several publications. The earliest reference known to me is Saks and Kidd (1980–1).

in the law and he supports his case with an alleged paradox which results from its use. Suppose that an issue to be decided in a court of law is made up of two component issues both of which have to be established for the case to succeed. Since such matters can rarely be settled with certainty the civil standard of proof requires only that the matter shall be decided 'on the balance of probabilities'. It seems reasonable to interpret this as meaning 'with probability greater than 0.5'. Imagine that a witness whose reliability (probability of telling the truth) is 0.7 testifies in favour of the case on the first issue and a second witness of the same reliability does likewise on the second. On Cohen's criterion the action would succeed because both the components have been established 'on the balance of probabilities'.

Now let us suppose that the two witnesses testify independently—meaning that our view of the reliability of the second witness is unaffected by what the first says. The statistician now comes along and says the case has to be judged as a whole and that the reliability of the combined testimony is $0.7 \times 0.7 = 0.49$ and as this is less than 0.5 the case is not proved. The alleged paradox is that even when each component is proved separately, by a substantial margin, the case as a whole fails. Using probability rules seems to make the task of the plaintiff harder. How can it be that having established both necessary parts the mere act of considering them together leads to the opposite conclusion?

The paradox disappears when subject to careful scrutiny, as Dawid (1987) clearly shows, but it illustrates yet again how easy it is to go astray when handling uncertainty. There is no need to go into the details here but the root of the trouble lies in the fact that we, and Cohen, easily confuse reliability of the witness, 0.7 in this example, with the probability of the truth of the event reported. That this cannot be right is clear if we were to consider a claim that a witch had been sighted flying on a broomstick. Even if a usually reliable witness reported this we would be very strongly disposed to disbelief on this particular occasion and certainly would not assign the event a probability as high as 0.7. In fact it turns out we could only legitimately apply the 0.7 to the event if we had believed beforehand that it was as likely as not (that is, had probability 0.5). But is this not just what it should be if we were to come to the matter with an open mind? Perhaps, but if so our prior probability for the two components taken together would have then had to be 0.5 × 0.5 = 0.25. Yet if we came to the whole issue with an open mind should that probability also not be 0.5 as for the two components taken separately? The way out of this inconsistency lies in the discovery that evidence for events is properly measured by relative probabilities and then it emerges that two witnesses, however unreliable, are always worth more than either taken separately. As long as our prior probabilities were consistent with one another the two approaches would not lead to different conclusions. Dawid goes on to investigate the further claim that by decomposing wholes into as many components as possible one makes it more and more difficult to establish a case. He is able to show that the degree of subdivision actually makes very little difference and that rather than make it harder it actually makes it a little easier. Cohen has other objections which need to be carefully weighed but I remain to be convinced that they are fatal.

INFERENCE FROM PROBABILITIES

It might seem that when we have calculated the probability of some matter of interest our job is virtually done. If it were possible to calculate a numerical probability that St Paul wrote the epistle to the Galatians or that God exists surely all that remains is to decide whether or not it is close enough to zero or one to justify belief in the proposition. In some cases this may be so but often it is not quite so simple.

There are, broadly speaking, two sorts of probability on which we may attempt to base inferences. First there are those which give us directly the probability of the truth of some hypothesis, like God's existence, given certain evidence derived from the natural world. The tool for arriving at such probabilities (assuming they are not just 'estimated' subjectively) is Bayes' rule which, when used in this context, is known among philosophers as Confirmation Theory. This, as we have seen, involves what we called prior probabilities and these pose certain difficulties so we first see how far we can go without them.

The second kind of probability is of an event given some hypothesis about the nature of the world. The probability that a certain enzyme could be assembled 'at random' in a soup of amino acids is one such example. If such a probability is very small it is tempting to reject the conditioning hypothesis on the grounds that what has happened is almost impossible if that hypothesis is true. However, this is not legitimate because the event may be equally (or, even less) probable on all other conceivable hypotheses. The usual example used to make this point concerns dealing a hand of 13 cards from a pack of 52 playing cards. The probability of getting any possible hand is the same and is very small indeed.[6] It would be absurd to reject the hypothesis that the pack had been thoroughly shuffled on the grounds that my hand was exceedingly improbable given that hypothesis. The reason is that the same would be true of any other hand and one of them *must* be dealt. A similar type of example arose in an argument, to be discussed later, by Sir John Eccles about his own uniqueness (in Popper and Eccles, 1983: 559). The probability of a person with his particular genetic composition (given that of his parents) is very small indeed but the same would be true of any other combination so the improbability of his existence given a random association of genes from the two parents does not require the rejection of that hypothesis.

Suppose now that one such combination, though exceedingly improbable on a given hypothesis, was many times

---

[6] About 1 in 6 million million.

larger than the probability of the event on all other hypotheses. It would then be reasonable to say that the evidence favoured the given hypothesis. This might be termed the 'Sherlock Holmes principle' because of its similarity to the great detective's dictum that when all other possible explanations have been eliminated the one remaining, however improbable, must be true. We have extended the principle slightly by saying that the other explanations are much less probable rather than impossible but the logic is essentially the same.

All of this provides us with the rudiments of a rule of inference which we may formalize as it relates to two hypotheses. One may be the hypothesis of interest, such as 'God exists', and the other its negation. Suppose we have some data and wish to say which hypothesis is favoured on that evidence. The rule says that we should calculate (or estimate) the probability of obtaining those data on each hypothesis and judge the two hypotheses by the relative sizes of the two probabilities. This can conveniently be done by expressing the result as a likelihood or 'odds' ratio. An example will help to make the matter clear.

Let us consider a slightly more elaborate version of the multiple-choice test we used earlier. Instead of asking some simple factual question suppose we now ask the child to find the answer to some mathematical problem such as finding a square root. A child who does not know the method will have to guess the answer and with five to choose from we may assume, as before, that the chance of getting it right given that they do not know the method is $1/5$. If they do know how to do the sum they may still get the wrong answer by making a mistake in the calculation. (The 'wrong' answers in multiple-choice tests are often those which would be arrived at making the 'natural' mistakes.) For the sake of argument let us say that the chance that a person who knows the method will get the right answer is $4/5$ and therefore $1/5$ that they will make a mistake. Suppose now that a child does the test and gets the right answer. What can we say about the plausibility of the two hypotheses? According to the above figures a child who knows the method is four times as likely to give the right answer as one who does not. We can then say that the evidence favours the 'knowing' hypothesis by a likelihood ratio of 4 to 1. The word 'likelihood' here is being used in a special sense. When we compare the probabilities of various events under the same hypothesis we call the quantities probabilities. When we compare the probabilities of the same event under different hypotheses we refer to them as *likelihoods*. This is a very useful verbal distinction which helps to avoid logical confusion. In a simple case like the multiple-choice question what is achieved by this quantification may seem modest. Its real power only becomes apparent when we consider what effect further evidence might have on the point at issue.

Imagine that the child is now set a further problem whose solution depends on knowledge of the same method. For the moment we suppose that the correctness of the first answer has no bearing on the second. The data now consist of two independent pieces of evidence. Suppose both answers are correct. The probability of two correct answers given that the method is known is, by the multiplication rule, $4/5 \times 4/5 = 16/25$. In the same way the probability of getting both right given lack of knowledge is $1/5 \times 1/5 = 1/25$. The likelihood ratio is now 16 in favour of knowledge which is also the product of the individual ratios for the two tests. This shows us how evidence accumulates, namely by *multiplying* likelihood ratios. If the child had got one question right and the other wrong the two likelihood ratios would have been 4 and $1/4$ which when multiplied give a figure of 1. This is what intuition would suggest since the two results point equally in opposite directions.

It may well be that in an example like this the outcomes are not independent. If a 'knower' makes a mistake the first time he or she may be more likely to make the same mistake again. In that case the second probability must be computed conditional on the first outcome. For example, we must ask on the second occasion, 'What is the probability that a candidate who knows the method *and* who got the item wrong the first time will also get it wrong the second time?' It is that conditional probability that is relevant for the second likelihood ratio. The general conclusion that evidence accumulates by multiplying likelihood ratios stands. The weight of evidence in favour of one hypothesis as against the other is expressed numerically by this likelihood ratio—which is not, of course, itself a probability. Most of us would like to go further than this and would prefer the answer to be expressed as a probability that one or the other hypothesis is true. Bayes' rule tells us what is required for this to be possible.

We continue considering the choice between two hypotheses which in the interests of brevity we label H1 and H2. It will be sufficient for our purposes if we can find their relative probabilities—that is, how many times more likely one is than the other. The result that we require follows immediately from Bayes' rule which, we recall, says that the posterior probability of a hypothesis is proportional to its prior probability multiplied by the likelihood. It follows therefore that the ratio of the posterior probabilities is equal to the ratio of the prior probabilities multiplied by the ratio of the likelihoods. To convert a likelihood ratio into a probability ratio we therefore have to multiply it by the prior probability ratio.

Although this result is easily stated it is not so easily implemented. The difficulty, as we noted earlier, is in knowing how to assess the prior probabilities. In the matter of God's existence, for example, it is far from clear how we could form a judgement prior to having any evidence at all! We shall return to this question at the appropriate point but first we illustrate how the rule may still be useful even if we are unsure what the prior probabilities ought to be.

Suppose for the sake of argument that we have a likelihood ratio of 10. If the two hypotheses were thought to be equally probable a priori then the rule says that H1 is ten times more probable than H2. If H1 were believed to be ten times as likely as H2 a priori then when that information is 'added' to that of the likelihood the odds in favour of H1 become 100 to 1. On the other hand if the prior evidence favours H2 so strongly that the prior probability ratio is 1/100 the posterior ratio becomes 1/10. Thus although the evidence of our data favours H1 it is not sufficient to outweigh the very strong prior evidence the other way. The following example will help to show how this sort of reasoning works out in practice.

Suppose we are considering the possible existence of a monster in Loch Ness in Scotland. This is something on which we might well have some prior view based on media reports. Suppose next that a large luminous shape is spotted from the air at dusk moving in a zig-zag fashion across the loch. Let us suppose also that a photograph is taken which confirms that the sighting was not an illusion. What can we now say about the probability that a monster exists? The rule tells us that two other probabilities are relevant: one is our prior probability that the monster exists. The second is the probability, on each hypothesis, of observing a luminous shape moving in a zig-zag fashion from the height at which the helicopter was flying. If there is, indeed, a monster in the loch we would not be very surprised that it should be moving in this fashion or that it should be luminous. The probability of our observation given that a monster exists is presumably rather high. What figure we assign does not matter too much but, for the sake of argument, let us say we judge it to be 0.90. If no monster exists we *would* be rather surprised at the reported sighting. It seems extremely unlikely that any known aquatic creature would give rise to such an observation but we have to reckon with the fact that it might have been an optical illusion created by the moon or car headlights or a fisherman, for example. After an exhaustive consideration of these matters let us suppose we decide that in the absence of a monster the chance of a combination of factors to produce the illusion is, say, 0.001. (It must be very small or the phenomenon would have often been observed before.)

The two conditional probabilities, or likelihoods, are of the kind we have met before and if we interpreted them, ignoring prior probabilities, we would be strongly inclined to favour the monster hypothesis. After all, what was observed is only to be expected if the hypothesis is true but it would be a rather rare occurrence otherwise. Rather than believe that a very rare event had occurred we might prefer to believe that a monster existed. How is this conclusion affected by the introduction of prior probabilities? The answer is contained in the following formula.

$$\frac{\text{Posterior probability of a monster}}{\text{Posterior probability of no monster}} =$$

$$\frac{0.90 \times \text{prior probability of a monster}}{0.001 \times \text{prior probability of no monster}}$$

If we felt neutral beforehand and so reckoned the two prior probabilities were about equal we would have to conclude that a posteriori the odds on the existence of a monster were 900 to 1 (0.90 to 0.001) and this would be convincing. Suppose, on the other hand, that we were extremely sceptical and were almost convinced that there was no monster. So as not to be totally impervious to new evidence we allow that there is a small chance that a monster exists but we are not prepared to give it a probability of more than 1 in 10,000. This means that the prior probability of no monster is 10,000 times larger than that of a monster and the posterior probability ratio now becomes 900/10,000. The posterior odds are now 100 to 9, or about 10 to 1, against the monster hypothesis. The ditherer would be easily persuaded by the sighting but the sceptic would not be. This is what we would have expected but what the rule does for us is to quantify the uncertainties to a degree. I say 'to a degree' because the introduction of numerical values for the prior and conditional probabilities might seem highly questionable. If further sightings were made quite independently of the first each would contribute a new likelihood ratio which would, by multiplication, move the probability ratio towards certainty one way or the other. The sceptic, once having chosen the prior probabilities, would have to accept whatever the rule ultimately yields. It is not legitimate to go back and revise one's prior probabilities in the light of the evidence in order to resist the conclusion to which the evidence increasingly points.

There is another way of judging hypotheses which we shall meet a number of times which is not directly covered by the discussion so far. This is by using what is known as a test of significance. Here one identifies a set of outcomes which, collectively, would be very improbable if the hypothesis under test were true. If the actual outcome is in this set then the hypothesis is rejected on the grounds that given the choice of believing that such a rare event had occurred or that the hypothesis is false the latter is much to be preferred. At first sight this seems to fall into the error of ignoring the fact that all other possible hypotheses may be no more probable. But this is not the case because the critical set is chosen precisely because it contains outcomes which are judged to be much more likely on some other hypothesis. Such critical sets are, in fact, often chosen on the basis of likelihood ratios and so the 'significance probability' may be regarded as an alternative way of scaling likelihood ratios in probability terms without having to invoke prior probabilities. Statisticians are divided on the merits of these two approaches but all are agreed on the relevance of likelihood ratios. This will be sufficient for our purposes since the degree of sophistication achieved in most theological discourse which uses probability ideas falls far short of the ideal.

The foregoing discussion brings to the fore a point which has the potential to cause a good deal of trouble. Because posterior probabilities are obtained by multiplying likelihoods by prior probabilities all evidence in favour of any hypothesis can be completely nullified if one's prior probability happens to be zero. It is thus vital if any progress is to be made to establish that a hypothesis could conceivably be true. In the case of such matters as virgin birth or bodily resurrection this first essential step is also the most difficult and hence will involve what may seem a disproportionate effort. We therefore explore the issue in the next chapter along with another threat to progress arising from the apparent randomness in our own reasoning processes.

3
The Credibility Barrier

Although we have described a formal procedure by which uncertain evidence can, in principle at least, be accumulated in a coherent way there is one vital matter which threatens to abort the whole project at the outset. Many people never get beyond this initial hurdle and so rarely come to grips with the substance of the argument. It is simply that in a scientific culture religious claims seem to be so preposterous as to be unworthy of serious consideration. This amounts to saying that the prior probability is zero or, at any rate, so small as to effectively wipe out any evidence no matter how weighty; no amount of evidence can turn an impossibility into a possibility. The late Baroness Wootton was not alone when she said that in her student days she 'came to see that Christian dogmas were intellectually completely incredible'.[1] She saw no chance of reconciling them with what we know the world to be.

An essential first step on the road to certainty is to establish that the proposition being entertained is not, literally, incredible. Some would argue that if one adopts the Bayesian paradigm then one must be prepared to allow some prior probability to any hypothesis, however implausible it may seem. Only in this way does it become possible to get the argument off the ground. Indeed, if we allow that all rational knowledge is, to a greater or lesser extent, uncertain, then

---

[1] I cannot trace the source of the quotation. Among contemporary popularizers of science there are many who speak in equally categorical terms. A list of names would include Carl Sagan, Richard Dawkins, Peter Atkins, and Victor Stenger.

surely nothing should be ruled out a priori. This may be so in some cases but it is easy to find examples where such a way of proceeding is patently wrong. Suppose, for example, that the hypothesis under investigation is either self-contradictory or stands in conflict with something known to be true for certain. In neither case can the hypothesis be anything other than false and it would be irrational to assign it a non-zero probability. It is for just such reasons that many, like Baroness Wootton, refuse to entertain the claims of religion. They regard them as in direct contradiction to the known facts about the world which science has revealed. Although certainty may be hard to achieve, hypotheses can certainly be falsified. In that case it would be sheer perversity to allow them even the tiniest prior probability; they are simply false and there is no more to be said. Dennett, whose views will be considered below, is one among many who would argue that some religious views are conceptually impossible under any scientific world-view.

In view of all this we must be prepared to demonstrate that any such claims to have falsified hypotheses for which we wish to build up a case are mistaken. When we consider out-of-the-body experiences and their relevance to the question of life after death in Chapter 5 we shall note that one investigator, at least, finds it quite inconceivable that life should exist apart from the brain. Unless the believer can give some account of how that might happen the debate cannot begin. It is not necessary to establish, at the outset, that such a proposition is at all likely. In a recent book Eccles (1989), who is a dualist (he would say an interactionist), suggests that mind and brain might be linked through what he calls psychons located at different points in the brain. A reviewer[2] dismisses this on the grounds that it is mere speculation, there being no evidence whatsoever for their existence. This objection misses the point. In the very nature of the case it is difficult to know how such linkages could be detected but

[2] D. Lloyd in *The Times Higher Education Supplement*, 13 July 1990.

what matters is that it is possible to conceive of a way in which the connection could occur. Without this one cannot begin to make a scientific case for dualism. Only when the possibility is granted by all participants in the argument can we go on to deal in probabilities. On the broader front believers cannot expect to gain a hearing unless they can propose a supernatural model which is entirely consistent with what science shows to be the case.

It might be objected that we are substituting mere speculation for rational enquiry. This is partly true but it is speculation with a purpose. It is the use of the imagination to construct possible worlds and selecting from among them those that are consistent with all that we already know. Of course, the fact that we may not be able to find a coherent model does not mean that none is to be found. Our imaginations may not be fertile enough to conceive of the way that things really are but at least we must try. Given that the supernatural dimension of any hypothesis is, inevitably, based on speculation it will be highly desirable to weed out the more far-fetched imaginings from the more promising candidates.

At various points in the book we shall have to dispose of the credibility issue before attending to the probability arguments. We have already touched on the question of life after death and we shall use that example later in the chapter to illustrate the kind of thing that is required. Other matters, such as virgin birth, resurrection, and some kinds of miracle need similar treatment and we shall deal with these as they arise.

There is another side to the crucial role of the prior probability. If the totally committed atheist can resist all the evidence that the believer can muster by the simple device of declaring that the prior probability is zero, so believers can similarly protect their position. By announcing that they have had a revelatory experience of such power that nothing can undermine the certainty which it creates in them, they too become immune to any accumulating evidence against their belief. By being certain of their own position they assign zero probability to its converse and so their position is secured.

This polarization is, of course, just what we find among so many groups of people. Being absolutely convinced of the rightness of their own stance they see no need to engage their opponents in rational argument. The weakness of such extreme positions, which the unbeliever is only too eager to point out to believers, is that the various certainties often seem to be incompatible. However, this criticism is somewhat blunted by the recognition that so far as the existence of a realm of reality beyond what can be directly apprehended by the senses is concerned, most believers are at one.

At this point the atheist is at a disadvantage. If there is a supernatural realm it is entirely reasonable to suppose that some people, at least, might have an intuitive awareness of its existence. By ruling out any other source of knowledge beyond the material world, the atheist cannot claim any such private source of knowledge on which to build the case for atheism. The claim that any supernaturalist account of reality stands in direct contradiction to what we certainly know is therefore at the heart of the atheist's case. The need to overcome the credibility barrier is thus vital if the believer is to make headway.

It may appear that we have conceded too much to science by setting it up as a provider of certainties by which religious claims can be falsified. Is not scientific knowledge a cumulative inductive process leading to a provisional rather than a final view of the way that things are? In strict logic it must, indeed, be allowed that this is so, but the compelling nature of the scientific world-view derives from the interlocking of a vast number of well-attested facts into an immensely impressive and coherent framework. It is true that there are many gaps and unexplained areas and that viewpoints will change. But scientific progress typically proceeds by incorporating existing knowledge into a broader framework rather than by rejecting it. That the earth is not flat, that it is millions of years old, that the galaxy is only one among many, that there are such things as genes which carry the coded information for reproduction are truths as near to certainties as we can ever hope for. The apologist who fails to take the scientific enterprise seriously is riding for a fall.

CHANCE

The traditional bedrock of the intellectual defence of belief has been the supposed incompleteness of the scientific account of reality. It was the seeming impossibility of conceiving how a universe such as this could have come into being, how life could have emerged or how one could explain the richness of human experience without recourse to a designer and creator that has underpinned the believer's position in the realm of rational discourse. Slowly but surely, as we noted in Chapter 1, these certainties have been undermined until the point has been reached where it appears to many that there is no longer need or room for anyone or anything beyond what science can comprehend. If that is so any supernatural reality is superfluous and even if such were to exist it could have no relevance for us.

The thing which has replaced God in the scheme of things is chance. What at one time seemed to require the unseen hand of a superior being, in control, can now be seen to be the inevitable consequence of a multitude of chance happenings constrained and directed by the inherent properties of matter and the interactions between things. Chance is seen to be at work at all levels and at all stages of the evolutionary process. It is no longer viewed, by some, as necessary to invoke a creator for the origin of the universe which, itself, could have been a chance happening. The subsequent appearance of a habitable planet and the appearance of life on it are likewise the outcome of an evolutionary process in which chance has played a significant role. If chance is so central to the account of how we come to be here it is essential to be clear about what the term means. Can it bear the enormous weight which current atheistic claims place upon it?

WHAT IS CHANCE?

This question takes us back to the prior question: what is probability? In the last chapter we noted that there were various ways of measuring probability and the one which we identified as being relevant for our purposes saw it as a measure of degree of belief. This could be measured, for example, by observing the risks which people are willing to take in making choices among uncertain events. The discussion of chance takes us back to the other methods which are appropriate in situations such as coin tossing. The outcome of tossing a coin is a chance event in the sense that its outcome cannot be predicted with certainty. Some such events cannot be predicted simply because we do not have enough information about the causal factors. Others appear to be unpredictable in principle and we do not know what to look for as a causal agent. Radioactive decay is the well-known example but such things as the accidental happenings which lead to genetic mutations are, for all practical purposes, in the same category. The point is not that such things are not caused but rather that there is no means of knowing the causal mechanism and hence no means of predicting with certainty.

Some Christians would claim, quite correctly, that the fallacy in the argument that chance has replaced God lies in regarding chance as an agent whereas, in truth, it arises from the lack of an identifiable cause. They would go on to claim that the causal agent is God and that he is in total control of each individual happening. Chance thus arises solely from our ignorance about what is necessarily beyond our reach. The counter-argument is that the properties of matter, the laws of motion, and so on which are inherent in the material world are sufficient to generate the interactions which, because of their complexity, defy our comprehension.

The believer's argument here establishes the credibility of a supernatural explanation in the sense that it *could* be true and hence moves the argument on to the plane where probability arguments can be brought into play.

A better argument, I believe, is that the hand of the causal agent is to be seen not in the myriads of individual chance happenings themselves but in the regularities of their collective behaviour. This view was taken by Peacocke (1979) and worked out in some detail in Bartholomew (1984). Such a view makes it easier to provide a place for free will, offers a more hopeful approach to the problem of evil, and, most importantly, provides a more subtle and majestic view of God. Chance according to this view of things is not an alternative to God but a manifestation of a particular mode of God's working.

It might seem then that we have met the minimal requirement of establishing a supernatural model of some sort in harmony with the scientific world-view. Thus far I believe this to be so but there is one further credibility barrier which is not so easily overcome. This concerns the role of chance in our own make-up and the implications which this has for our own thought processes by which we acquire knowledge.

There are in fact, two barriers here. One is the claim that self-consciousness is an ultimately meaningless epiphenomenon of brain activity. Any religion worthy of serious attention regards humanity as having a distinctive quality and value. The gap between God and man as usually understood may be great but that between God and matter is even greater. An account of things which so diminishes what it means to be human goes a long way to falsifying any hypothesis which sees humanity as the crown of creation.

The second barrier undermines the trustworthiness of those very reasoning processes on which all rational discourse is predicated.

CHANCE AND THE SELF

The attempt to study our own nature scientifically presents us with a qualitatively different situation in that we are both the subject and object of enquiry. Most writers on the subject assume a position of lofty detachment and pronounce on the nature of things as though they were not part of the same world. As we shall see, such a stance is prone to lead to self-defeating arguments but, unless we are to abandon the quest at the outset, there is no alternative. We should, nevertheless, be alert to the hazard and be prepared to call a halt when the limits of science are reached.

Recently there has been a spate of literature on the mind–body problem which is rapidly moving the subject to the head of the agenda in the science and religion debate. Dennett (1991: 26) writes,

Human consciousness is just about the last surviving mystery. A mystery is a phenomenon that people don't know how to think about—yet. There have been other great mysteries: the mystery of the origin of the universe, the mystery of life and reproduction, the mystery of the design to be found in nature, the mysteries of time, space and gravity. These were not just areas of scientific ignorance, but of utter bafflement and wonder. We do not yet have the final answers to any of the questions of cosmology and particle physics, molecular genetics and evolutionary theory, but we do know how to think about them. The mysteries haven't vanished, but they have been tamed.

In his book *Consciousness Explained* Dennett aims to do for consciousness what he believes has already been done for the other 'mysteries' of science. He regards the triumph of physicalism as an accomplished fact and hence sees his task as to provide an account of how human consciousness could have arisen in the course of evolution. He is particularly concerned to challenge the view, which has a deep hold on all of us, that there is a centre of control where brain activity comes together and from which the whole operation of thought and feeling is co-ordinated. In contrast, Dennett proposes what he calls a 'Multiple Drafts' theory of what goes on in the brain. According to this there are many strands of activity originating from the various channels of sensory input, which take place in parallel, and what emerges is the result of selection from this mass of activity. He uses the word 'pandemonium' to describe the near-chaotic nature of this activity in order to emphasize the contrast with the picture of a well-structured bureaucracy under the control of 'the self'.

Such an account does not fit easily with traditional views of the self, or soul, but neither is it clear in what sense it can be said to be an explanation. We might well concur with Stuart Sutherland, a cognitive scientist, in a review of yet another book purporting to explain consciousness, when he said[3]

he appears to be no nearer to a solution than Francis Crick, Daniel Dennett, Michael Lockwood, Roger Penrose, Uncle Tom Cobbleigh and all. The real difficulty with consciousness is that nobody, not even the worthies named above, has succeeded in stating the problem. They should ask not 'What is the answer?' but 'What is the question?'.

Dennett writes as a philosopher but the challenge which we face is most sharply focused in the field of artificial intelligence and especially in the writing of Marvin Minsky. He claims that free will is an illusion created by a combination of law and chance. Rather as Jacques Monod claimed to have buried for ever the idea of a providential God acting in the evolutionary process, so Minsky (1987) has done the same for the realm of mind and with matching eloquence. His book *The Society of Mind* is a distillation of a life's work; it consists of a sequence of one-page essays in which he sets out his ideas on what minds are and how they work. Towards the end of the book he comes to the question of the freedom of the will. First he makes an observation which reflects our common experience (p. 306):

[3] Review of *A History of Mind* by N. Humphrey (Chatto & Windus) in *The Times Higher Education Supplement*, 3 July 1992.

We each believe that we possess an Ego, Self or Final Center of Control, from which we choose what we shall do at every fork in the road of time. To be sure we sometimes have the sense of being dragged along despite ourselves, by internal processes which, though they come from within our minds, nevertheless seem to work against our wishes. But on the whole we still feel that we can choose what we shall do.

But this, he goes on to claim, is an illusion, albeit a necessary one:

According to the modern scientific view, there is simply no room at all for 'freedom of the human will'. Everything that happens in our universe is either completely determined by what's already happened in the past or else depends, in part, on random chance. Everything, including that which happens in our brains, depends on these and only these:

A set of fixed, deterministic laws. A purely random set of accidents.

There can be no room on either side for any third alternative. Whatever actions we may 'choose', they cannot make the slightest change in what might otherwise have been *because those rigid, natural laws already caused the states of mind that caused us to decide that way.* And if that choice was made by chance—it still leaves nothing for us to decide.

The grammatical loophole which seems to be offered by the 'in part' of the second sentence is quickly closed when Minsky goes on to say that 'freedom of the will' is something we imagine to protect ourselves from the unacceptability of the idea that Cause and Chance are the sole determinants of our belief and action. The Chance and Necessity which Monod saw as sufficient to account for the origin of life here becomes the Chance and Cause which for Minsky is all that is needed to account for thought.

If this is the modern scientific view and if it is substantially correct then most theology of any kind is no more than random noise—a technical term which hardly needs translating! It would still be conceivable that a God should have created such a world for his own amusement but no theology worthy of the name would be possible. Minsky is certainly not alone in taking this view though, in passing, we note that what he says, if his own account is taken seriously, is no more than the product of cause and chance in his particular brain.

We have focused on the question of free will because it is at this point that we feel our special status in the scheme of things is most threatened. Minsky put the challenge in its most pointed form because he not only sweeps God aside but makes the worlds of thought and feeling, of art, literature, and music no more than meaningless by-products. He has thereby removed one of the main planks in the apologist's platform. When science seemed to be solely a matter of law it was very difficult to believe that the spontaneity and creativity revealed in these distinctively human activities were no more than the outworkings of a deterministic machine. It could then be credibly argued that something extra was needed to do justice to experience. Now, when chance has been added to law, science has acquired greater explanatory power. For if mind is no more than a machine into which chance introduces variety and novelty then the outstanding gap in knowledge left by deterministic science is closed. The final demise of the God-of-the-gaps is thus in sight if not already accomplished.

All of this is a far cry from the traditional Christian view of the self as an autonomous and responsible being capable of entering into a living and eternal relationship with a creator God who is actively involved in the life of the human community. We therefore have to consider whether the supernatural hypothesis has been demolished. Unless we can dispose of Minsky's contention all else falls. We shall therefore begin by examining the logic of his argument in more detail. The central question is whether the truth of the statements he makes can be reconciled with what those same statements imply about the brain which is making them.

A LOGICAL CONUNDRUM

It is as well to be clear from the start on the near absurdity of the situation in which we find ourselves. We are using our own mind to reach conclusions about itself. Minsky is one of those who makes God-like pronouncements about minds in general. But we can no more do this than we can escape from our own shadow. If Minsky is right it is hard to see how anything that he says, or anything that we say about what he says . . . and so on, could have any real meaning. Therein lies the logical problem.

If the utterances of minds are the result of the interplay of blind determinism and blind chance then it is not clear what relationship these utterances bear to the real world they purport to describe. Minsky tells us that the convictions we have about our own autonomy, though they seem real enough to us, are in fact illusory. But on what grounds could Minsky himself believe that his pronouncements have meaning since, on his own account, what he says is solely determined partly by causal laws and partly by 'random chance and therefore illusory'? Since it would be a contradiction in terms to suppose that the latter contained any meaning at all, his utterances, at best, could only be a garbled account of the actual state of the world. If the deep conviction which the rest of us have that we have free will is simply a defence mechanism constructed by the mind to shield it from the truth about itself may not Minsky's deep conviction about the true nature of mind be, by the same token, a defence mechanism against some reality which he cannot face? What is sauce for the goose is sauce for the gander.

The position we find ourselves in is rather like the classical Epimenides paradox concerning statements of the kind, 'I am lying.' If the statement is true then what it says renders it false and vice versa. In our case it is a matter of whether a statement is false or meaningless and so when Minsky says that everything we utter is the result of cause and chance and owes nothing to an autonomous self he is caught in the same trap. Either what he says about the nature of mind is true in which case the fact that he should happen to say it signifies nothing, or it is false. In short, there is no way that he or we could know that what he says is true.

But is there any reason for believing that it might be true

even though there is no way of knowing? One could argue that scientific method has proved to be a strikingly successful way for the human race to learn about its environment and prosper. Any group of people which follows its precepts and shares its benefits will expect to have a selective advantage. One might therefore expect a consensus to arise in the scientific community about what is actually the case. This is, in fact, what appears to have happened in the past. Thus even though, on his own account, Minsky is a partly random automaton the fact that he and others of the scientific community who have shared his insights have come to similar conclusions is a sufficient reason for believing that they may be right. In other words it is reasonable to expect the evolutionary process to generate thought patterns in its most successful products which accurately describe the mechanism which generates them. This may be so but we must probe it further to see whether it explains behaviour and whether it is internally coherent. Of course, our decision to do this, if Minsky is right, is not a free choice but the response of one automaton to another. On the other hand, if what he claims is false we are free to regard ourselves as thinking beings capable of discovering something about the way things really are. It is on that presumption that we shall proceed. Granting Minsky's point, for the moment, that it is legitimate for a random automaton to discuss its own nature let us examine his argument in more detail. He says that we think of the mind as consisting of three regions. One concerns those activities in which causal relationships operate. This is not in dispute; there are many brain activities in which cause and effect can be clearly seen to operate. When a loud noise, for example, impinges on the ear, impulses are transmitted to the brain, muscles are activated, memories are brought to the surface, and so on. We can understand how this sort of thing happens from our knowledge of brain anatomy, the behaviour of electrical circuits, and the way that muscles function.

Secondly there is the region of chance happenings which appear to have no such antecedents and are in no sense a result of 'our willing'. These are things which just happen. Finally there is the 'myth of the third alternative' which we call free will. This is something we create because we find that all our thinking is being 'taken away from us' so to speak. (Though why the 'we' of Minsky's construction should be concerned about this is left unexplained.) According to Minsky the third alternative has been gradually eroded as, with increasing knowledge, more and more of the activities which it contains have had to be allocated to the categories of Cause or Chance. We cannot live with the truth thus revealed, he says, because too much of what we do and think revolves around these old beliefs. All questions of responsibility and virtue, good and evil depend upon the myth and so we are virtually forced to adhere to the myth even though we 'know' it to be false. This reminds us again of the God-of-the-gaps argument which sees the world of experience as divided into two categories. In one are those events which can be explained by science; in the other are those left over for which God has to be invoked as the explanation. As science extends its range the territory of this God is diminished until, today, very little remains and that which does is in a precarious state. Minsky would have free will go the same way but his task is much more difficult. Unless we can define our terms more clearly the shuffling of activities between categories is unconvincing.

The point at issue is how one is to distinguish between the Chance and Free Will categories in a scientific manner. At the very least there has to be some definition of a chance event before we can assert that some happening can be so described. By definition, chance events and acts of free will (if they exist) are unpredictable even in principle because if they were not they would fall into the causal category. How then do we distinguish between events which 'just happen' and any which are the products of autonomous selves? One possibility is that the question does not arise because neither kind of event actually occurs. That would mean that the brain is completely deterministic and that the unpredictability we find arises only from our incomplete knowledge. A more sophisticated approach might seek to show that any system's knowledge of itself was bound to be incomplete. The idea that apparently random events might really be completely determined is given credence by the modern mathematical theory of chaos. This shows how quite simple causal mechanisms can give rise to chaotic behaviour. The reason why it is so difficult to predict them is that it is virtually impossible to obtain knowledge of the initial conditions from which the processes start which is precise enough to make predictions possible. This shows the common distinction which is drawn between the predictable and the unpredictable to be highly suspect. Nevertheless it is very difficult to believe that all human feelings and achievements are as meaningless as this explanation would imply. If genuinely unpredictable events are allowed then we have to return to the question of how they might arise. To say, with Minsky, that they are due to random chance explains nothing because chance is not a causal agent. The best we can do in scientific terms is to *define* them by the lack of any assignable cause. But if this is so there is no scientific way in which we can distinguish between Minsky's second and third categories and hence no rational way in which we could move activities from one category to the other. It is therefore not clear on what basis Minsky rests his claim that the advance of science has gradually eroded the 'mythical' third category. There is no scientific basis for ruling out the notion of mind as the origin of independent sources of action. Indeed it should rather be argued that it is the 'random chance' category that should be called into question since the notion of mind is a coherent 'explanation' of unpredictability in human behaviour whereas 'chance' is no more than an admission of defeat. Minsky's distinction between pure chance and free will is, therefore, unsustainable. What purports to be an explanation is no more than a description. It would, however, be premature, I think to dismiss the role of pure chance in brain activity as easily as that. In Bartholomew (1984) I left open the question of whether

such genuinely random events occur anywhere but concluded that there certainly were events which should be
treated *as if* they were purely random. This was because
regarding them to be individually directed to some end
would serve no explanatory purpose. All that mattered was
their collective properties which were guaranteed by the
underlying randomness. This represented an efficient and
elegant way of creating an environment with the requisite
amount of flexibility to make life, in its fullest sense, possible.
I suspect that much the same is true of the functioning of the
brain. It may well be that the variation introduced by effectively random neural events makes for efficiency in operation
and contributes to the creativity which particularly distinguishes human thought. It does not seem, to me, to be
sufficient to explain all of human experience, not least my
conviction that this particular discussion is worthwhile. One
can, however, challenge Minsky's claim on the grounds that
he is confusing scientific and non-scientific categories. If
what he is saying is true it implies that there is no reason to
take him seriously!

'BEYOND THE REACH OF SCIENCE'

This phrase from Brian Pippard's Eddington Memorial lecture goes to the heart of the matter (Pippard, 1988). The
argument is simply that the notion of 'mind' is outside the
realm of science because science is concerned with objective,
publicly observable phenomena whereas mind is essentially a
subjective experience. The mind cannot observe itself and
without that science is impossible. Mind is therefore beyond
the reach of science. This point has a long pedigree in the
writings of philosophers. Thomas Nagel explored the issue in
a famous article entitled 'What is it like to be a bat?'[4] Being
conscious is all to do with 'knowing what it is like to be . . .'

---

[4] Reprinted in Hofstadter and Dennett (1982: 391–403).

and the fact that we cannot enter into another's experience demonstrates the problem we are up against.

The dilemma which this poses for science, especially neurophysiology and psychology, has been discussed by Fenwick and Lorimer (1989) who argued that there is a need for a new kind of qualitative science. The trouble with existing modes of scientific thinking is that they implicitly exclude consciousness and mind from the framework in which they operate. When faced with the undoubted fact of the thinker's own self-consciousness they must inevitably be led to the same conclusion as Minsky—that there is no place in modern scientific thought for the idea of a freely choosing autonomous mind because it has been excluded by definition. In the words of Johnson-Laird (1983), 'Any scientific theory of the mind has to treat it as an automaton.'

In one sense Minsky must be correct but the trouble arises when he reaches the point of saying that the freely willing self does not exist. At that point he begs the central question of whether anything can exist which is incapable of explication in scientific terms. Adherence to a God-of-the-gaps is a hazardous undertaking if all the gaps in scientific knowledge are capable of being closed. But if, in the nature of the case, there are things which are beyond the reach of science and if those things turn out to be those which concern us most deeply then the God perceived in that gap may well have more substance and durability than his ephemeral predecessor!

In conclusion, then, we may say that the artificial intelligence perspective as exemplified by Minsky fails to justify the assignment of a zero prior probability to the supernatural hypothesis because the essential core of that hypothesis lies beyond the reach of science. In particular, we cannot distinguish, in principle, between a purely random event and one which arises from the exercise of free human choice. Both involve the essential ingredient of unpredictability. This does not rule out the contention of Dennett, Minsky, and many other workers that consciousness may, in fact, not need any explanation beyond the purely physical properties of the brain. What it does do, and is intended to do, is to keep the door open for the supernatural dimension by showing that the scientific account does not preclude it.

It is not, in any event, necessary for the believer to insist that the 'true self' or 'soul' is a non-material entity somehow embedded in the body. The case would be met if the self, no matter how it had arisen, were to transcend its material base and be capable of an independent existence in some other context. Such a possibility is essential if 'the resurrection of the body and the life everlasting' are to be given more than a symbolic meaning. Although such a belief is by no means a necessary part of theistic or, even, Christian belief, there are many who would agree with St Paul when he said, 'If it is for this life only that Christ has given us hope, we are of all people most to be pitied' (1 Cor. 15: 19). In the next section we shall therefore consider whether the belief in life beyond death is credible. This will serve not only as a natural sequel to the Artificial Intelligence view of life but will exemplify what is involved in overcoming the credibility barrier.

LIFE BEYOND DEATH

This is an ideal case study because, to those imbued with the outlook of a materialist culture, the finality of a funeral appears to be an irrefutable argument. The total dissolution of the body, apart from which we have no experience of human life, seems to mark such a fundamental discontinuity that any hope of survival seems so much wishful thinking.

Up to a point the Christian apologist's task is relatively easy and it is useful to rehearse the line of argument which orthodoxy would offer. Whatever general arguments there might be based on the sense of incompleteness which many feel about this life, or whatever, the key element of the case would be based on the life and resurrection of Jesus. His person speaks of another realm of reality beyond this from which he came and to which he returned. The conviction of his initially sceptical disciples that he was, indeed, alive after his crucifixion transformed them into a force which turned the world upside down. If God could effect the transformation from the temporal to the eternal in the case of Jesus then he is capable of doing so for us. Furthermore he is both willing and able to do so.

In barest outline this is the main thrust of the Christian case and, in its own terms, it is a powerful one. But its credibility depends on the things reported as having actually happened. The willingness of the present-day sceptic to accept that they did depends critically on the possibility that they *could* have happened. We shall discuss the credibility of the resurrection in Chapter 4 but here we are concerned with the more general question of whether it is conceivable that such a transition could be possible for ordinary mortals. The trouble is not in establishing whether a 'spiritual' world could exist. That is certainly possible because in the nature of the case there can be no direct evidence via the senses one way or the other. What matters is the means of transition or transformation that might be involved in moving from one to the other.

As so often happens, Lewis Carroll captures the essence of the problem in the story of the Cheshire cat. In *Alice in Wonderland* Alice is confronted by the grinning Cheshire cat. As she watches, the cat gradually disappears but the grin remains only to be later reunited with the cat. In Wonderland you can have the grin without the cat and this is what the believer seems to want of the self. But in real life the self appears to be inseparably linked to the brain and it is meaningless to speak of the former as if it had a separate identity.

How then are we to effect the separation between the self and its physical basis? There are several ways, but if they take us into territory beyond the reach of science how can their credibility be established in the absence of empirical evidence? Are we not reduced to mere speculation? There is, of course, no lack of speculative theories from astrology to the more bizarre beliefs in extra-terrestrial influences which all assert that the way things are is not entirely comprehended by science. We must be careful not to open the door to the arbitrary and irrational antics of pedlars of such nonsense. Some phenomena can be accommodated by extensions of existing science, others may be incompatible with any science.

If any such extension of the realm of knowledge beyond the reach of science is to be possible it seems necessary to me to base it on the following premiss already enunciated in Chapter 1. We repeat: that with which science cannot cope is not a 'separate world' but part of the one world. The natural and the supernatural are one in essence and the distinction which we draw between them is a function of our cognitive process and not in the nature of reality itself. This means that the two aspects thus distinguished interact with one another and therefore, in principle at least, the existence of the one could be inferred from the other. We have begun with that experience which appears to fit least easily into the scientific framework, namely our own personal autonomy. In line with the programme just outlined we have to consider how the boundaries of knowledge might be enlarged to provide a more satisfactory account without in any way compromising the purely scientific view.

One of the most hopeful lines of accounting for human self-consciousness is to say that it is an 'emergent' phenomenon. In opposition to a reductionist view of the world this says that as thresholds of complexity are passed new phenomena appear which are not wholly explicable in terms of more elementary structures. Thus biology is not entirely reducible to chemistry and neither is psychology simply a matter of biology. New tools and categories are needed as we move up the scale of complexity. According to this view life, consciousness, and self-consciousness are such emergent phenomena which have to be accepted as new entities. Just how this could be possible is obviously a very difficult question but computer science provides some analogies and clues which hold some appeal for theologians trying to find a place for the soul. A key idea is in the distinction between computer hardware and software. The hardware is the set of circuits, transistors, and so forth which make up the computer. The software is the set of instructions, or code, which makes the computer do things. Since the brain shares many of the attributes of a computer it is natural to equate the mind with the program—the software. The analogy is particularly close in the case of a robot. On a car production line welding may be done automatically by a robot which senses the position of the parts to be joined and carries through the rest of the operation just like a human operator. The goal of much work in robotics and artificial intelligence is to do things which humans do on an ever-increasing scale of complexity. What are termed expert systems can assist in medical diagnosis and provide advice on eligibility for state benefits in a way which imitates and often betters their human counterparts. It is the belief that this work can be extended to the higher realms of human activities which inspires the view that mind is to brain as computer software is to hardware. This raises the obvious question of where the code comes from and who conceived the purpose which the execution of the code expresses. The answer has to be that it evolved and, in part, is transmitted from one generation to the next in the DNA. As the organism responds to its environment the program is modified and as it has increased in complexity so it has attained a measure of self-understanding and the power of self-modification.

Whether or not a satisfactory account of mind can be developed along these lines remains open to question, though the efforts of Hofstadter and Dennett (1982) in that direction are a heroic attempt. Nevertheless it is instructive to see whether a scientific account on these lines has any prospect of harmonizing with a Christian orthodoxy which speaks of a life which transcends the physical body.

Suppose that the human self consists of a body of information, memories, behaviour patterns, decision rules, feelings, and so on. This information could be coded in various ways and the code need not depend on the medium in which it is 'written'. Words can be expressed using letters of a variety of alphabets or Morse code; they can be recorded as holes in metal, ink on paper, or variations in a magnetic field. The message is not to be identified with the medium, it lies in the structure—the way in which the elements are related to one another. In the same way, so the argument goes, the mind is the program which runs on the brain. The program is not a thing or a substance which resides in the computer or brain but a structured body of information which 'animates' the hardware.

Up to a point this view translates quite naturally into theological language. One can conceive of the same code surviving the death of its body, of being stored in some fashion and of being made to run on a totally different kind of hardware. Daniel Dennett offers his readers just this possibility of immortality. The biochemical basis of the brain may not be the only type of hardware capable of running a 'mind'. If the code could be transferred to some other, more permanent, kind of hardware it might become eternal. This is wholly in line with the incarnational emphasis of Christianity according to which being needs a medium of expression. St Paul's teaching on the need for spiritual bodies appropriate to their environment shows a firmer grasp of the realities than the disembodied spirit idea of much popular piety.[5] The resurrection and ascension of Christ would be interpreted as a demonstration of the transition from one mode of existence to another with the resurrection body being an intermediate but transitory stage showing to the disciples the continuity between the earthly and the heavenly. One could go on to entertain the idea of the communion of saints as a developing

[5] Strawson (1959) concludes his chapter on 'Persons' with the words, 'No doubt it is for this reason that the orthodox have wisely insisted on the resurrection of the body.' He begins his analysis of the idea of a person with the two questions: 'Why are one's states of consciousness ascribed to anything at all?' and 'Why are they ascribed to the very same thing as certain corporeal characteristics . . .?' This leads him to the conclusion that disembodied survival as an individual is ultimately no different from the cessation of experience altogether. This view of the matter fits well with the line taken here.

and intermingling of individuals with the mind of God sharing in that environment which constitutes his essential being.

   Although this scenario has its attractions it raises some
difficult questions which should, at least, make one pause.
We have already noted, by implication, that it is far from
obvious that a code, however subtle, is sufficient to account
for the total person. Penrose (1989) is one who doubts very
much whether this could be the case. But leaving that aside
our troubles are not over. If, as the theory requires, the code
which represents 'me' can be copied and stored there would
be the possibility of several identical 'clones' of 'me' existing.
But is not my experienced uniqueness an essential part of
being a person so that the existence of two versions would
render my very existence meaningless? Such questions are
entertainingly aired in Dennett's essay 'Where am I?' in
Hofstadter and Dennett (1982). Possibly no self can remain
static, so that two distinct beings would develop under different environments as with identical twins—but which of
them would be me? Then there is the question of how the
copying is done. One idea, which avoids the possibility of
multiple copies, is to think of the self as having a 'positive'
and a 'negative' aspect. As the self develops in the brain it
might induce a matching pattern in the basic 'stuff' of existence not subject to the decay of the body. Indeed the act of
living might then be more picturesquely seen as the writing
of a message on the page of eternity.

   What seems to be lacking above all in this account of
things is a fully rounded picture of what we feel ourselves to
be. This may be because we have an overblown sense of our
own importance, but then that sort of sense is rather a
remarkable thing for a dynamic stock of information to have!

   The traditional, if not wholly scriptural, way of accounting for ourselves is by reference to the soul conceived of as
some immortal essence constituting the real person. The
popular picture is of an insubstantial self linked to the body
at conception and set free by death. Such dualism is out of
favour and scarcely acknowledged in scientific circles. It

bristles with problems such as how and when the self becomes linked with the individual, whether and how it develops, what it consists of, how it interacts with the brain, and so on. To the hardline materialist all this looks like the invention of a totally unnecessary hypothesis merely to prop up outmoded religious beliefs. However, when we recognize that the confidence of Minsky, Dennett, and those like them is based on no more than the equally insecure hypothesis that the scientific account *must* be sufficient it seems that the honours are equally shared.

Dualism, or interactionism as they call it, is advocated by Popper and Eccles (1983) in their book *The Self and Its Brain*. Their two-pronged approach is from their respective disciplines of philosophy and neuroscience and leads to the conclusion that the self is not to be identified with the brain but rather interacts with it. Popper does not like asking 'what is?' questions and he does not think it useful to ask what the self is—and he certainly does not think of it as a 'substance'. Indeed, neither author gives much attention to the origin of, or, for that matter, the destiny of the soul/self. Their basic reason for espousing interactionism is the scientific one that it provides a more satisfying account of the way things are than any of the competing theories.

At one point, however, Eccles introduces a probability argument for his own supernatural origin. As the authors conclude their dialogue Eccles turns to the question of the origin of the self. Popper had taken the view that the self was an emergent phenomenon—a kind of spin-off from the highly developed brain which has a sufficiently independent existence to act on the brain. Eccles takes up this point as follows (p. 559):

My position is this. I believe that my personal uniqueness, that is my own experienced self-consciousness, is not accounted for by this emergent explanation of the coming-to-be of my own self. It is the experienced uniqueness that is not so explained. Genetic uniqueness will not do. It can be asserted that I have my experienced uniqueness because my brain is built by the genetic instructions of a quite unique genetic code, my genome with its 30,000 or so genes (Dobzhansky, personal communication) strung along the immense double helix of the human DNA with its 3.5×10^9 nucleotide pairs. It has to be recognized that with 30,000 genes there is a chance of $10^{10,000}$ against that uniqueness being achieved. That is, if my uniqueness is tied to the genetic uniqueness that built my brain, then the odds against myself existing in my experienced uniqueness are $10^{10,000}$ against.

So I am constrained to believe that there is what we might call a supernatural origin of my unique self-conscious mind or my unique selfhood or soul; and that gives rise of course to a whole new set of problems. How does my soul come to be in liaison with my brain that has an evolutionary origin? By this idea of a supernatural creation I escape from the incredible improbability that the uniqueness of my own self is genetically determined.

At first sight this argument sounds like another example of what I called the significance test argument in Bartholomew (1984: ch. 3) or what others have called the bridge-hand fallacy. It is that if some event, the chance of getting someone with my genetic composition, is exceedingly small then we can neglect the possibility of it happening by chance. The fallacy lies in the fact, already noted, that if all other possible outcomes, however many there might be, are equally improbable (or nearly so) then one *must* occur. One should therefore not be surprised to find such a rare event occurring. It is indeed highly unlikely that the individual called John Eccles should have existed but it was nevertheless certain that, given the act of conception and subsequent survival, someone had to exist in his place and it was no less likely to be him than any of the other possibilities.

However, on closer examination, I believe Eccles's argument is more subtle. His particular self-consciousness is linked to the outcome of that particular genetic combination. Why does he experience himself to be that particular individual and not someone else? If my self-consciousness is a result of my particular brain having appeared it is simply incredible that of all the possible conscious selves that might have existed I happen to be around. In essence John Eccles is saying that the emergent hypothesis makes it virtually certain that *he* would never have existed.

We might be able to avoid the fallacy by making explicit what seems to be implicit, namely that my own self-conscious mind is not so improbable—inevitable even, whereas my brain is an exceedingly improbable occurrence. This then seems to make it essential for there to have been some external involvement in the linking of the self which I experience to this particular brain.

Popper's rather modest reply is that since the emergence of life is so improbable anyway (though this might be questioned) we have nothing worthy of being called an explanation and, by the same token, we have no explanation for the emergence of the human brain. We might then be content to acknowledge the deep mystery of life and leave it at that.

Whether or not one is convinced by their case for interactionism, and we have barely scratched the surface of it, one thing at least seems very clear. We should not lightly dismiss the interactionist hypothesis despite its many difficulties especially when we remember that the burden of the opposition's case is based not on empirical evidence but on the assumption that there is nothing beyond the reach of science.

This brings us to the end of the first stage of our investigation. Up to this point our concern has been with defining the problem and describing and illustrating the approach. In the next four chapters we shall assess the strength of the evidence in a variety of fields over which the battles of belief have traditionally been fought. Inevitably, the question of God's existence takes centre stage and it is one, moreover, on which probability arguments have increasingly been brought to bear. For many Christians the Bible is the foundation of faith and yet its nature, historicity, and meaning have never been more hotly debated. Whether or not the attempt to recognize the uncertainties involved and to weigh them objectively is universally welcomed the task could hardly be more necessary. Miracles have been one of the touchstones of the debate between belief and unbelief. Although some

Christians find them something of an embarrassment and seek to move the ground of the argument elsewhere, the unbeliever shows an understandable reluctance to let go of such a potent weapon. Probability has been of the essence of much of the debate over several centuries and thus provides a good starting point for Part II.

The paranormal, treated in Chapter 5, may seem an odd bedfellow for the more central and weighty topics of the other chapters. It earns its place for two reasons. Surprising though it may seem, the heterogeneous collection of topics spanned by this term appear to have a considerable popular appeal. Inspection of the shelves of many serious bookshops will reveal that more space is devoted to 'the occult', 'mind and spirit', and suchlike than to the whole of religion and theology. Many people appear to find it promises to satisfy their hunger for the supernatural in a way that more traditional religion does not. The credibility of these beliefs bears examination if only because the thing which they and traditional religion agree on is that materialism does not provide an adequate explanation of the world. The second reason for including the paranormal is that it is much easier (though still difficult) to test its claims in a scientific manner.

Part II

4
Miracles

The subject of miracles provides a good starting point for our discussion because it has long been a matter of dispute and is beset by uncertainties of many kinds. David Hume, Charles Babbage, and C. S. Lewis are part of a long line of distinguished contributors to the debate and there is no sign of diminishing interest as the review of Keller and Keller (1969) testifies. Our first concern will be with the strength of the evidence for miracles and with the implications which they might have for the content of supernatural belief. There are secondary issues having to do with what miracles might tell us about the character of God or the divinity of Jesus and with how our prior views on these questions might affect our interpretation of the evidence. These various strands are interwoven but we shall focus throughout on the main issue.

A main plank in the Christian claim that Jesus was divine has always been, until recently, that he performed miracles. His exercise of divine power was seen as evidence of his divine nature. Latterly, what was once seen as the main strength of the apologist's case has become a considerable liability. The scientific revolution has left us deeply suspicious of anything which appears to transgress the orderly pattern of nature. Those theologians who wish to retain the miraculous as an essential element of the Christian faith have had to move from attack to defence, and often seem to be engaged in a salvage operation in which the precise nature of the happening is deliberately left obscure beneath an unconvincing theological superstructure.

Among believers there is disagreement about whether miracles could happen, whether they should happen and about whether they actually have happened. Given that there is a degree of uncertainty under all those heads it is not surprising that probability language should have been brought into play on both sides of the argument and it is this aspect which will be given special prominence in this chapter. No progress can be made unless we are clear what we mean by a miracle, so we begin with definitions.

Theological definitions of miracles usually begin (e.g. Richardson, 1950) with the meanings of the words commonly translated as miracle; power, wonder, or sign, for example. Macquarrie (1977) proposes a minimalist definition of a miracle as something which excites wonder. There is no lack of such events to judge by the efforts of the newspaper headline writers. Wonder-drugs and miracle-rescues abound and, without question, such things are real. But for our present purposes they are peripheral to the main issue because they do not call into question the scientific consensus. There is no suggestion that these things contravene the laws of nature. They usually refer to some new discovery in which the potential of nature is realized or, perhaps, to some rather remarkable coincidence as when a passing ship happens to come across a survivor of a wreck. They certainly excite wonder but they do not call for any special explanation outside the known laws of nature. Of course, there are many occurrences where this conclusion might be disputed and 'significant' coincidences provide a good example. Though it might be allowed that the event in question *could* have happened naturally the probability of it doing so is so remote as to call for some other explanation. The evaluation of such claims is clearly a probability matter and we shall return to it below.

The main kind of miracle which is relevant to us is the sort of event which appears to call for some kind of supernatural explanation. Even here the definition is not straightforward and so, to sharpen the issue, we begin with a collection of definitions.

Hume (1777), who may be said to have started it all, defines a miracle thus: 'A miracle may be accurately defined, a transgression of a law of nature by a particular volition of the Deity, or by the interposition of some invisible agent.' Lewis (1960: 7) gives what he calls a crude and popular definition: 'I use the word *Miracle* to mean an interference with nature by a supernatural power.' He then goes on to explain very clearly how the natural and the supernatural are to be distinguished for this purpose.

Swinburne (1971, 1976) gives three criteria which must be met for an event to be classed as a miracle.

1. The event must have some religious significance.
2. It should constitute a 'violation' of natural laws.
3. It should be brought about by God or gods.

Macquarrie (1977: 247) goes beyond his minimal definition as follows: 'It is believed that God is in the event in some special way, that he is the author of it, and intends to achieve some special end by it.'

The common and essential element in these definitions is that a miracle is an act by some power external to the natural world. If, therefore, something happens which cannot be explained by the natural processes of the world and which cannot be attributed to human agency then there is a prima facie case for supposing that a miracle has occurred. In practice it may be impossible to be sure because of our ignorance of the circumstances and of the scope of natural law; many everyday happenings such as satellite communication would have been clear examples of the miraculous if they could have been demonstrated two centuries ago. Nevertheless some of the events recorded in the gospels, such as the turning of the water into wine, the raising of Lazarus, or the virgin birth are, if taken at face value, so far outside the range of what is normal as to be clearly in the category of miracle.

Although the definitions set out above agree in the essential point they differ in one fundamental matter and this concerns whether a miracle involves the 'suspension' or 'breaking' of a natural law. Hume and Swinburne explicitly say that it does and in this they are expressing the popular conception and the one, moreover, which poses the greatest difficulty for the scientifically informed person. Macquarrie makes no mention of natural law and his view, expressed elsewhere in the chapter from which the definition is taken, is that no such transgressions are possible. This, of course, raises serious questions about whether many of the events recorded as miracles could actually have happened as described. Lewis likewise does not refer directly to natural law and he goes on to explain that when performing miracles God does not violate his own laws. This is a crucial point which is essential, in my view, if the idea of miracle is to be seriously entertained within the scientific world-view. We must therefore digress for a moment to examine more carefully what this involves.

Lewis's use of the word 'interference' is unfortunate in that it raises theological difficulties to which we come later. The question for the moment is whether it makes any sort of sense to think of multiplying loaves and fishes or turning water into wine as acts which could be accomplished by divine power within the framework of natural law.

First we follow Lewis in noting that events can be 'explained' in one of two ways. First they may be natural outcomes of some physical process which can be understood in terms of known laws. For example, the weather today can be explained, in principle at least, by the preceding state of the atmosphere and so forth; the growth of a plant by conditions of soil, temperature, and such like. There is nothing miraculous about the occurrence of a thunderstorm or the blooming of a pansy. Secondly there are also happenings in the world which cannot be explained in this way but which are certainly not miracles either. Left to its own devices nature could not assemble the materials required to make a motor car and move the resulting ton of metal from Manchester to Perth. It requires human 'intervention'. If the wallet which we left on the shop counter turns up later through the letter box we may regard it as a miracle in the minimalist sense but it certainly does not require us to invoke the divine hand. We assume that it is there because some person carried it there. The law of gravity is not broken when the wallet is lifted from the mat and placed in our pocket. When seeking an explanation for any event we naturally apportion responsibility between the nature of things as science reveals them and the participation of human agents. In some cases, as in changes in climate (as opposed to weather), the interaction between the two may be subtle and difficult to disentangle but that they provide a full explanation is not in doubt.

Lewis's contention is that there is a third agency at work in the world and hence that there may be some events which would not, and, perhaps, could not, have occurred without the involvement of what he would call supernatural agency. One could think of this agent as standing back from the world for most of the time and occasionally intervening to achieve some particular end or to give some clear 'sign' of his presence. It is this notion of occasional interference which, to many, is theologically objectionable. In any case it is more plausible to think of God as continually acting in a manner which interacts with the two other agencies without 'overriding' or 'transgressing' either of them. One might expect the divine agency to be largely, perhaps exclusively, acting in association with human agents but, in any case, it would be rather rarely that the divine component would be so dominant that there would be clear evidence of his involvement.

To illustrate the point let us imagine ourselves to be alone on a desert island. From time to time things will appear on the beach. Often they will be there because the tide and the wind have washed them onto the shore. No other agency has to be invoked to explain their presence. Occasionally it may be more difficult to believe that they have been simply washed up; they may be too heavy to float or too far above high-water mark. Then we might conclude that a bird had dropped them or some animal living on the island had carried them there. Marks might appear in the sand which we would put down to the action of pebbles or creatures dragging sticks along the beach. They might be explained either by the action of the sea alone or by a combination of sea, wind and bird activity. Suppose now that one day we find the embers of a fire. Could it be that sticks have come together at this point by known agencies and could a piece of broken glass have also happened to be there in such a position that it focused the rays of the sun to ignite the wood? All of this is possible but a rather more plausible explanation is that a third agent has been at work who possesses knowledge of how to make fire and has the means to do it. If there really is another person on the island some of the traces of his presence will be ambiguous; bones, feathers, fruit stones, for example, could all be explained without recourse to belief in this person's existence. Others, like the remains of the fire, will be harder to explain away. Finally there may be some signs so clear as to compel belief in the second person; a message written in the sand, for example.

ARE MIRACLES POSSIBLE?

We now have a rough idea of how the activity of an unobserved agent might give rise to otherwise unexplainable events without the need to suppose that any natural law has been broken. In one sense such events are no more miraculous than are the things that we do ourselves. What gives them their special character is that the divine component of the action is unusually conspicuous. The question now is whether such a view can be sustained in the face of the arguments against miracles. These fall into three categories as follows.

1. Theological objections of the kind which say that though God might be able to perform miracles it

would be inconsistent with his nature, as deduced from other sources.

2. Scientific objections which claim that some alleged miracles, at least, do require the breaking of physical laws and so conflict with the scientific view that such laws are immutable.

3. Historical objections which turn on whether the events in question actually happened. These will usually centre on the fallibility of human testimony and its transmission.

The first two of these have to do with the prior probability of a miracle. They say, essentially, that there are other things which we know about the constitution of the world which rule out the possibility of the miraculous. On the theological side it is sometimes held that miracles would be evidence of poor design. If a god has to intervene to keep things on the rails then this shows a lack of foresight on his part. He should have anticipated the difficulty and provided for it at the design stage. His failure to do this is a contradiction of his supposed nature. In other words the notion of an all-powerful, all-seeing God who overlooks flaws in the system which have to be corrected by miracles is self-contradictory. To those who view matters from this angle there seems something rather out-of-character about *ad hoc* tinkering with the system which for the most part runs with remarkable smoothness. Put in yet another way it is very improbable that God, if he exists, would act in that way.

A somewhat similar objection is that the idea of intervention from outside belongs to a mythological outlook which has now been superseded. 'It is objectionable', says Macquarrie (1977: 249), 'because it goes back to the mythological outlook and expects God to manifest himself and prove himself in some extraordinary sensible phenomena.' That this is not his way is shown, for example, by the refusal of Jesus to throw himself from the pinnacle of the temple and by his obvious reluctance to allow his miracles to be publicized. Again, the argument is that miracles would be out of character.

The maintenance of either of these positions clearly requires some deft theological footwork. The existence and character of God have to be established independently of any particular acts by reference to knowledge of a more general kind. One has to explain why Jesus would have been concerned with limiting publicity about the miracles if there had been nothing to publicize in the first place. And following Macquarrie, who holds that a purely natural event can be a miracle in the sense of having a revelatory quality, one has to identify how that revelatory quality is to be distinguished from other interpretations which might be put upon events.

This is not to say that a coherent account cannot be given along these lines but we must be careful to avoid the logical fallacy of forming our concept of God on the supposition that miracles do not happen and then using that conclusion to deduce that they cannot happen. The probability that God is the kind of being who would not wish to perform miracles is of crucial importance to the theological objection and this must first be established from fallible data. An essentially similar point was made by C. S. Lewis in the context of scientific objections but with less justification as we shall now see.

On the scientific side the difficulty is simply stated. Science shows the world to be an orderly place in which everything can, in principle, be explained in terms of laws of nature. Wine may turn into vinegar under certain circumstances but there is no conceivable way in which water alone could be turned into wine. To accept such happenings as factual would undermine the whole basis of science by showing that the laws were not really laws at all. Given the tremendous success of the scientific enterprise and the countless number of occasions on which its predictions have been borne out it would be irrational to entertain the possibility of miracles. If the Gospel miracles are approached from this standpoint three conclusions are possible: that some natural happening has been embellished or exaggerated to the point where it appears miraculous; that the account is fictitious, or, that though there may be no explanation within our present knowledge, there must be some natural explanation which will, no doubt, come to light as scientific knowledge grows. Whichever turns out to be the case the inviolability of the laws of nature must be accepted as the bedrock of truth.

Historical objections are less concerned with what is a priori possible than with what beliefs can be justified by the data to hand. If it can be established that at least one miraculous event has occurred then the question of the possibility of miracles is settled. The event becomes a fact and if it does not fit into the scientific or theological schemes of things then that is too bad. But the trouble is that it is very difficult, if not impossible, to establish whether such an event really has occurred. There are two major obstacles. First, something may actually have happened but only appeared to be miraculous because of our limited understanding. Children may be persuaded that the magician really does bring rabbits out of thin air but adults 'know' that what appears to be magic is merely an illusion even though they may have no idea of how it is done. Our ancestors would have found it quite inconceivable that we should be able to speak to our friends on the other side of the world. Since there is no reason to suppose that our knowledge of how the world works is complete there is always the possibility that some natural event will appear miraculous to us.

The second obstacle is that of human testimony. Unless we actually witness them ourselves we only know about the many alleged miraculous events because someone reported them. Yet we know that eye-witnesses are unreliable; that stories, especially unusual ones, become embroidered and distorted as they are passed on, and that some reported events are pure fabrications designed to reassure or mislead. Whether the motives are good or bad the scope for corruption is almost unlimited. For this reason most human organizations have elaborate procedures for keeping records of their meetings and for ensuring that they are agreed by the members present. Can we then say anything about the probability that a reported miracle really happened?

We shall now pursue the scientific and historical objections through the arguments of three of the principal protagonists, Hume, Babbage, and Lewis.

PROBABILITY ARGUMENTS FOR AND AGAINST MIRACLES

For someone like C. S. Lewis who insisted that miracles do not involve breaking laws of nature the scientific dogma is no threat. It is true that there may be an acute difficulty about showing how the miracle in question could have been engineered within the scientific framework but that is a different matter. Nevertheless in his chapter 'On Probability' in his book *Miracles* (Lewis, 1960) he produces an argument which purports to show that the scientific approach cannot, in fact, exclude miracles. He starts with the question of how we know that nature is uniform and answers it by saying that we can have no such knowledge. For however often the same linking of cause and effect has been witnessed the number of cases that we and the rest of humanity, past and present, have observed is but a tiny fraction of the total occurrences. On the evidence of experience alone we cannot therefore deduce with certainty that nature always behaves in the same way. That part of the argument is familiar and unexceptionable but the trouble arises at the next step when he asks 'Can we say that uniformity is at any rate very probable?' (p. 106). Common sense would certainly suggest that we can say precisely that and all of us certainly behave as if that is what we believe. But Lewis claims that we can make no probability statement of any kind about the uniformity of nature. The reason for this, he claims, is that the whole idea of probability depends on the principle being true and thus without assuming it to be true in the first place no probability calculation is possible. The crux of his argument lies in the necessity of assuming that the laws operate in the same way for those events that we do not observe as for those that we do.

Or, in the case of the familiar example, the proportion of tosses of a coin falling tails can only be interpreted as a measure of the probability that any other tossing will result in a tail if we assume that the world of the projected toss is the same in all essentials as the one which has yielded the past experience. This argument is sound as far as it goes but the question is whether there is any empirical evidence for believing in uniformity. Lewis claimed that there was not and could not be any such evidence.

We can show the fallacy in his argument by taking Lewis's own example. 'Unless Nature always goes on in the same way, the fact that a thing had happened ten million times would not make it a whit more probable that it would happen again' (p. 106). Imagine that we ask the question after the first five million or so occurrences which, one would have thought, would be enough to justify us at least in entertaining the hypothesis that it will always occur. Suppose we then proceed to observe the next few million occasions. Each further occurrence provides a test of the hypothesis that nature is uniform in regard to this event. By the ten millionth occurrence the hypothesis would have been put to the test several million more times and each time it would have been vindicated. This adds up to a very considerable weight of evidence in favour of uniformity. The translation of this into probability language is an example of an argument going back to Laplace where his so-called 'Law of Succession' was used to justify belief that the sun will rise tomorrow given its unfailing record of rising in the past.

There is a quite different probability justification for believing in the uniformity of nature due to Harrod (1956). This does not seem to have been widely recognized but it aims to show that if we observe any uniformity continuing for a period of time then there is a frequency justification for believing that it will continue for a short time longer with high probability. Any uniformity which has endured for as long as the regularities of nature is thus virtually certain to continue for some time to come. Whichever line we follow the uniformity of nature is not therefore an unsupported assumption necessary for calculating any probability but something which is inferred from observation. Lewis anticipates this kind of objection by saying that 'It is no good saying "Each fresh experience confirms our belief in uniformity and therefore we reasonably expect that it will always be confirmed" for that argument works only on the assumption that the future will resemble the past' (p. 106). But our experience *has* provided us with evidence that what has happened in the past will happen in the future, for each occurrence is an example of just that. Lewis's contention therefore falls.[1]

Of course Lewis was well aware of the fact that we do believe in the uniformity of nature and he did not wish to dispute that there are good grounds for it. The question is 'What are those grounds?' if they are not to be found within the sort of probability theory which he has just ruled out of court. His answer is that our confidence is derived from an 'innate sense of the fitness of things' and that this derives from the fact that it reflects the character of the God who has made us and all things. If the natural is all there is there would be no such justification. Indeed the whole scientific enterprise presupposes just such a metaphysic. This is strongly reminiscent of the alogical probability of Tennant (1930) which is real and rational though not subject to quantification and which forms the basis of science. Lewis himself quotes Sir Arthur Eddington on the same theme. This sort of probability is very much akin to trust or faith as those terms are used in religious belief. It is a commitment to a particular approach to nature which derives its strength from the way it fits with something inside us. In taking this view Lewis aligns himself with those who think that what they often call mathematical probability is insufficient to cope with all kinds of uncertainty. This is an arguable position but I am unaware of any

---

[1] It can be argued that what has happened is equally consistent with the hypothesis that nature has been uniform up to the present but will cease to be from now on. However, unless one has some ground for claiming that the present moment is special in some way it seems to me that Harrod's argument works.

demonstration that there are uncertain events which cannot be fitted into one or other of the categories we considered in Chapter 2.

All of this leads Lewis to the conclusion that nature is uniform and reliable almost all the time and this reflects its origin in rational spirit. But this does not exclude the possibility that from time to time God will act outside this framework but entirely 'in character'. In assessing the truth of a miracle we therefore apply the same test as we do in science by appeal to the innate sense of the fitness of things.

It seems to me that there is a fundamental ambiguity about Lewis's position. On the one hand he asserts, categorically, that a miracle does not require any breaking of natural law. On the other he is at pains to establish that nature is not absolutely uniform, which is tantamount to saying that occasionally nature does not conform to past regularities. In effect he defines a law to be an 'almost but not quite always' kind of thing which is not what most of us think of when we use the word. But if he is saying that God can do things within the framework of law which would not be possible without his intervention then he does not need to show that exceptions can occur. My raising of a glass in apparent defiance of the law of gravity involves no more a breaking of that law than would a miracle such as stilling a storm. What makes such things miracles is not their 'going against nature' but the fact that they are acts of God. But do such things actually happen?

The question of whether miracles have actually happened brings us into an area of debate with a long pedigree going back to David Hume's celebrated essay on miracles. His approach was not to directly consider the chance that the miracle occurred but to compare it with the chance that nature had gone out of its course. It was a matter, he thought, of weighing one unusual event against another, 'whether it be more probable, that this person should either deceive or be deceived, or that the fact which he relates should really have happened' (p. 116). In Hume's judgement our

experience of the regularity of nature was so securely
founded as to make the chance of the miracle virtually zero.
In contrast, the fallibility of witnesses is such that the chance
of that event being incorrectly reported, for whatever reason,
is far from negligible. Faced with this choice Hume was in no
doubt that we should opt for error on the part of the witness
and conclude that miracles do not occur.

Thomas Paine puts the matter somewhat more colour-
fully. 'Is it more probable that nature should go out of her
course, or that a man should tell a lie? We have never seen in
our time, nature go out of her course, but we have good reason to believe that millions of lies have been told in the same
time; it is therefore millions to one that the reporter of a miracle tells a lie' (Paine, 1795: 55). Here we recognize the kind
of argument which we anticipated in Chapter 2. Judgements
are being made on the basis of the relative values of probabilities but it remains to be seen whether the rules are being
correctly applied.

Hume, in fact, went further by claiming that 'no human
testimony can have such force as to prove a miracle' (p. 127).
As we shall shortly see it is not easy to give a precise interpretation of this statement but Hume clearly thought that the
cumulative effect of the testimony of many individuals
would still not be sufficient to outweigh the miniscule probability of the miracle really having happened. This is the
point at which probability arguments can be brought to bear
to some effect and many attempts have been made. One of
the first was by the Revd Dr Richard Price who produced an
argument which, though ingenious, has not found favour
with modern commentators.[2] A more successful attempt was
made by Charles Babbage, the father of the computer.

Before looking at what he did let us try to get an intuitive
idea of what is at issue. We generally feel that the credibility
of a reported event is increased if several people tell the same
story. As Archbishop Richard Whately remarked, 'That

---

[2] See e.g. Owen (1987) and Dawid and Gillies (1989).

when many coincide in their testimony (where no previous concert can have taken place) the probability resulting from the concurrence does not rest on the veracity of each considered separately, but on the improbability of such agreement taking place by chance.'[3] The case for believing in the resurrection is widely seen to be strengthened by the fact that the Gospels report many 'sightings'. But we have to be careful as was Richard Whately when he added the caveat, 'where no previous concert can have taken place'. It is not unknown for witnesses to agree among themselves to tell the same story and then their combined testimony cuts no ice at all. Indeed the very similarity of their stories may alert us to the possibility of prior collusion and so reduce rather than increase the probability of their story. This illustrates why we were at pains to emphasize the importance of the independence of events when calculating the probability of a conjunction. In the present context some would claim that independence of testimony is impossible because witnesses share a common culture which will, to some extent at least, colour what they see and report. Professor T. Lewis[4] nicely illustrates this point from the New England witch trials of the seventeenth century. Four individuals supported the statement of one Samuel Aves: 'I do Testifie that I have seen Margaret Rule in her Afflictions from the Invisible World, lifted up from her Bed . . . by an Invisible force . . . when . . . a strong Person hath thrown his whole weight across her to pull her down.' Though one may be intrigued and puzzled by the motives and mental processes which underlay such testimonies few of us would think that the addition of extra names in support of the statement does anything further to convince us that Margaret Rule did in fact levitate from her bed.

This brings us back to the question dealt with in Chapter 2 of how the testimony of witnesses may be 'added up'. How

---

[3] Quoted in Badham and Badham (1982) who, in turn, refer to the preface of R. Crookhall, *What Happens When You Die?* (1978).

[4] In a contribution to the discussion of Bartholomew (1988).

many independent witnesses would be needed to convince us that a flying saucer had hovered over Wimbledon Common? We need to know whether six witnesses are twice as valuable, in some sense, as three witnesses. If witnesses disagree how do we weigh the testimony of one group against another?

As we know, questions of this kind can be answered by elementary probability calculations though we should have no illusions about what can be achieved in practice. In reality there are so many complications that it is virtually impossible to apply the results to particular cases. Nevertheless we can establish a few general ground rules which will help to inform our judgement. It is well to remind ourselves that human judgement of probabilities in these circumstances is particularly prone to error.

Charles Babbage wished to refute Hume's claim that no amount of human testimony could overcome the sheer improbability of a miracle. He did this by showing that however improbable a miracle was judged to be, one could always specify a finite number of independent witnesses whose cumulative testimony would outweigh the extreme improbability of the miracle occurring. One difficulty he faced was to translate Hume's assertion into terms sufficiently precise to enable the calculation to begin. I set out the options he considered in Bartholomew (1988) but it will serve our present purposes to consider the third and simplest. This concerns the probability that n witnesses will concur in a falsehood. The argument is that we should compare two small probabilities, the one relating to the improbability that the miracle actually occurred and the other to the chance that the n independent witnesses have colluded in reporting falsely that the miracle had occurred. Even though both probabilities will be very small one of the possibilities must be true and so, Babbage would have argued, we should opt for the one which is least unlikely. Suppose that any witness tells the truth with probability p; it follows that any one will lie with probability $(1 - p)$. We must now work out the probability that all *n* individuals will be lying. If they report without any prior collusion the chance that they will agree in this falsehood is $(1 - p)^n$. The size of this probability depends on both *p* and *n* in a manner which is illustrated by Table 1.

TABLE 1. *Chance that n independent witnesses will concur in a falsehood*

p/n	2	4	8	16	64
1/10	.81	.66	.43	.19	.001
1/4	.56	.32	.10	.01	.000
1/2	.25	.06	.004	.000	.000
3/4	.06	.004	.000	.000	.000
9/10	.01	.000	.000	.000	.000

It is immediately clear that the chance in question diminishes rapidly with *n* and, as we might guess from the table, can be made as small as we please, for any *p*, by making the number of witnesses large enough. This is the point which lies at the root of Babbage's quarrel with Hume. Hume had claimed (so Babbage thought) that no matter how large *n* was the chance of concurring in a falsehood would always exceed the chance that the miracle really happened. Unless the miracle is judged to be absolutely impossible, so that its probability is precisely zero, this is not true. Furthermore, Babbage was able to show that even if the chance of a miracle was very small indeed *n* would not need to be particularly large. To illustrate the point he supposed that $p = 10/11$ and for rather obscure reasons chose the chance of a miracle occurring as 1 in 10^{12} (one in a million million). In that case it is easy to show that only 12 independent witnesses would be required. Hume's argument is thus refuted, but before drawing the conclusion that the occurrence of miracles can be rendered credible by this line of reasoning we need to look at the Babbage argument more carefully. (The other two interpretations which Babbage put on Hume's argument lead to a similar conclusion.)

One obvious weakness is that we have assumed that all witnesses are equally truthful; in practice some will be more truthful than others. It turns out that allowing p to vary from one individual to another does not affect the essentials of the analysis; it is still true that by making the number of witnesses sufficiently large the probability of them all concurring in a falsehood can be made as small as we please.

A much more serious objection is that, in practice, witnesses are unlikely to be independent. Even if there is no overt collusion there may well be common cultural or social ties between witnesses which lead them to react in a similar way. Will our conclusion stand up in these circumstances? Not necessarily, as is easily seen by taking the extreme case where there is supposed to be a total dependence between witnesses; what one says, they all say. The testimony of sixteen is then worth no more than one and sheer numbers count for nothing. In general the answer depends on the degree of dependence but providing that it is not certain that an individual is lying, given that the others are lying, an increase in the number of witnesses will decrease the chance that they will all concur in the falsehood. The trouble is that the number may have to be very large for the chance to become negligible. Put rather imprecisely, there has to be a good measure of independence among a fair number of witnesses for their cumulative testimony to be overwhelming.

But there are further objections to the argument. The probability that a person tells the truth may well depend on what actually happened. A witness of a real miracle might be deterred from reporting it as such because he 'could not believe his eyes' or for fear of ridicule. Equally, wishful thinking might easily lead someone to see a miracle where none existed. Further, since a miracle is considerably more newsworthy than any unremarkable event, those who come forward with such reports may well be less trustworthy and so calculations like Babbage's could easily overestimate the value of their combined testimony.

Rosenbaum[5] pointed out that Babbage's argument can be turned round by supposing that n witnesses concur in reporting the alleged miracle in terms which clearly indicate that it was not a miracle. Since the prior probability that it was not a miracle is presumably much higher then the number of independent witnesses required to establish its credibility is much less. A few people arguing that it was not would thus outweigh a larger number on the other side.

Notwithstanding all of these qualifications it is pertinent to ask whether, in the light of our earlier discussion of principles, Hume, Paine, and Babbage were comparing the right probabilities. So far we have taken it for granted that they were. Let us therefore look at the problem from first principles. There are two complementary hypotheses between which we wish to choose: either there exists a God capable of performing miracles or there does not. In the latter case the probability of anything that happens must be calculated on the supposition that the laws of nature alone are operative. Our guide as to what to do is Bayes' rule, according to which we would want to calculate the posterior probability of each hypothesis and make that our basis of judgement. If God exists this posterior probability is proportional to the product of our prior probability that he exists and the likelihood, which in this case is the probability that n witnesses agree in reporting the miraculous event. The former (the probability of a miraculous event having occurred) is allowed by both sides to be very small. The likelihood is presumably very close to, if not actually equal to, one, since if God performs the miracle there would be no reason to question the testimony of witnesses to that effect. The posterior probability in this case is therefore, for all practical purposes, equal to the prior probability. The posterior probability of the alternative hypothesis—that a miracle-performing God does not exist—is effectively equal to the likelihood because, given that the prior probability that God exists is very small, the

---

[5] In a contribution to the discussion of Bartholomew (1988).

alternative must have probability very close to one. The likelihood is the probability that the witnesses concur in a falsehood since on this hypothesis the miracle could not have
occurred and so the witnesses could not be telling the truth.
The comparison which Babbage chose to make was therefore
the right one. It should be added that this Bayesian justification of Babbage's argument is not the one given in several
modern treatments of the subject[6] though all come to much
the same conclusion. It does seem to me the most natural and
it agrees in essentials with that of Dawid and Gillies (1989).

All of this may leave the reader wondering whether any
progress can be made at all on this front. It appears that in
striving to bring more precision and rigour into the assessment of historical evidence (albeit of a rather limited kind)
we have merely exposed our reasoning to criticism at every
turn. This is true and to be welcomed. A main purpose of this
book is to demonstrate how vulnerable is the manner of
much of our informal reasoning on uncertain matters. But
the conclusion to be drawn is not entirely negative. It is true
that under very general circumstances, which can be
specified, the credibility of a reported event does increase
with the number of witnesses and that if we can satisfy ourselves that there is a reasonable degree of independence
between them the cumulative value of their testimony
mounts up very rapidly indeed. It follows that in assessing the
value of combined testimony it is of crucial importance to
investigate common influences or interactions between individuals. Even more important, perhaps, is the fact that
sufficient testimony of high quality can outweigh very strong
disbelief in the possibility of miracles. The other main conclusion from our analysis is that much depends on the prior
probability. This, as we shall see later, turns out to be the
Achilles' heel of so many attempts to express beliefs about
God in terms of probabilities and we defer further consideration of the matter.

---

[6] For example, Sobel (1987) and Owen (1987).

We cannot claim that the credibility of the multitude of alleged miracles has been tested according to the logic of probability but we have delineated the ground on which a case must be made. There are two areas on which there is more to be said. As far as miracles recorded in the Bible are concerned there are questions about the general reliability of the text and this topic will be taken up in Chapter 7.

Secondly there are the phenomena usually considered under the heading of the paranormal. Strictly speaking the paranormal does not fall within the field of miracle as we have defined it but it does concern events which appear to be beyond the reach of science and therefore is of direct relevance to the existence of a supernatural dimension of reality. We shall look at this area in the following chapter.

COINCIDENCES

A Mr George D. Bryson happened to be passing through Louisville, Kentucky, for the first time in his life and registered at a local hotel. As a joke he asked whether there was any mail for him and was surprised to be given a letter addressed to Mr George D. Bryson, Room 307, the room that he had just been given. It turned out that the previous occupant of the room had exactly the same name. Both Mr Brysons eventually met and were able to convince one another that they both existed. Coincidences like this reported by Weaver (1963) undoubtedly occur but do they call for any special explanation? Are they in any sense miracles? Clearly they do not contravene any law of nature so there is no question of a conflict with science and so in that sense, at least, they are not miracles. But are they so improbable that some agency outside the normal working of nature must be invoked to explain them?

Of a rather different kind is the following coincidence reported by Koestler (1972) and retold by Inglis (1990) relating to a young architect who in 1971 had narrowly escaped death when attempting suicide by throwing himself in front of a London underground train. It turned out that a passenger on the train had pulled the emergency handle just in time to avert the disaster. Attempts at suicide in this manner occur from time to time and so do false alarms with the emergency system. (A passenger on the train could not possibly see what was happening in front of the train.) As Koestler's informant remarked, 'If one had precise figures for suicides by this method at this station, the incidence of "false alarm" calls by passengers etc, etc, a calculation of statistical probability could be made, but one supposes that the chances are infinitesimally small.' Can one argue in this case that because the conjunction of the two events was so highly unlikely to have occurred by chance that some other agent must have been at work? Did some external being or force act at that moment to stop the train through the agency of the passenger who operated the braking system? The short answer, of course, is that we do not and, perhaps, cannot know. But if it could be shown that such events occurred more frequently then one would expect 'by chance' there would be good grounds for believing that there was something 'going on'. While Koestler was aware that such evidence was needed (and was not available) he was not deterred from speculating that meaningful coincidences as he would call them arose from what, following Jung, Kammerer, and others, he called an a-causal principle. That is, coincidental events can be linked in some manner which lies outside the world of cause and effect with which science deals.

Coincidences like these are by no means unusual though usually they are less dramatic. Inglis (1990) lists many such, ranging from the trite to the truly remarkable. The question for us is whether such happenings can be accommodated within the scientific world-view and, if not, whether they are indicative of an unseen hand at work. On the face of it 'significant' coincidences such as the train incident appear to be ideal candidates for miracles in the sense that C. S. Lewis defined them for they seem to point to the hand of a divine agent operating within the framework of natural law. The Bryson coincidence does not seem to carry any particular meaning and Weaver himself had no doubt that it was just one of those things which are bound to happen sooner or later. In order to get our thinking clear it may help to begin with the definition with which Diaconis and Mosteller (1989) begin their discussion of coincidences.

A coincidence is a surprising concurrence of events, perceived as meaningfully related, with no apparent causal connection.

Notice the inclusion of the phrase 'meaningfully related' which sharpens the focus to those events which might call for some extra-scientific explanation. These authors go on to discuss a number of reasons why such concurrences might not be so surprising after all. These fall broadly into two categories which we might call the psychological and the mathematical. In the former the coincidence lies in the eye of the beholder, so to speak, and in the latter in the nature of the events themselves.

Diaconis and Mosteller quote results showing how we can easily be misled into attaching undue significance to our experiences. For example, things which happen to ourselves seem far more surprising than those that happen to others. Our memories are very selective and things are more likely to be recalled from memory if they match something in present experience. Coming across a new word or idea a second time shortly after meeting it for the first time is a familiar enough experience. A day or two after talking in conversation about the French revolutionary calendar based on ten months I saw an article about it in a newspaper. Many other less interesting coincidences doubtless pass unnoticed. Even though it is usually impossible to calculate numerical odds for such happenings we should be aware that psychological factors will tend to make them seem more remarkable than they really are.

On the mathematical side a similar conclusion applies. In

Chapter 2, for example, we saw how the coincidence of two people in a room having a common birthday was much more probable than most of us suppose. A whole class of such things may be subsumed under what Diaconis and Mosteller dub 'the law of truly large numbers'. This states that in a sufficiently large population any outrageous thing is likely to happen. They point out that if a coincidence happens to one person in a million each day then in a country with a population of 250 million we should expect 250 occurrences a day and close to 100,000 a year.

All of this should make us wary of attributing remarkable coincidences to the hand of God. Indeed, if, as we argued earlier, miracles are part of God's normal activity taking place within the framework of natural law they may rarely stand out from the normal run of events. However, there is one further point to be made. We have implicitly adopted the view that the hand of God should not be invoked as an explanation if what has happened can be perfectly well explained without it. This may be a sound rational principle but Diaconis and Mosteller (1989) give an example from the work of the psychologist B. F. Skinner which should give us pause for thought. The question is, 'Did Shakespeare intentionally use alliteration when he wrote poetry?' They quote the line 'full fathom five thy father lies' as evidence that the answer is obvious. But Skinner showed that in the case of the 's' sound there is no need to invoke intentionality on the author's part. He counted the number of times that sound occurred in each line of the sonnets and compared the resulting frequency distribution with what it would have been if Shakespeare had been totally unconcerned with alliteration. The two were in close agreement! The proper conclusion is not that Shakespeare did not intentionally use alliteration but that in the corpus of his poetry it does not occur often enough to be detectable through the variation in his normal usage.

The conclusion to be drawn from this discussion of coincidences is clear and simple. God may very well be at work in some of the events which we call coincidences and if so they might properly be called miracles. However it is very unlikely that we would be able to demonstrate that this was so by probability arguments. The enormous variety of such happenings and the vast amount of time and effort needed to collect the necessary data put it beyond reach.

Christians would in any case be well advised to tread cautiously in this area. Many apparently miraculous happenings of a coincidental kind raise serious questions about the character of the agent who, it is alleged, causes them. Suppose God had wished to save the architect who jumped into the path of the train. Are we to suppose that he did not foresee what was going to happen and forestall the act in some less dramatic way? Why was this man singled out from the many others who succeed in their attempts? No doubt answers can be found to such questions but the theological objections to their being regarded as miracles may be at least as great as those derived from science or probability.

Before we leave the subject of coincidences there is one closely related kind of event in which believers have a special interest. This concerns alleged answers to prayer.[7] If someone prays for the healing of another and if at that time a change in the patient's condition occurs it is natural to conclude that the prayer was instrumental in effecting the cure. If it was not, then the coincidence of the two events in time is very remarkable. Now such coincidences have occurred very often in the realm of healing and elsewhere. Archbishop William Temple's reported remark that 'When I pray coincidences happen; when I don't, they don't', may not be based on the counting of cases but does reflect a common

---

[7] The notion of coincidence is analysed from a philosophical point of view by Owens (1992). According to him a coincidence arises when the events involved result from independent causal chains. The separate events thus have causes but, because of the independence, there is no *explanation* for their coincidence. In the cases of interest to us there is an *apparent* dependence between the causal chains involved—due to God's alleged action—and we are concerned with whether probability arguments can help us to determine whether it is real. One of the examples used by Owens in his analysis of the issue concerns answers to prayer.

experience. It is worth asking whether the reality of answers to prayer of this kind can be given statistical support. Galton (1872) conducted a retrospective study on prayer for long life. He noted that royalty have their length of life prayed for more often than others of similar socio-economic status yet on the whole their lives seemed to have been noticeably shorter (more recent data might not support this). Barnard described[8] a small experiment in which he had participated to test the efficacy of prayer for healing. Twelve matched pairs of patients were obtained and one of each pair was prayed for by a group willing to pray for the speedy recovery of a named person not directly acquainted with the group. The cases were taken sequentially and the trial was 'double blind' (meaning that neither patients nor their carers knew who was being prayed for). The first six responded to prayer, the next five did not and the last was inconclusive. Barnard concluded that if prayer had any effect it was likely to be small though he noted that his results had no bearing on the case where the person prayed for is directly known to persons praying. It is clearly possible in principle to design such experiments and, with difficulty, to carry them out in practice. However, a moment's thought will show how difficult it is to interpret the results. Suppose first that the result is entirely negative. The believer will argue that the fact that the exercise is an experiment vitiates the results. 'You are not to put the Lord your God to the test' (Luke 4: 12) would be sufficient to refute the results. God could not be expected to behave 'normally' if he was being put on trial. Next, consider the position when the result of the experiment was strongly positive in that healing always followed prayer. This would be more consistent with some so far undiscovered natural law or a puppet-style God than with a free agent. The outcome most favourable to divine involvement would perhaps be a better than chance outcome but one falling short of automatic response. Once again we see that there is a subtlety to

---

[8] In a contribution to the discussion of Bartholomew (1988). Further references and comment will be found in Kruskal (1988).

these questions which is rarely noticed at the superficial level at which such arguments are usually conducted.

No discussion of miracles would be complete, for Christians at least, which overlooked what they see as the two central acts of God in the world. If the divine nature and bodily resurrection of Jesus were firmly established most of the problems of the lesser miracles would seem trivial by comparison. The chief problem there is in establishing the prior credibility.

INCARNATION AND RESURRECTION

These two supreme miracles continue to be the subject of vigorous debate especially within the Christian community. A recent treatment by Montefiore (1992) sets out the evidence in an accessible way and uses probability language in assessing it. For example, when dealing with the view that the two events are mythical with no historical foundation (p. 153), Montefiore recognizes that neither proof nor disproof is possible in such cases but claims that the mythical interpretation can be shown to be improbable. However this may be, the evidence which he considers is concerned with what we called the 'likelihood' part of the calculation whereas the crux of the matter here, it seems to me, concerns the prior probability. It is the sheer unbelievability, as it seems, of these two claims which is the great stumbling block on the road to belief. The world as we know it appears to allow no room for such things to happen. Some people, such as Dawkins, are amazed that anything so local as the happenings concerning a man in Palestine two thousand years ago should have the cosmic significance claimed for them by Christian apologists. For such critics the wide sweep of the history of nature with its awe-inspiring beauty and order make it very hard to see why so much importance should be attached to a single historical oddity. And yet it is the very particularity of the incarnation which the Christian most wishes to defend. If Jesus was an ordinary man conceived in the usual way and dying a criminal's death one must have sympathy with the critic who fails to see why this particular life should be singled out as the key to the interpretation of the cosmos. If one were told that after his death his followers became convinced that he was, in some sense alive, even though his bones mouldered in the earth, the apologist's task is still an uphill one. The problem lies in the difficulty of explaining how the supernatural realm relates to the natural. Those who, by abandoning the supernatural elements of the incarnation and resurrection, believe that they have freed the doctrines from scientific criticism may, in reality, be laying up further trouble by making it difficult to justify attaching any ultimate significance to the life of Jesus. But is the alternative of giving a more literal interpretation to these central events a serious option? Does it not fly in the face of all that we know about the world and how it works? It is only after we have established the credibility of these events as historical happenings, in some sense, that we can follow Montefiore in weighing the evidence about whether they actually happened. It is on the prior credibility aspect that we shall therefore concentrate.

I think that the virgin birth and the bodily resurrection have to be considered individually and we take them in turn. Unlike the resurrection the conception of Jesus is not an event which could have been readily verified by observers had they been present. In principle, perhaps, one could imagine a genetic analysis of some kind which might have ruled out a human father but that, of itself, would not imply divine parentage. Furthermore, even if the story of the annunciation is taken in its most literal sense there is still the historical impossibility of verifying what was actually said or meant. The most we can do is to consider what physical happening could have occurred which would justify the phrase 'conceived by the Holy Ghost'. In this case it seems better to start at the other end. This was a doctrine formulated in retrospect by people who had become convinced that Jesus was more than human. They believed that God had come among them in the person of Jesus and they must, inevitably, have asked themselves what that implied about his origins. Since the rest of us depend for what we are on our parents it would have seemed obvious that God must have been involved in the genesis of this particular person. It was beyond question that Mary was his mother and therefore God's role must have been on the father's side. Since God acts in the world through the person of the Holy Spirit, he must have been the means through which the divine life entered the human stream.

The facts of the case, so far as they are available to us, are that a remarkable individual lived who behaved in such an unusual way that those close to him believed that he was divine. These facts depend, of course, on fallible human testimony but they are well attested and there is nothing implausible about them at the descriptive level. The inference drawn from the facts by the early Christians was that the Holy Spirit played the role of father in his conception. They did this without the knowledge which we now have about the details of procreation but there was nothing in the doctrine as they formulated it which went against their understanding of how these things happen.

The question for modern Christians is twofold. Were the early Christians right in their belief that there was more to Jesus than could be accounted for in human terms? And, if so, was their 'biological' explanation a correct and complete one?

The answer to the first question is closely tied up with the other alleged supernatural happening to which we shall shortly come. It also depends on the credence we give to accounts of miracles and the life-changing encounter to which many then and since have testified. Let us, for the moment, accept that this part of the case is made and that the first question can be answered affirmatively. We are then in the same position as our predecessors and are called upon to explain what made Jesus uniquely different. The easy options such as, for example, the dualistic account in which the divine logos indwells the human body, fall foul of theological objections which are ultimately rooted in a failure to do justice to the facts. Something more intimate and fundamental is called for. The traditional 'explanation' of virgin birth offers an uncomplicated account which guarantees the theological essence of what the facts seem to demand, but it does not say what actually happened. Today's scientific objection is that it is extremely difficult to see how it could have happened, though the force of that argument is much diminished when we recognize that we are talking about a unique event. If such things happened frequently we would not be surprised by them and would, by now, be able to give a tolerably accurate account of how they occurred. But events which happen repeatedly, even if rarely, could not qualify for consideration because they do not have the unique quality which the facts require. In a strict sense, therefore, the mode of conception of Jesus lies beyond the reach of scientific enquiry which cannot generalize from unique events. The argument that this is not the way that things happen in the world is thus not applicable in this case.

But, in fairness to doubters, we must press the matter further. Did a Y-chromosome materialize from 'nowhere' to create the first cell of the embryo or did some divine manipulation take place on raw material provided by the mother which then played the same role as the male sperm? These and other similar explanations may be possible, even if highly improbable. If one or other were true a declaration of belief in the virgin birth would be no more than literal truth.

Personally I do not incline to explanations of this kind even though I think that most of the objections founder on the rock of uniqueness. Neither am I attracted by the kind of explanation which locates the 'specialness' in a divine selection of the chosen sperm and/or egg to yield a special character in the offspring though that, in a real sense, would give to God a central role.

I do not see how either type of explanation could adequately account for belief that the incarnation expresses the essence of God in the full sense which traditional doctrine requires. Any kind of genetic or other manipulation at conception would essentially involve the same kind of raw materials as give rise to the rest of us. We would still be faced with the question of what was the qualitative difference which distinguishes the Son of God from the rest of his people. We are all unique in the sense that no two of us have the same make-up but that does not make us 'windows into God' in the sense that Jesus is claimed to be.

Ultimately I think we can give no explanation of what happened in scientific terms since we have neither the tools nor the concepts to do so. But I do believe that we can indicate the direction in which the heart of the mystery lies. We should look, perhaps, not at the building blocks of life but rather at what makes *us* more than the sum of the molecules which presently constitute what the world recognizes as ourselves. What we are is constrained by, but not wholly determined by, our genetic inheritance and our environment. Our essential being is fashioned by a subtle interplay between both these and, if the religious interpretation is true, with the ultimate reality which we call God in whom 'we live and move' (Acts 17: 28). What kind of entity that rich interplay produces is impossible to locate in the realm of human thinking but the greater God's role the more God-like we become. In the case of Jesus one might suppose that, from the very beginning, God was the determinative formative factor in creating a person whose Godward 'side' was completely open, making him what we are only potentially.

This leaves open the biological questions but asserts that reality can only be fully understood in terms of a supernatural realm which is beyond our means of knowing but which is intimately related to the world we know. If things which happen there help to constitute what we observe here it is inevitable that we shall not be able to fully specify the nature of things.

The affirmation of the virgin birth is thus a statement that

God acted in a unique way to make Jesus a manifestation of himself in human terms. To describe that role by analogy with that of the human father may very well be as close as we can get to the truth of the matter.

The impasse into which discussions of this topic commonly lead is a result of demanding a full explanation from within the world of science. If there is another dimension of the world of equal importance but beyond our reach which affects the way things are then that must be part of the explanation and, by definition, it cannot be expressed in scientific language. If something on these lines is true the evidence which would count for or against the doctrine lies less in the physical act of procreation than the qualitative difference between him and us. The total event has a natural and a supernatural aspect and what God's unique self-disclosure in this person requires on the supernatural side lies beyond our reach. All that we can say, if the view of miracle advocated here is accepted, is that it must not require something which is physically impossible.

In the case of the resurrection the sharpest division is within the believing community and it again concerns what is actually supposed to have happened. The non-Christian who believes in some sort of afterlife would not see any particular difficulty in supposing that Jesus survived death in the same way that everyone else does. The unbeliever who denies any kind of survival would hardly want to spend time arguing about whether or not a physical body was left behind. For the Christian the question is whether to take the record at its face value and to accept that the tomb was empty or to suppose that the resurrection did not involve the physical body.

Unlike the virgin birth, the resurrection was claimed to be a publicly observable event and there is historical testimony which is relevant to the issue. So far as we know the body was never produced and so there must be some ground for believing that the belief of the early disciples was well founded. However, most of those who reject the bodily

resurrection appear to do so on the grounds that it is scientifically impossible that a dead body should come back to
life and later be translated to another sphere leaving no trace.
Since the theological implications of going along with this
seem to be minimal, some might argue that it would be more
sensible to abandon the incredible part of the story and
emphasize what really matters which is that Jesus lives. What
happened to the physical body is then a matter of relative
indifference as David Jenkins, the former Bishop of Durham,
has often pointed out. Indeed even if the resurrection
appearances happened exactly as they are described in the
New Testament it is clear that the risen body behaved in a
rather unusual way. The appearance and disappearance of
Jesus without warning is not something which the disciples
had experienced before the crucifixion. The accounts are
certainly consistent with a process of weaning the disciples
from a dependence on a physical presence and bringing them
to the point where they could do without it. But that does
not necessarily require a physical continuity with the earthly
body. So what is all the fuss about?

Perhaps it does not matter as much as those in the
entrenched positions suppose but if it were true that the
human body of Jesus was transformed from the earthly to the
heavenly it would make a lot of other very thorny questions
easier to answer. For it would have demonstrated in a visual
way a continuity between the natural and the supernatural. It
would say something rather profound about the nature of
matter and its relationship to the ultimate nature of being. It
would show that the eternal could find expression in the
temporal and hence would radically shift the perspective in
which we view the boundary between the two.

If so much is at stake it would seem sensible to look carefully at the historical evidence since the facts must always take
precedence over our preconceptions. That evidence has
often been rehearsed and evaluated, Montefiore being a
recent example, and this is not the place to repeat it in detail.
It has two aspects. The primary one is that there are various

documents which relate that the event happened and that there were many witnesses. The second, which though indirect is perhaps more compelling, is the difficulty of explaining the existence of such a durable and widespread institution as the Christian church if the event which is supposed to have given rise to it never happened. How much weight should be given to these two kinds of evidence is certainly debatable but it is surely unreasonable to dismiss them out of hand on the strictly unscientific ground that what is described could not have happened. The claim that belief in bodily resurrection is unscientific needs justification. If Jesus Christ was what orthodoxy claims, he was not 'as other men' and hence there is no reason for assuming that what is true for all others was true for him. Hence there is no ground for pronouncing on the possibility of the resurrection from a scientific standpoint. It is beyond the reach of science and so the question must be settled by other means. This assertion may not go unchallenged because if, as the creeds assert, he was fully human it should not be possible for things to happen to him that could not happen to anyone else. But to be fully human is not the same as being no more than human as a denial of resurrection would require.

The essential point being made is not that there must have been a bodily resurrection but that there is and can be no good scientific argument for denying it. To make that case one would also have to assert that Jesus was no more than human or to put it another way that a divine being could not exist. This, in turn, would imply that the whole of reality is encompassed by science which, as we shall have more than one occasion to emphasize later, is not a scientific statement.

CONCLUSION

We seem to keep returning to the same dilemma. Whether or not we think the evidence for miracles is strong depends on the prior beliefs which we bring to the question. If there is more to reality than can be apprehended by the senses we should not be surprised to find events within our experience which fall outside the competence of science to explain fully. If, on the other hand, the materialist is right after all, Christianity, and most other religions, even in the attenuated form of their more radical varieties, are simply an illusion and no amount of evidence can render the impossible remotely probable. We have to make a choice and the only rational way to do so is to decide which of the two versions of reality seems to do the greater justice to the sum total of the collective human experience.

Our principal conclusions may be briefly listed as follows:

1. The evidence that the world is lawful is extremely strong. Miracles, if they occur, will not go directly against these laws but may well go beyond them.

2. The strength of the evidence for a miracle as measured by its probability depends not only on the reported evidence but, more crucially perhaps, on our prior probability that a God capable of acting in the world exists.

3. It is therefore vital to establish that an alleged miracle is credible in the special sense that the facts do not demonstrate its impossibility.

4. Many surprising happenings which the credulous might readily regard as miracles are not remarkable at all and thus provide little evidence for divine involvement.

5. The logic of uncertain inference is, in principle, capable of measuring the evidential value of human testimony and other data but in practice its precepts have seldom been followed. Even if they are we have seen why it is likely to be difficult to obtain strong support for the miraculous.

These conclusions are frustrating for believer and unbeliever alike but they do not necessarily condemn us to perpetual agnosticism. There are other facets of the problem yet to consider and we shall later argue that probability alone is not a sufficient basis for commitment. Our next topic is also controversial, both in its content and in regard to its relevance for a belief in a supernatural reality. Nevertheless the varied field of the paranormal appears to bring us within sight of hard experimental evidence for the world beyond this which belief requires.

5
The Paranormal

Believers have often made great play in their apologetic with the alleged gaps in the scientific picture of the world which, in their view, point to the existence of God. In former times miracles were seen as the prime example of happenings which demonstrated the incompleteness of the scientific account. Today there is another set of phenomena which is also used as a basis for claiming that there is more to the world than science can reveal, often by those who are not conventionally religious. These we lump together under the title of the paranormal. This embraces a very motley collection of things such as telepathy, precognition and such means of extrasensory perception, together with astrology, spiritualism, and the occult generally. The latter would be judged by many to be beneath the notice of reputable scientists or theologians yet they engage the interest of much of the population at large if the popular newspapers and shelves of booksellers are anything to go by. To all of these we may add out-of-the-body experiences and the idea of formative causation put forward by Sheldrake (1987). These last, at least, have been the subject of serious, if somewhat heated, scientific discussion. The reason for dealing with such things here is twofold. First, unlike most alleged miracles, some of these phenomena are more accessible to scientific investigation and hence there is the prospect, at least, of basing belief on a surer foundation. To be sure the truths uncovered might seem rather trivial by comparison with the central concerns of theology but the enlargement of the realm of discourse which they would offer would make dialogue possible in places where none now takes place. Secondly very large numbers of people take these things seriously and in so far as much of their content is incompatible with orthodox belief Christians have an interest in exposing their fallacious character.

Even though some paranormal phenomena lend themselves to rigorous examination, the whole area is embedded in a sea of uncertainty. Telepathy, if it exists, is not something which can be demonstrated as readily as Archimedes' principle but appears as a weak signal against a very 'noisy' background. To establish firm conclusions requires careful regard for the principles of uncertain inference. In the case of some of the other phenomena where experiment is not possible and the data are scarce and of doubtful quality the discipline of the logic of uncertainty is even more necessary. Here, however, we are on familiar territory, statistically speaking, and the tools of inference are ready to hand. There is much more to go on than subjective beliefs however carefully framed these may be.

Both scientists and believers are bound to be somewhat ambivalent towards the paranormal and this is reflected by divisions in both camps. The Society for Psychical Research was founded in 1882 to bring a rigorous scientific approach to bear on paranormal phenomena and it has always included prominent scientists among its members. Professor J. B. Rhine established a major research tradition in extrasensory perception (ESP) in the department of psychology at Duke University, North Carolina, and there continues to be a modest academic research effort in the field, mainly in the United States, but marked in Britain by the establishment of the Arthur Koestler chair in the University of Edinburgh. Against this many scientists have shown hostility bordering on contempt for all such activities. T. H. Huxley declined to attend a seance on the grounds that he had better things to do and regarded it as the business of science to combat superstition and magic. When Sheldrake (1987) published his book advancing his hypothesis of formative causation, the journal *Nature* denounced it as introducing magic into scientific discussion and as the best candidate for burning for many years.

Theologians seem to have been less forthright perhaps because 'Christians too frequently have made no study of the subject at all, so that their prejudices are unconstrained by familiarity with any evidence.'[1] But again there is an obvious ambivalence. On the one hand the establishment of paranormal phenomena as an accepted part of the world-view would help in the overthrow of materialism and reductionist science, and as a result, perhaps, create a more friendly climate for the propagation of theism. On the other hand astrology, spiritualism, and the like are strange bedfellows for believers. The convinced believer is likely to be as dismissive as the scientist. Vicars have been known to ban astrologers from giving talks in parish halls to groups who would defend themselves by saying that it was only a harmless piece of fun. To be tainted with the smell of magic and superstition is more than most rational believers can stomach. Christianity is just as concerned to refute the absurdities of the occult as to challenge an overweening science.

It is clear that we must tread carefully and recognize that not all of the topics included under the 'paranormal' are to be taken with equal seriousness. Equally it is important to be very clear about our reasons for entering the territory in the first place. These can be conveniently brought into focus by a series of questions.

1. Are there any genuine paranormal events?
2. If so, do they result from undiscovered laws of nature?
3. If not, what do they tell us about what lies beyond the world of the senses?

As is immediately apparent these questions are not straightforward. The answer to the second question, for example, depends on how we define a paranormal event in

---

[1] From a review of J. J. Heaney, *The Sacred and the Psychic* (Paulist Press, 1984), by Michael Perry in *Theology* (Nov. 1985), 485.

answer to the first question. Nevertheless, they will serve to get us started and we shall proceed in stages. First we attempt to clarify the issues at a general level and then go on to consider particular topics to see how the tentative conclusions we arrive at stand up in practice. The topics we shall cover vary considerably in the prior credibility which their claims might be accorded, they are: astrology, formative causation, telepathy, and out-of-the-body and near-death experiences.

SOME GENERAL CONSIDERATIONS

There is no doubt at all that many apparently inexplicable things do occur. Wilson (1985) and Koestler (1972) are two among many authors who have given numerous examples involving such things as communication with the dead, absence from the body, and significant coincidences. Soal and Bateman (1954) gave an account of people who appeared to possess telepathic powers. What is equally true is that some at least of those cases were subsequently shown to have involved conscious or unconscious fraud. This is hardly to be wondered at given the celebrity status which attends anyone who can demonstrate remarkable powers. Of itself, this does not justify the dismissal of all such occurrences but it does underline the need for an above-average degree of caution when approaching these matters.

The obvious first step in any enquiry is to establish whether there is a natural explanation for the phenomenon in question. After all, magicians make their living by illusion. By the manipulation of their props and their interaction with the audience they produce effects which appear to be contrary to nature but in reality we know they are not. If anyone claims to exercise paranormal powers we shall first want to establish that no trickery is involved. For example, if a person reports an 'out-of-the-body experience' in which they claim to have witnessed an operation performed on themselves while under a general anaesthetic, it will not do for them to give a vague description which could have been concocted from general knowledge of what goes on on such occasions. To be convincing there would need to be reports, confirmed by those present, of happenings peculiar to their operation which they could not possibly have known about without being present to observe it. Even then there might be the possibility, however remote, that a dreamed or invented account might quite fortuitously have coincided with reality.

If we can satisfy ourselves on that point (and, as we shall see, this may be impossible in a strict sense) the next step is to enquire if there might be a natural explanation involving undiscovered laws of nature. Many things which in the past would have been classed as paranormal now hold no mysteries for us. The transmission of pictures of the surfaces of distant planets to earth is inexplicable unless we know that radio waves can be propagated over long distances through empty space. Is there anything analogous, one might ask, which would account for the transmission of images between one person and another in the absence of sensory contact of any kind? It was in this spirit that the pioneers of research into extrasensory perception approached their work. Like the early scientists, they turned away from phenomena on the grand scale and began to experiment with very simple things under closely controlled conditions. For example, they used sets of cards, the size of playing cards, displaying simple symbols: a plus sign, a square, a circle, a five-pointed star, and wavy lines, in one case. Subjects were invited to say which card was being viewed by an experimenter hidden behind a screen. One might have hoped, and still hopes perhaps, that a programme of research on these lines might gradually push back the frontiers of science to the point where some, if not all, paranormal phenomena were brought within its scope.

At this point we may pause to raise the theological question, 'Would such a *new science* have any implications for theology?' C. T. Oram, then secretary of the Society for

Psychical Research, seemed to think so when he chided me for making no reference to such research in Bartholomew (1988). My reply was that if psychical phenomena were to be brought within the province of science there would be no essential change. We would simply know that the lawfulness which we observe in so much of our experience extended rather further than we now believe. I *might* have added that such knowledge *might* be held to count against a theistic view of the world by suggesting that things which have hitherto been attributed to God's action could now be explained without recourse to him. One of the gaps in our knowledge then would have been closed and the need for God as an explanation that much reduced.

This is an unduly harsh view in the sense that it dwells on the negative aspect. More positively one could see psychical research contributing to religious belief in two ways. If, for example, survival of death could be established the view that the 'self' has no existence apart from the brain would be untenable. This would fall far short of a vindication of Christian belief in the resurrection of the body and the life everlasting but it would contribute to a general world-view which was more hospitable to such tenets. Secondly, psychical research could illuminate what is loosely called our 'spiritual' aspect. By being concerned with what on most reckonings would be counted as the higher human attributes such research might give insight into human religious experience, prayer, and even the work of the Holy Spirit.

To some extent similar considerations apply to the other topics to be considered below and we shall deal with them as they arise. First there is a further general point to be considered. Once we get away from the mundane matters of card guessing which lend themselves to laboratory investigation we face another problem shared by the softer end of more traditional science. The question is how we can ever establish anything on a sound scientific footing if controlled experimentation is either impossible or undesirable. Apparitions, premonitions, and such like, if they are genuine, could not be engineered because they are initiated, one presumes, by some agency beyond those who experience them. One can only observe and carefully record what happens and then examine the evidence for clues as to its origin and nature. If we cannot conduct experiments under properly controlled conditions then we can never be certain that the causal links have been accurately identified. Scientific investigations which have to rely on observation of what happens in the course of nature can never attain to the near certainties of the experimental sciences. That leaves us in the familiar situation of having to make judgements using criteria of credibility, coherence, and probability which, however much we may wish it to be otherwise, is our lot on almost all matters of real importance.

ASTROLOGY

We take this first because of the four topics to be covered it is relatively easy to test some of its predictions in a fairly rigorous fashion. Furthermore there is a substantial body of what appears to be hard statistical evidence that there is something to be explained and yet its claims can hardly be taken seriously by thinking people. It is thus a useful example for illustrating the methodological questions which arise when approaching the paranormal scientifically.

Astrologers claim that individual personality is related to the time of birth or, more exactly, to the relative positions of the sun and planets at that time. To most rational people it seems absurd to suppose that the conjunctions of heavenly bodies at a particular moment of time could affect the destiny of an individual. So far as genetic make-up is concerned one would have thought that the moment of conception would be more relevant and common sense would suggest that there were environmental influences nearer to home than the solar system which ought to be more significant. To give any credence to the idea at all it would be necessary either to endow the heavenly bodies with some kind of intelligence or to regard their positions as indicative of other psychic influences. Neither seems very likely. Nevertheless it is curious that astrology maintains such a hold on the popular mind in a society which is supposedly so permeated by scientific ideology that religious belief has withered. This interest is not limited to mass circulation magazines and newspapers. The Guardian newspaper reported at length a study by Alan Smithers who wrote under a headline, 'Do the stars shape our ends after all?' 'The study has turned up a mass of extraordinary data. Much of it cannot be explained.'[2] Like T. H. Huxley in the matter of seances we could dismiss this evidence without examination, but that hardly seems conducive either to establishing the truth or combating error. Leaving aside the important question of whether there may be any psychological effects, good or bad, from the practice of astrology it is a simple question of fact whether or not individual characteristics are related to birth date. The question then is whether the facts, whatever they turn out to be, can be explained without recourse to the supernatural in some shape or form.

There have been two major studies of astrological claims which merit attention on account of the large numbers of cases involved. They, at least, offer the prospect of being able to make a worthwhile statistical analysis of any alleged effects. The first is due to Gauquelin (1984) who reports the results of his investigations carried out over many years, initially in France but then in the United States and elsewhere. He claimed to be a 'trained psychologist' and he adopted a suitably critical standpoint though this was linked to an enthusiasm for astrology going back to childhood. The aspect of astrology which lends itself to statistical investigation concerns the effect of birth signs on personality. In France time of birth is included in the birth register and this makes it

---

[2] The series of articles appeared in the *Guardian* in March 1984. I have been unable to discover whether the material was subsequently published elsewhere. Efforts to contact the author were unsuccessful.

possible to determine the position of the various planets at the time of birth. The possibility of relating this to personality depends on being able to obtain sufficient information about people whose birth details are available. The ideal way of investigating this would be to do a prospective study. That is, one would take a sample of births and follow those individuals throughout their lives recording such information about them as would enable an assessment of personality to be made. In practice this would take a lifetime to do and so Gauquelin took the more practical course of conducting a retrospective study. Here one takes a sample of individuals for whom a wealth of biographical information is already available and enquires about their birth times. Such people will, of course, be among the more distinguished and able members of society and in no sense representative. However, if there were no connection at all between birth sign and subsequent career one would expect soldiers, for example, to have the same distribution across the various possible birth signs as the population at large. If this turns out not to be the case then an explanation is called for.

Occupation is a relatively easy thing to obtain and much of Gauquelin's work is concerned with the relationship between birth sign and occupation. However, we know that the choice of occupation depends upon many accidental happenings and is, by no means, a perfect indicator of the underlying personality which the birth sign is alleged to influence. Gauquelin therefore explored this point using Eysenck's three dimensions of personality and showed to his own satisfaction that occupation is an acceptable proxy for personality. In view of the indirect nature of the linkage one would not expect there to be a strong relationship between birth sign and occupation but even a weak relationship would call for explanation.

Gauquelin did, in fact, find some such relationships of which the most conspicuous is, perhaps, the so-called 'mars effect' according to which those in 'warlike' occupations are more likely to have been born when the planet Mars was in the ascendant than are members of the population at large. This effect was replicated in Belgium and the United States on large samples and became a main ground for Gauquelin's belief that there is a scientific basis for some astrological claims.

The fact that occupation is readily available opens the possibility of testing for a link between this and date of birth using very large samples. Date of birth alone is of less astrological interest because it is also necessary to know the time of day if the position of the planets is to be determined. Nevertheless if there were a link between birth date and occupation it might be held to point to a linkage unknown to science.

With the help of the Koestler Foundation and the Guardian newspaper (see n. 2) Professor Alan Smithers was able to analyse data on a 10 per cent random sample of the 'economically active' British population obtained from the 1971 Census of Population. The sample comprised 1,461,874 men and 842,799 women covering 223 occupational groups. His first aim was to see how birth dates were distributed throughout the year and, in particular, whether there were different patterns for different occupational groups. In the population at large the distribution is not uniform. For both men and women there is a peak in the spring and a trough in the autumn, the maximum variation from the mean being about 7 per cent of the average. However, the overall pattern conceals as much as it reveals because different social and occupational groups show interesting deviations from the average. Members of the Registrar General's social classes I and II (the highest in terms of prestige) show relatively more births in the spring than the population at large. Does this mean that those born at that time of year owe their subsequent success to the stars? Hardly; there are many more mundane reasons why this might be so. Birth follows about nine months after conception and this, to a degree, is planned and one might hazard a guess that such planning might be more common and effective among those in the higher social classes who tend to have children who achieve high occupational status. One can think of many reasons why the spring might be thought to be a good time to have children of which the beginning of the tax year in April, in the United Kingdom at least, might be one. The converse is also true. Members of classes IV and V show an excess of births in the late summer and autumn which, we note, is about nine months after the Christmas and New Year holiday period. This has a certain plausibility if opportunity rather than planning was the dominant determinant of conception.

As one would expect these class variations reappear to a large extent in the individual occupational groups which make up the classes though there are exceptions. In no case are the variations from the population average very large, often being less that 1 or 2 per cent, but given the very large numbers of cases even such small differences can be statistically significant and therefore require an explanation. That being said it is perfectly clear that the influence of the stars comes a long way down the list of possible explanations. The time of conception and subsequent growth to maturity are complex biological and social processes and it is not surprising that they should operate differently in different subgroups of the population. Some of the variations thrown up by Smithers's analysis are intriguing and provide demanding challenges to social researchers. A great deal more work would have to be done in order to eliminate the more earthly hypotheses to account for the differences before resorting to the heavenly.

Smithers made one further test which is more specifically related to the claims of astrology. Astrologers would claim more than the analysis described so far assumes. They would argue that not only is the personality related to the birth date but that the particular character of the sign under which a person is born has a specific effect on the individual. Thus the personality and hence, to some extent, the occupation, will be influenced by the supposed character of the sign. Smithers found that the information given in *Teach Yourself Astrology* was not precise enough so he consulted the president of the Astrological Association who enlisted the help of other senior practitioners. The aim was to predict which occupations were likely to be linked with which birth signs. In many cases the predictions were not supported by the data. There were two cases, however, where there was a rather striking agreement. One, based on the 35,000 nurses in the sample, showed an oscillating pattern of deviations. Nurses were more likely relatively speaking to have been born under the alternating signs beginning with Taurus and less likely under the intermediate signs. This had been predicted on the grounds that the alternate signs beginning with Taurus are, to the astrologer, feminine or supportive signs and hence likely to predispose someone to serve in the caring professions. A similar result was found in the much smaller group of trade-union officials (742) except that with them it was the masculine or assertive signs which led to the excess of births.

This effect is certainly not seasonal and it is not immediately easy to see any other explanation for this peculiar, albeit small, pattern of variation. The obvious question is whether the effect is real. After all with so many occupational groups one would expect a few unusual patterns. Smithers claims that the pattern is statistically significant though it is not possible to check this from the data given. I assume he means that the comparison is being made with the whole of social class II to which nurses belong but this may not be the relevant population. We know that the social classes differ significantly among themselves and so, it appears, do individual occupational categories within classes. All we can say is that occupational categories appear to differ among themselves. One would like to see data from other samples and especially from another census before taking the matter further. Unusual patterns like this are sometimes statistical artefacts. If, for example, nursing schools had a minimum age of entry and took in new recruits at two-monthly intervals and always selected the oldest among the applicants allowing no second chances a somewhat similar pattern would emerge.

This seems highly unlikely but its possibility illustrates the point at issue.

There are two more points to be added. Even if all possible explanations that we can think of for these two particular anomalies fail, it remains the case that the astrologers were often wrong. What is remarkable is not that they were right in two cases but that they were not right in all cases. A good deal of special pleading would be needed to rehabilitate the reputation of the profession in the face of this evidence.

The second point is more fundamental. When all is said and done what we are left with in these two studies is an association between two things. There is a tendency, for example, for people born at particular times to be in particular occupations. The interpretation that astrologers wish to put upon this association requires that there be a causal link between the two and that it runs from birth date to the occupation. At first sight this seems natural because it is of the essence of causation that cause comes before effect. But we are not dealing here with a physical system but with people making choices. It is perfectly conceivable that, for some people at any rate, choice of occupation is influenced by the fact that they have 'adopted' the self-image wished upon them by astrologers. A person born under Mars who reads horoscopes from an early age may come to think of themselves as 'warlike' and hence look more favourably on a military career. It would only be necessary for this to happen on a small scale since the effect, at best, is only a small one.

In principle one could, perhaps, test this hypothesis though it would be extremely difficult to do so in practice. However, until it is eliminated as an explanation it remains a much more likely explanation than the astrological claim that there is a causal link between the state of the heavens when we are born and our personality.

Suppose, finally, that there were no earthly explanation for successful astrological predictions, would we be compelled to accept the influence of heavenly bodies on human destiny? Not necessarily. There might be some other external power directing our ends whose intentions happened to mirror the movements of the solar system to some degree. We would then have reached the conclusion that there was a source of action beyond what could be explained within the scientific framework, but theists, at least, would see the object of their belief as an altogether more plausible explanation. It thus might just be the case that the scientific investigation of astrological claims would lead us to stumble on some sign of the supernatural but there are other potentially more rewarding ways. Failing any such discovery the refutation of occult claims is more favourable to mainstream belief than their acceptance.

FORMATIVE CAUSATION

The New Science of Life proposed by Sheldrake (1987) offers one of those new perspectives on life which invites theological reflection. In a sense it gives a new impulse to those lines of enquiry which have seen telepathy and the other subjects of parapsychology as providing a *rapprochement* between science and religion. In both cases they achieve their appeal by claiming that the mechanistic and materialistic world of traditional science is myopic and fails to see reality on a broader scale. It appeals to the sense of mystery and wonder by showing that physics, molecular biology, and so forth have not plumbed the depths of reality and may, even, be overlooking what is most important. Not surprisingly Sheldrake's particular contribution attracted the plaudits of the like of Arthur Koestler and other such persons who have sniped at science from the sidelines for many years. Not surprisingly either it provoked the scorn of many traditional scientists reinforced, no doubt, by the motley collection of its supporters and by Sheldrake's own religious interests.

However, Sheldrake claims that, unlike many fringe areas of science (but like telepathy, to which we come later), his theory is testable and therefore refutable, and therefore, in

Popper's sense at least, science. Sheldrake does not claim that his theory is true but simply that if it were, numerous presently inexplicable things would make sense. There is therefore an incentive to put it to the experimental test. Those scientists who take exception to the idea, and the journal *Nature* has been particularly scathing, appear to take the view that acceptance of the theory would overthrow most of the well-tested harvest of traditional science. That is, it could not be fitted in, as a missing piece of a jigsaw, but rather would undermine the whole basis of scientific knowledge. This is somewhat surprising coming from scientists since nothing can take away the vast base of empirical evidence on which conventional science rests. Any revision of the current view would have to incorporate existing models of the world otherwise it would not pass the essential test of scientific acceptability. Whether or not formative causation eventually survives testing, Sheldrake is surely right when he claims that it would supplement rather than supplant existing knowledge.

What then is the hypothesis of formative causation and why has it created such a stir? Sheldrake argues that the formation of all structures from molecules and crystals to living things is not pre-programmed; that there are often alternatives, none of which is particularly favoured. With living things his contention is that the proliferation and diversification of cells and their function is not wholly determined by the genes. The hypothesis of formative causation says that the line of development is more likely to follow the same path as on previous occasions. It is a 'beaten track' type of theory which says that it is easier for future development to follow paths beaten out by others. This is conceived to happen through the agency of *morphic resonance* by which existing paths are beaten out in some kind of 'field' which influences those who come after. This effect is envisaged not to be active in time or space. It therefore permits influences to be felt without regard to distance or time. In particular the past influences the future by changing the probabilities of different lines of development in such a way as to make those which have frequently been used in the past more likely in the future. This is not to deny the role of the coded instructions in the DNA but rather to add another causal origin for things. There is some experimental evidence which is held to support this theory (and some which does not) and this all relates to learning in man or animals. Thus it is argued that if a large number of rats learn some trick then others, presented with the same problem, will find it easier to learn as they follow 'the beaten track'. In the case of people the nature of the hypothesis is well illustrated by the proposal to test it by presenting human subjects with apparently meaningless words in a foreign language (Turkish or Japanese, say). One form would be, say, a nursery rhyme which would have been repeated countless times and the other something quite meaningless. To the subject, ignorant of Turkish or Japanese, both would appear equally meaningless but, if the hypothesis were correct, they would find it easier to learn the genuine nursery rhyme by virtue of the fact that it had been previously repeated so often. It would, so to speak, be so deeply engraved in the nature of things that other learners would find the tracks easier to follow than would be the case for the real nonsense composition. Experiments have been conducted based on this kind of idea with some, but by no means conclusive, evidence in support of the hypothesis. Even when positive results are obtained the conclusion does not necessarily follow. If the passages were learnt by oral repetition there might be a rhythm characteristic of nursery rhymes which made them easier to learn. One would need to ensure as far as possible that the meaningless control shared the same features. The full account is contained in Sheldrake (1987) together with a variety of extracts from reviews, criticism, and so forth of the theory which have appeared since it was first proposed.

Is this something which theologians ought to get excited about? Its proposal that causative actions outside the ordinary linkages of traditional science and unbounded by time or space has a certain appeal. Theologians have had increasing difficulty in finding a plausible way of fitting God's action in the world into the scheme of things. The notion that there are influences hitherto unknown to science is a straw to grasp at even if not a fully equipped life-raft. The picture of a world with unsuspected depths is not merely a well-placed blow at presumptuous scientists but a positive indication that God may not have been banished from his world after all.

It is certainly something which theologians should be interested in if they have any care for producing a theology which is congruent with the world as it really is. But it does not produce an inherently more supernatural view of the world and Sheldrake makes no such claim for it. It is a natural rather than a supernatural theory. It says that the world is a more complicated place than we had supposed; that there are other forces and influences at work which we had not suspected. But it does not question that these are amenable to scientific study and of being ultimately incorporated into the scientific world-view. It does not see the hand of God directly at work in determining the forms which things take. Rather it is the way that things were that helps to make things what they are. It is thus a process of self-formation. This richer and deeper view of the world, if it were true, might well enhance and deepen one's wonder at the creation and thus of the creator but it does not make him more accessible or his ways more transparent. The theory is about past patterns of development and behaviour becoming so deeply ingrained that they help to determine how things are. It says nothing about how the initial choices were made and Sheldrake recognizes that this theory, and science in general, leaves such matters open. Here there is room for divine involvement but science can say nothing on such matters.

If, as I believe, the truth of Sheldrake's hypothesis has little bearing on the credibility of theism it remains to consider whether it would help us to understand how things such as prayer might act or how the thoughts of God might express themselves in the created order. It might throw some light on the nature of our own being, on the mind–body problem and the possible continuity of selves beyond death and time.

Although Sheldrake proposes that formative causation operates at all levels from the lowest forms of matter to the highest it is at the highest level that the experimental work has been done (and it is difficult to think how it *could* be done at lower levels). If the learning of a rhyme or the recognition of a pattern can somehow be facilitated by the fact that others have 'gone that way before' then some interesting possibilities become apparent. For example, if the mind of God were to create a kind of resonance, his thought might become our thoughts and his 'will' might somehow be the grain of the universe making it easier to live his way than to cut across the grain. It might become easier to live the good life in the community of believers because of their harmony with God and with one another. It might explain the claim I heard made by a member of the Prayer Book Society that the oft-repeated prayers of that English classic had a special quality derived from their constant use. It might also explain the Pauline dilemma, 'The good which I want to do . . .' (Rom. 7: 19), since the evil ways of previous generations might leave so beaten a track of evil as to make it easier to do evil than good. It would also help to explain, if that were thought to be necessary, how the evil thoughts and deeds of earlier generations might influence their successors. How 'the sins of the fathers' might be 'visited on the children', and so on. The influence without limit of time and space likewise would give a scientific framework within which to think about the interaction of the temporal and the eternal, of the communion of saints, and possibly even the resurrection of the body and life everlasting.

All of this stimulates the imagination and enables one to see that what, within one framework of reference, might seem incredible is seen in a different light entirely when that frame has a new dimension added to it. It does not mean that any of this is true. That is a matter which can only be settled within science so far as that is ever possible. So far as our methodological approach to uncertainty is concerned we have aimed to show that formative causation does not fail the test of prior credibility. Whether or not it stands up to further empirical testing remains to be seen but even if it does its implications for a supernatural view of the world are marginal.

EXTRASENSORY PERCEPTION

Do we have powers of knowing things or influencing what happens beyond the five senses? Parapsychology aims to investigate so-called paranormal phenomena within a rigorous scientific framework. If such extrasensory perception (ESP) really exists it sets existing science in a broader setting and makes the supernatural claims of religion less remote from the world of science. It may be this very fact which lies behind the fierce opposition of some scientists to the very idea of research into these matters. There is a Committee for Scientific Investigation of Claims of the Paranormal which proclaims its belief that paranormal phenomena are worthy of scientific attention only to the extent that scientists can fight the growing interest in them.[3] The fact that the subject is so hotly disputed serves, at the very least, as a reminder that the evidence needs very careful evaluation and that the language of probability rather than certainty is appropriate.

The realm of the paranormal spans an enormous range. At one extreme we have the conduct of laboratory experiments on card guessing where the object is to see whether some individuals, at least, have the power to do better than if they were simply guessing. This approach into what is popularly known as telepathy has now developed into a major research field with a full panoply of publications including several learned journals. At the other extreme is a whole range of phenomena relating to the human psyche and the possibility

---

[3] *The New Skepticism* (Kurtz (1993)) is by a founding member of the committee.

of its existence apart from the body. We shall look fairly briefly in this and the following section at both extremes with a view to assessing the current state of knowledge and its possible implications for belief in the supernatural.

Beginning with the more mundane end of the spectrum it appears to be widely believed that there is good scientific evidence for the existence of the paranormal. Perry (1984) reports the results of a *Times* questionnaire on the paranormal in 1980 based on 1,314 respondents; 51 per cent thought ESP was an established fact and 33 per cent thought it a likely possibility. (He also noted that in another survey of leaders in the scientific establishment only 29 per cent of all respondents fell into these two categories.) In June 1990 a Gallup Poll in the United States gave a figure of 49 per cent who believed in ESP. These figures for the general public compare with Diaconis's estimate (de Groot, 1986) that between 80 and 90 per cent of a class of Stanford freshmen put up their hand when asked how many took 'this stuff seriously' (p. 324). However, the burden of the talk which Diaconis was giving was to show that in spite of the substantial literature and the apparent scientific respectability of the enterprise there was, in fact, no hard evidence for the existence of ESP, the psi-effect, as it is sometimes called. Persi Diaconis is exceptionally well placed to judge in these matters having having started life as a professional magician and subsequently having become an eminent mathematical statistician. In an earlier article published in *Science* (Diaconis, 1978) he had reported on being present at a number of demonstrations by individuals who were believed to have extrasensory powers. In two notable cases he had identified the use of sleight of hand (with a pack of cards), and lack of proper control, among other things sufficient to discredit the scientific value of the results. By 1986 he was able to report further experience with such experiments which has convinced him that there was no experimental evidence sufficient to justify the inference that ESP exists.

Is this a correct reading of the evidence? An important

characteristic of a good scientific experiment is that its effects are repeatable; similar experiments by different people in different places at different times should yield the same results. The problem with so many psychic experiments, as with many allegedly psychic individuals, is that the effect cannot be repeated or the subject's ability declines. There are good reasons why this might be so which have nothing to do with frauds on the part of experimenter or subject. Selective reporting is one reason. Even if there is no ESP there will, purely by chance, always be a few cases where the subject's guesses exceed the chance expectation by a significant amount. These are the ones which get reported while the many non-significant results are forgotten. The reported level of statistical significance is therefore wrong. The point can be made using a simple illustration involving the tossing of a single coin. Suppose we toss a coin which, it is claimed, possesses a greater than average propensity to fall tails. If we make a number of trials, fixed in advance, we would find support for our expectation if there were significantly more tails than heads. Significance here would be judged in the conventional way by determining a critical proportion of tails which would only rarely be exceeded if the propensities were, in fact, equal. But suppose, instead, we keep a running tally of the proportion of tails and, at each trial, make the same test and choose to stop as soon as we get a significant result. (Although it is not obvious, this will happen sooner or later if only we continue long enough.) By this means we can guarantee that we shall get a result which supports the hypothesis. This would be cheating, of course, but it indicates how a tendency to stop 'while the going is good' can easily lead to illusory significance.

If it were possible to find a psychic experiment which had been reported many times in many places with results favourable to ESP then the case for ESP would be immeasurably strengthened. The nearest approach to this ideal, so far, appears to be what are known as *ganzfeld* experiments. The idea behind these is that if ESP exists it must be a relatively weak effect otherwise it would be more readily apparent. The best chance of detecting it therefore seems to lie in excluding other stimuli and this is attempted by removing all normal auditory and visual stimuli from the subject. Under such carefully controlled conditions attempts are made to transmit information telepathically between sender and subject. In one version this involves predicting a list of 20 outcomes in the correct order. If the subject is guessing, one would expect a 5 per cent success rate, whereas it is reported that the success rate is between 50 and 60 per cent. There are almost 50 such experiments on record and this, one would have thought, would be sufficient to put the matter beyond reasonable doubt. Diaconis claims (de Groot, 1986: 324) that when the matter was looked into closely by the psychologist Roy Hyman, his friend and fellow magician, the excess over guessing vanished. This is not actually the case, at least as far as the debate in a symposium published in *Research in Parapsychology* (1982) is concerned. Hyman (1982) enumerates a variety of shortcomings in the reported experiments and estimates what allowance should be made for their effect on the success ratio. Contrary to Diaconis's assertion, he only claims a narrowing of the gap between observation and expectation, not its elimination. He considers that the overall percentage success rate is nearer to 25 per cent than the 50 per cent claimed. In a response to Hyman's criticism Charles Honorton took up many of the points and claimed to have refuted some of them. One particularly important matter concerns the number of unreported unsuccessful experiments. If this number were large the effect exhibited by those reported would be much diluted, perhaps to the point of non-significance.

The most recent authoritative and up-to-date review of the subject, with special attention to the *ganzfeld* experiments, has been given by Utts (1991). This includes contributions from most of the main protagonists in the debate with a reply by the author. Utts concludes that there is an anomalous effect which requires an explanation but whether or not it can be attributed to ESP remains an open question. It would be impossible to summarize what is itself an effective summary of a wealth of evidence, but two aspects of the argument may be highlighted. First the notion of what is actually being asked for when replication is demanded is often far from clear. This takes us into deep statistical water where intuition is an uncertain guide but, roughly speaking, if the ESP effect is small one would not expect it to show up as a statistically significant effect in every experiment. This fact makes it important to be clear about how the results of many experiments should be combined. This is often known as meta-analysis and links in with the general question of how uncertain information 'adds up'. The second noteworthy element of Utts's paper, especially the discussion part, is the recognition of the role of Bayes' rule in the process of inference. As we would expect from our earlier discussions of the matter, the degree of belief in ESP justified by the *ganzfeld* experiments depends on the prior probabilities and the determined sceptic will be harder to convince than the agnostic. Nevertheless, as Bayarri and Berger[4] show in their contribution, the odds in favour of some anomalous effect are quite large over quite a wide spectrum of prior beliefs.

All that can safely be said at this stage is that the evidence is not yet overwhelming. The more recent reported results,[5] which have yet to be replicated, appear, even to some sceptics, to have overcome most earlier objections to the conduct and design of the experiments but it will be some time yet before remaining doubts can be overcome. It is premature therefore to look to parapsychology for firm scientific evidence of realities beyond the current reach of science.

It is worth spending a moment to return to the theological implications of settling the matter one way or the other.

---

[4] Contribution to the discussion of Utts (1991).

[5] In McCrone (1993) and a report on work by Daryl Bem in the *Independent*, 15 Feb. 1993, due to be published in the *Psychological Bulletin*. Susan Blackmore, a long-time sceptic, was less sceptical in a book review in *New Scientist*, 11 July 1992, p. 43.

If the existence of ESP were to be clearly established by scientific methods it would become part of natural science. It might not be easy to find convincing models of the mind which explain how thought and images might be transmitted between individuals but the same sort of thing could have been said of gravity acting at a distance. Of itself ESP would say nothing directly, for example, about the possible existence of God. However, by establishing the possibility of the non-physical perception of reality it would offer a way of understanding how a supernatural being might interact with the physical world, and thereby add credibility to religious claims.

When we move towards the other end of the spectrum the implications for theology become much more important but at the same time the task of evaluating the claims which are made becomes even more intractable. In the final section we therefore turn to a paranormal phenomenon which relates in a much more direct way to what Christians believe.

OUT-OF-THE-BODY AND NEAR-DEATH EXPERIENCES

Telepathy stands at one extreme of the spectrum of paranormal phenomena. In principle it can be investigated by scientific procedures under controlled laboratory conditions. The results are rarely, if ever, spectacular and mostly involve very modest deviations from what could be expected if the subject had been guessing. If the phenomenon is a real one it is somewhat uncertain in its operation and limited in its effects. The theological implications are likewise limited though one should not ignore the significance of discovering an extrasensory dimension to reality by scientific means.

At the other end of the spectrum stand a variety of phenomena which seem to have a much more immediate relevance to theological claims. These relate to the experience of the self being separated from its body and able to view what is happening to it from outside. Such experiences may be linked with a close approach to death where the subject sees the efforts being made to resuscitate their unconscious body. This sort of phenomenon is closely related to experiences known as near-death experiences which are sometimes recounted by those who have been close to death. There is now a large number of well-attested cases on record which share certain common features conveniently summarized in an editorial in the *Lancet* in 1978.[6]

Amongst the experiences many have described are an initial period of distress followed by profound calm and joy; out-of-the-body experiences with the sense of watching resuscitation events from a distance; the sensation of moving rapidly down a tunnel or along a road, accompanied by a loud buzzing or ringing noise or hearing beautiful music; recognizing friends and relatives who have died previously; a rapid review of pleasant incidents from throughout the life as a panoramic playback (in perhaps twelve per cent of cases); a sense of approaching a border or frontier and being sent back; and being annoyed or disappointed at having to return from such a pleasant experience—'I tried not to come back', in one patient's words. Some describe frank transcendental experiences and many state that they will never fear death again. Similar stories have been reported from the victims of accidents, falls, drowning, anaphylaxis and cardiac or respiratory arrest.

The question which these experiences pose is whether they provide good evidence for the existence of a self distinct from the physical body untouched by physical death. Note first of all that these are not claimed to be beyond-death experiences. Indeed if we define death as the point beyond which no return is possible it is clear that no such evidence could ever be reported. There are, of course, reports of ghostly appearances from beyond the grave and messages relayed from the dead via mediums but they are not the sort of thing we are concerned with here. We are hearing, as it were, reports of happenings at the frontier of rational enquiry and are asking whether what we hear is indicative of a reality beyond.

[6] Quoted in Badham and Badham (1982: 71).

There seems to be little possibility, even if it were desirable, of conducting experiments in this field. We are therefore in the realm of observational science where we must largely rely on what can be deduced from a reported happening over which we have no direct control. There is a sense, however, in which a limited kind of experimentation might be possible. The evaluation of a claim that a person witnessed happenings from outside their body while they were unconscious depends crucially on being able to establish that things were 'seen' which could not possibly have been in the subject's store of memories. It has been suggested, for example, that if symbols of some kind were painted in intensive care units in positions where no patient 'in-the-body' could possibly see them then accurate reporting of them would be powerful evidence of some means of perception outside the body.[7] As it is there are many reports in which the accounts are remarkably convincing even if they fall short of absolute proof. It is not part of our purpose here to assemble and evaluate such case studies. A useful starting point for explanation of this territory is in Badham and Badham (1982). Our concern will be to consider whether these experiences might be wholly explicable within the framework of conventional science.

There is no dispute that near-death experiences do occur on quite a wide scale in many cultures and that they may have a profound influence on a person's subsequent activity and behaviour. In spite of that, many scientists remain deeply sceptical about the reality of the contact with another world. This has to be set alongside the total conviction of the subjects that what they experienced was, if anything, more real than everyday experience. This may leave the interested spectator in a state of considerable uncertainty. Faced with two parties, one of whom is convinced that something is true and the other who is very doubtful, it is clearly important to

---

[7] A recent report in the *Independent* said that this had now been done at the Institute of Psychiatry in London.

establish the logic by which each reaches his or her conclusion.

Susan Blackmore, a psychologist who has made a careful study of the paranormal, is among those who believe that all the well-attested cases of near-death experiences on record can be explained without reference to anything beyond the reach of science (see Blackmore 1988 and 1993). She allows that there are reported cases which would bring her conclusion into question but that none has yet survived close examination.

Blackmore starts from the extra-scientific point that she cannot make any logical sense of the idea of a self, soul, or spirit distinct from the body. (We might note in passing that the coherence of this notion has also exercised philosophers who appear to be divided on the matter.) This motivates her search for a psychological or physiological explanation for the phenomena which are reported. She has attempted to understand what might be happening in the dying brain and to relate this to the perceptions of the subject.

Among the psychological explanations is one which links the 'tunnel' element of so many near-death experiences with the process of birth. Birth is a universal experience and it might plausibly be argued that such primary experiences would be deeply lodged in the brain only to resurface in the final extremity. The passage through the birth canal might somehow be linked with the final departure through a tunnel. Whatever credibility such a theory might have is seriously undermined by a survey of 254 people carried out by Blackmore. If the theory were true people born by Caesarian section should not have tunnel experiences. The survey showed that they do and that the incidence does not depend on the mode of birth.

It does appear to be possible to account for the sensation of being in a tunnel with a light at the end in terms of the function of the visual cortex of the brain. This phenomenon is not peculiar to near-death experiences but can be induced by drugs or can occur naturally in such conditions as migraine or epilepsy. The thing which all these have in common is that they induce a highly excitable state in the visual cortex. Such hyperactivity is believed to destabilize the uniform state producing bands of activity which would appear as concentric rings or spirals in the outside world. The light is likewise accounted for in terms of the intensity of neuronal activity.

As an explanation this account is somewhat deficient. It merely establishes that a certain kind of brain activity is associated with certain experiences. The implication, of course, is that the brain activity *causes* the experiences but this begs the question. It presupposes that all experiences are a consequence of brain function. This is just what many brain scientists do appear to think but we have already noted the dubious status of such a view in Chapter 3. An association between two phenomena does not imply a causal link and even if one does exist this is not sufficient to specify its direction. Suppose, in this case, that the direction of causation is the other way round—from experience to brain activity. If this is not the case, sometimes at least, then our sense of being able to implement our wills is an illusion. Approaching the phenomenon from this direction we should have to explain what was happening to the self near to death which might generate this sort of brain activity. Blackmore's commitment to physicalism requires the line of causation to run from brain to experience, but there is nothing in the empirical evidence which requires this.

Blackmore's own explanation goes rather deeper than a mere attempt to link experiences with brain activity. She focuses on the appearance of 'reality' which attends these experiences and which evidently accounts for the certainty which subjects seem to have about what has happened to them. Her central idea is that the self is a 'construct' built by the brain. (Just what this means is difficult to pin down but, for the moment, we let is pass.) Our world is likewise a construct of the brain. What seems real to us is then the best model that the brain can find at the time. Under normal conditions the brain constructs 'the world' from the stimuli received through the senses. In the final stages of life when the brain processes are degrading there will be very little input from the senses so the brain will not be able to construct a satisfactory model of the world. It will, however, construct other models from memories and whatever things are being tossed around. One or other of these models will be judged best by the brain and thus will have the appearance of 'reality'. Given also that there are good physiological reasons for supposing that tunnels, bright lights, and the sense of taking a bird's-eye view are likely to be floating around in the brain it would not be surprising to find them incorporated into the model.

The fact that subsequent behaviour may be transformed by such an experience can also be explained by the theory. Having experienced another world the subject is able to see the 'normal' world in a more detached way which makes it seem less important. Money, power, and such like no longer have the same hold upon us and we become nicer people. Such transformations occur, of course, in many people who have not come through a near-death experience nor, so far as one can judge, suffered any brain disturbance. What mystics may be able to do with practice and effort is achieved more dramatically as death approaches. Powerful preaching or emotional upheavals of a traumatic kind may also have the same effect.

It has to be added that there are still some things left unexplained. Why should the experiences be associated with profound feelings of peace and joy? The 'unreal' worlds that we experience in dreaming, when there is also little sensory input, are often chaotic, absurd, and sometimes frustrating or frightening. What is special about terminal experiences which gives them such a different character and why should the behavioural changes be so beneficial? Freed from the constraints and inhibitions of the present world and having had a vision of the unimportance of its conventions and practices one might even predict that the subject might return to a life of self-indulgence and anti-social conduct. It still has to be explained why detachment of itself produces such beneficial effects unless they have some intrinsic worth which is more clearly perceived from a detached viewpoint.

Although Blackmore's interpretation is vulnerable to criticisms of this kind I believe it is flawed at a more fundamental level. Indeed, it falls foul of the very obstacle which it seeks to avoid. Blackmore starts from her inability to conceive of the duality implied by talk of self and brain. However, she is then led to an alternative duality which seems no less difficult to comprehend. What is the nature of this 'self' which the brain 'constructs'. A model is some kind of representation of something else. A model of the world is presumably some pattern of brain activity whose elements stand in the same relationship to one another as do the corresponding elements of the world 'out there'. But that world could only be apprehended by us if our 'self' can somehow recognize these brain patterns and attach meaning to them. This self, we are told, is another construct of the same brain represented, presumably, by a different pattern of brain activity. What we experience is thus the mutual interaction of these two activities going on in the brain. There has to be, however, a fundamental distinction between the two since one is able to identify itself as 'me'. In other words one is subjective and the other objective or, at any rate, one is 'more subjective' than the other. The fundamental difficulty with this kind of reasoning is that the construct in the brain identified with me has to be both subject and object since it has to be able to describe itself.

In a near-death experience the brain is struggling to make a coherent model of the world out of the 'bits and pieces' of raw material still available. The other model which is 'me' is presumably what is scanning the various world models on offer. But if the world modelling aspect of the brain is faltering, the 'self' part has to remain sufficiently intact to carry out its model selection function. This would require a kind of protected status denied to the other model. Paradoxically Blackmore's model makes much more sense if one adopts Sir

John Eccles's thoroughgoing dualism according to which the self is 'plugged into' the brain and reads brain states (as expounded by him in Popper and Eccles, 1983). This resolves the confusion between subjective and objective. On this view the experiences may seem more real for the simple reason that they are more real.

It seems to me that attempts to give a scientific account of the human phenomenon are doomed to fail. The notion of the self as a model constructed by a piece of neural machinery has no more meaning or coherence than the idea of a soul. The essential difference is that the model is indissolubly joined to the brain and can therefore have no separate existence. It is hard to see how this, of itself, can count as an argument in favour of the model hypothesis. I agree with Pippard (1988) that knowledge of the nature of the self is beyond the reach of science. Science is about what is objectively observable and the self cannot be simultaneously observer and observed. Materialist attempts to get round this are bound to leave a hole through which the banished subjectivity which characterized the self will reappear.

None of this is to deny the value of genuinely scientific research which seeks to understand brain function and to link experiences with brain activity. But if you believe that there is no reality outside what can be comprehended by science then you must explain why there is a region within our experience which science cannot handle. If you believe that the world of the senses is embedded within a deeper reality it is hardly surprising that one's perceptions of that other world should become more acute as the sensory input of this world recedes.

In the course of this discussion of near-death experiences we have had no occasion to introduce probability ideas directly because the uncertainty does not lie in the data. The problem lies, as so often, in the prior credibility and the coherence of the hypotheses which are entertained as possible explanations for the undisputed facts. In this case some find any notion of a self in some way distinct from the brain as quite inconceivable. However our argument here is that the alternatives are simply not coherent and therefore not credible. This appears to leave us with a body of evidence with no explanation in sight.

SUMMARY

In brief, we may summarize our conclusions on the very mixed variety of paranormal phenomena covered in this chapter as follows.

The claim that planetary motions influence human personality is exceedingly improbable on the current scientific world-view, the more so since it does not appeal to supposed extrasensory human powers but to the configuration of inanimate objects. The substantial empirical evidence produced by Gauquelin and Smithers is either negative or falls far short of what is needed to establish the claim. There is something to be explained but there is every indication that the explanation lies within science. In so far as astrology postulates a world beyond science which is antipathetic to Christian orthodoxy this conclusion removes a distraction and leaves us free to concentrate on more serious challenges to belief.

The hypothesis of formative causation is a more serious contribution to the search for something beyond science as presently understood but it remains a hypothesis. It certainly does not merit the scorn poured upon it from some scientific quarters and it does not constitute a threat to the scientific world-view. On the other hand it is rather marginal to the central issues at stake between belief and unbelief. If future research were to support the hypothesis it would illuminate some theological questions but its greatest value might be in the changed climate of thought rather than in its substantive contribution.

Extrasensory perception, again, remains unproven, though there is clearly a large volume of very suggestive evidence. The fundamental difficulty is that human experimenters have to set up watertight experiments for human subjects. It may never be possible to ensure that the experimenters are smarter than the subjects! The best hope may lie in automated experimental procedures and this is the direction in which current research is moving. Whatever the outcome the theological implications of the card guessing type of exercise are minimal. Of much greater interest are those phenomena which involve feelings and judgements, but as we move in that direction the problems of adequate control become extremely difficult. This may well be an area where the limits of rigorous scientific enquiry are quickly reached.

Out-of-the-body and near-death experiences are of most immediate relevance to the central concern of this book. Here there is no argument about their existence; the question is whether they can be explained in physiological or psychological terms without the need to invoke the supernatural. Blackmore has provided a scientific 'explanation' but I have argued that it actually explains nothing since it begs the question. It starts with the assumption that the phenomena must have a purely physical explanation and then constructs an account of what it might be. I contend that it is basically incoherent because it cannot distinguish the subjective and objective aspects of our experience and, furthermore, that this would be true of any purely physical account. In my view this points to reality beyond the reach of science. It does not, of course, prove that these experiences are what they claim to be, merely that there is not, and probably never can be, a complete scientific explanation.

6

Is God's Existence Probable?

There can be few people who are totally indifferent to the question of whether God exists. Judging by the results of periodical polls on the subject many people seem willing to express an opinion on the matter, one way or the other. On what evidence they base their opinion is seldom enquired into, but one suspects that relatively few people today are absolutely convinced atheists or theists. A degree of ill-defined agnosticism might better describe the position of the generality of people. Even among those who are distinguished in their own fields one often finds remarkably unsophisticated ideas about God. In Western society at least, theism seems to have been virtually universal in the 'ages of faith' but that consensus has disintegrated for reasons which have been briefly outlined in Chapter 1. On the philosophical side the so-called 'proofs' of God's existence have been found wanting. Rival philosophies, such as humanism, in which religious phenomena are explained in naturalistic ways, to their protagonist's satisfaction, have taken a deep hold. The breaking down of geographical and cultural isolation which makes the diversity of religions and gods common knowledge has tended to relativize all belief systems. But above all, in the West at least, the scientific revolution has so enlarged and altered our world-view that the signs of God's presence in everyday happenings have been pushed farther and farther back until his role is both inconspicuous and, for most people, irrelevant.

To some extent the question of God's existence has lain behind much of the discussion in Chapters 4 and 5. Miracles, almost by definition, are acts of God, and to the extent that these occur such an agent may be inferred. As already noted this was, until relatively recently, a main plank in the apologist's platform. In the case of the paranormal, although the link with divinity is much weaker, the existence of such phenomena would add a new dimension to the world of science and so tend to deepen the sense of wonder at the world and make the case for a divine originator more compelling.

Wherever people stand in the plurality of positions now available most would probably agree that the question had meaning and admitted the answer yes or no—even though they themselves might be unsure what it was. In other words it is a sensible question to ask and is worth trying to answer. When one approaches the question today account must be taken of the fact that some philosophers think the matter is more complicated; that before an attempt is made to give an answer it must first be established whether the question is meaningful—or, more generally, what meaning can be attached to it. This hinges, of course, on what we mean by the name God. We are told, for example, that we cannot think of him as one being among others albeit with a capital 'B', instead we must refer to his Being, the very source of all being.

We shall not get side-tracked into debating such issues, important though they are. We are concerned with whether or not there exists a fundamental reality to which the universe as known to science owes its origin and nature. If it could be satisfactorily established that 'this is not all there is' and that 'what there is' requires for its explanation some fundamental reality which is personal and purposeful we would have dealt implicitly with the question of meaning.

There is, however, another aspect which is rather more important for our purposes. The mere existence of some first cause or ultimate reality is not of much practical interest. What those who enquire into God's existence are really interested in is whether our world expresses God's purpose and what part, if any, they have in the scheme of things. Here, therefore, we shall be equally interested in the existence of a God of that more specific but interesting kind who is concerned with the world and what happens in it. Paradoxically, perhaps, this is a somewhat easier question to tackle since there is more empirical evidence to go on. The sum total of natural and human history and experience is available to reveal its divine origins and purpose if such exist.

Even within this framework a variety of 'gods' are possible. Most religions encourage us to think of one whose intentions are good rather than evil. But evidence of purposeful activity might come in the form of acts hostile to the perceived well-being of the human race.

One might have hoped that the matter could be simply settled by one simple irrefutable argument or 'proof'. For some people it is. As a result of some intense personal experience, some profound insight, or some wholly convincing argument they remain in no doubt. That there are such people is, of course, part of the evidence which has to be considered, but it is only a part because such conviction is not readily communicated. What is needed is a way by which the many arguments and evidences may be brought together and somehow 'added up' in an agreed fashion. Taken singly they may amount to very little but we need to give formal expression to our feeling that the cumulative effect of many such arguments can lead towards certainty. If proof of this were needed we only have to remind ourselves of the diametrically opposed conclusions reached by Richard Dawkins and the Archbishop of York as reported in Chapter 1.

The suggestion that probability theory is the tool we need will not go unchallenged and some will question whether the introduction of a scientific term such as 'probability' takes us much beyond the more traditional ways in which people have affirmed their belief. Words such as 'belief' itself, 'faith', and 'trust', all speak of an attachment of some kind to the idea of the existence of a supreme being and most would claim that this attachment is based on evidence. One can certainly have degrees of belief and of trust but what about faith? Faith is more often spoken of as being weak or strong. Its object is 'something' and, in a Christian context, would not be dependent solely on the individual but also on the object of faith as in a mutual holding of hands. It is a felt bond rather than a rational degree of belief—a disposition of the whole being rather than a state of mind. The same could be said of trust. It might fairly be said that one can have faith (or trust) in a *person* whereas belief relates to propositions (which may, of course, be *about* a person). A rational degree of belief in a proposition can, and must, be supported by reasoning based on evidence. An act of faith may be supported by evidence but is not directly dependent on evidence, indeed it may even fly in the face of the evidence.

Although this distinction can certainly be justified by common usage it is also true that, because belief involves commitment, the boundaries are so blurred in practice that the terms belief and faith are sometimes used interchangeably. Nevertheless the distinction is a useful one and we shall here regard *belief* as referring to propositions and as something which can exist in varying degrees. We are here concerned with what degree of belief in God's existence is justifiable and, in particular, with how the evidence can be marshalled and combined.

Doubts about the usefulness of formal probability reasoning are not confined to the borderlands of religious belief but apply more broadly. We have already mentioned, in Chapter 4, Tennant's 'a-logical' probability. He was quite clear that this was not the probability with which mathematicians and logicians deal but that its use was nevertheless valid in scientific induction and, by extension, in other fields as well. He described it as a 'non-rational, yet reasonable certitude determined psychologically'. This appears to mean that, in some spheres, at least, the brain/mind is capable of processing information and making judgements without the intervention of conscious control of the thinking process to make it conform to rules arrived at rationally. The reason for believing this to be so rests largely on the practice of scientists who develop a sense of the rightness of things without formalizing the processes by which they arrive at their conclusions. The success of science shows that people do arrive at the truth, in the face of uncertainty, without using a formal calculus for dealing with it. We have already noticed that C. S. Lewis saw this ability as a God-given faculty enabling us to recognize the truth when we see it.

There is doubtless an element of truth in this just as it is true that in the more mundane areas of life we often weigh up a situation correctly without regard to logic of probability, but it is pertinent to make two observations. The first is that we know that people at large are not very good at forming consistent probability judgements as the examples in Chapter 2 illustrate. This gives us reason to doubt that the confidence we feel in our own judgements is as securely founded as we think it to be. The second is that even if we do have a built-in capacity for arriving at reasonable certainty (or some of us, scientists especially) there is no reason to believe that such judgements are made in a rational way and hence that were they to be analysed in detail they would be seen to conform to the formal theory. Just as people can be trained to make better probability judgements so it is reasonable to suppose that the working scientist increasingly learns by experience to weigh the evidence appropriately. The trouble with the 'reasonable certitude determined psychologically' is that it is not readily communicable and thus open to examination. Without denying that the experienced scientist may be able to dispense with a formal mode of probability reasoning we shall nevertheless argue that the use of such reasoning can only help and not hinder the progress to knowledge. Tennant felt that his five arguments for God's existence had a cumulative effect which amounted to near certainty and most of us have similar feelings about things we believe in. However, when we come to see the broad spectrum of conclusions which reputable thinkers have reached on this most fundamental question of God's existence we may be forgiven for thinking that the time has come to give as much attention to the manner of reasoning as to the facts on which it is based.

Without wishing to deny the value of more intuitive approaches to the nature of ultimate reality our intention here is to try to answer the question posed by the chapter title. We shall proceed by critically examining a number of earlier attempts which have approached the question from different directions. In the following section we start with the contributions of Gaskin (1984) and Stannard (1989). Their use of probability arguments may be described as subjective and informal since they are essentially talking about degrees of belief and they do not invoke any formal rules. We then move on to Montefiore (1985) and Swinburne (1979) who, in varying degrees, adopt a more formal analysis and both reach very positive conclusions. Then we turn to Prozesky (1992) who uses probability ideas more explicitly. In the final section we turn to a group of scientists who use probabilities in relation to objective happenings which are held to bear rather more upon the purposefulness of God than upon his mere existence.

GASKIN AND STANNARD: REASONABLE BELIEF

The Quest for Eternity by Gaskin (1984) is a relatively recent attempt to return to the age-old question of God's existence which explicitly recognizes that the argument must be couched in terms of probabilities. He concludes that theism is coherent and therefore that it is meaningful to talk about its truth or falsity. On the latter he reaches the conclusion that the evidence is only such as to make it what he calls a 'weakly reasonable' belief. This judgement rests partly on the *kind* of arguments which can be adduced in its favour and partly on a balancing of the arguments for and against. In our terminology he allows that theism provides a credible hypothesis in that it gives some sort of explanation of the universe and what we find it in. But he finds that many of the arguments are circumstantial of the kind that 'things would be or could be thus if there were a God of the sort we believe in' (p. 178). This amounts to saying that the conditional probabilities (likelihoods) of various things which we observe in the world are not negligible. According to the principles set out earlier what we next have to do is look at the probabilities of those same things on the atheistic hypothesis. It is the relative values of these pairs which move us towards belief in one direction or the other. This, in fact, is effectively what Gaskin is doing when he talks of balancing arguments. He does this informally by setting out the pros and cons and some are implicitly given more weight than others. For example, for Gaskin the problem of evil clearly weighs heavily against theism, though, it should be added, only on the presumption that the God in question is good. Translated into our terminology he is saying that the probability of an evil world like ours is much greater if God does not exist than if he does.

But what, we must ask, is the rational basis of the judgement at which Gaskin finally arrives? There is no explicit adding up of the pieces of evidence nor can there be since no quantification is involved. What we have is Gaskin's judgement that if such a summation process were possible the answer would be that there would be a 'weak probability of truth'. But where would such a 'weak probability' fit into the scale of probability judgements listed in Chapter 2, and would most people agree in that placing? Again we ask, do the mental processes by which we weigh the evidence bear any resemblance to the rules for combining probabilities that we met in Chapter 2? The short answer, of course, is that we do not know but the minimum justification that we could seek, so far as I can see, would be an empirical one on the following lines. If a large number of rational people well versed in the philosophical issues were to consider the same evidence and to express their conclusions in similar terms independently then we might conclude that there was some unconscious mental processing going on which leads to valid conclusions. On past experience it does not seem very likely that such a consensus would emerge. If we believe that the question being asked is a matter of 'very great consequence', as Gaskin certainly does, then the way in which the evidence is to be combined and weighed is at least as important as the assembling of the data in the first place. It seems, so often, to be assumed that erudition in displaying the arguments and contemplation of them is the best that can be done. Whether or not it is, is the question with which this chapter is primarily concerned.

There has recently been a major contribution to the debate on belief in God which might be regarded as using informal probability arguments even though it makes hardly any explicit reference to the fact. This is *Grounds for Reasonable Belief* by Stannard (1989) and in this book he uses what might be termed a comparative method for establishing relative probability. This is quite commonly used in other fields and could be profitably applied to theological matters. The link with probability ideas is through the word 'reasonable' which Stannard defines in relation to belief as follows.

A conclusion is reasonable if it constitutes a position which can be held with intellectual honesty, that is to say, if it incorporates reasoning *as far as that is possible given the nature of the problem*, if it does not ignore contra-indications and if well-balanced judgement points to it being the more plausible of the various possible alternatives (p. 120 f.).

Apart from minor variations in terminology this is essentially the approach that I have been advocating. 'Not ignoring the contra-indications' and 'the more plausible' of Stannard's definition both indicate that it is relative probabilities that matter. The informal element lies in the need to form a well-balanced judgement and therein lies the rub. Stannard goes on to illustrate the kind of inductive argument on which reasonable belief may be founded and this is essentially a probability argument as the following quotation shows.

Reasonable belief is founded on *inductive* arguments. An inductive argument is such that acceptance of a given set of premises, while not leading inescapably to a particular conclusion, can lend support to it. Thus, for example, a set of premises might be: (i) 60% of the children in the school science class are boys; (ii) An individual named X is in the school science class. Conclusion: X is a boy. The conclusion does not follow inescapably; X could still be a girl. But the argument lends a measure of support to the conclusion. The conclusion is now more likely than it seemed in the absence of that piece of information (60% probability now instead of 50%). One should note also that inductive arguments can be cumulative. Thus, a further argument about X might be built on the premises: (i) Boys are twice as likely as girls to have dirty fingernails; (ii) X has dirty fingernails. Conclusion: X is a boy. Again the conclusion is not inescapable, but more probably true than not. Taken in conjunction with the first argument, the odds begin to mount that X is indeed a boy (p. 121).

Although these principles underlie the argument of much of his book they are not used in such explicit terms. However, the weighing of alternatives in the sense of ranking them according to their probability is a central theme of the argument. Stannard draws attention to the fact that we readily accept other things which are no better supported than is belief in God. There is, in particular, no proof for the existence of a physical reality or other minds and yet all science and most everyday activity proceeds on this assumption. If we can understand why even people of a sceptical turn of mind are prepared to accept that there is a physical reality but not a spiritual reality we may gain some insight into how uncertainties are assessed. Furthermore by identifying inconsistencies in the treatment of evidence under the two heads we may point the way to a more rational assessment of the case for belief in God.

This comparative method is familiar in the field of risk assessment. We noted earlier that people's subjective judgements about risk are often widely at variance with objectively calculated probabilities. Flying on scheduled air services is safer than driving a car (when considered on a proper comparative basis) but for most people the position seems to be reversed.[1] In part this misapprehension may have to do with the incomplete evidence available. Air crashes receive worldwide publicity and often involve large numbers of deaths whereas car accidents largely pass unnoticed. Such judgements may be radically altered if one is personally involved as witness or victim in either kind of accident even though nothing has changed objectively. But there may also be other reasons which have nothing to do with the real risk. For example, there appears to be some psychological evidence that one's feeling of greater security in a car is because, as the driver, one has a degree of control over the situation whereas in the plane one is in the hands of others.

It is common in the more intemperate outbursts in the science and religion debate to find the opponents' motives as well as their reasoning powers questioned. In an exchange between Mary Midgeley and Peter Atkins in the pages of the *New Scientist*, Atkins (1992) opened his article with the single word sentence 'Fear.' According to him it was the emotion rather than the reasoning which had to be targeted. It may well be that our finely balanced judgements in these matters are often contaminated by such extraneous and irrelevant considerations. All the more reason therefore to make the basis of our judgements as explicit as possible. The tactic of asking, 'Why, if you believe A, will you not believe B when the evidence for both is of much the same kind?' is a legitimate way of establishing the relative probabilities of beliefs. In the case of belief in God (or spiritual or supernatural reality), Stannard makes real progress along the road of uncertain inference.

---

[1] A discussion of these and related matters is given in Dowie and Lefrere (1980), especially in the contribution by Fischoff, Hohenemsu, Kasperson, and Kates. See also ch. 12 of Moore (1983) which also contains much else of relevance to the technical background of this book.

MONTEFIORE AND SWINBURNE: THE PROBABILITY OF GOD

Our next approach to the question of God's existence is the one which one might have expected to come at the beginning since it relates most closely to the question which is usually asked. What is the probability that God exists? If the matter cannot be settled with certainty one way or the other to everyone's satisfaction then surely we ought to be able to sum up our uncertainty in a probability. In this section we shall consider two major attempts to do this. The first is due to Montefiore (1985) whose conclusion we have already quoted. Since he is so very positive it is important to analyse his argument in some detail to see whether it measures up to the logical standards that probability theory requires. Only then can we say whether his conclusion is justified.

The evidence adduced by Montefiore falls into three parts. First there is the cosmological evidence having to do with the nature of the universe and, in particular, with the remarkable coincidences in its set-up which make life possible. (This is usually discussed in relation to the so-called anthropic principle.) Secondly there is the constancy of the physical environment which has enabled life to develop and evolve. Finally there are the special personal qualities and experiences of *homo sapiens*. Linked with the last two of these there is also the question of evolution with which Montefiore sees serious difficulties. That evolution has occurred is not the issue; the question is whether the combination of chance and necessity is sufficient to account for the emergence of life as we know it or whether, in addition, matter has some inherent quality or is subject to some divine direction. This last matter we treat separately.

We take the three types of evidence in turn. Montefiore lists eleven features of the physical universe whose values had to be 'just right' if life and ourselves were to be possible. The details are not germane to our present discussion but the bare list serves to focus our awareness of how formidable is the array of evidence. It is as follows:

1. The distribution of gases in the early universe.
2. The expansion in all directions of the primeval gases had to be uniform to within 1 part in 10^{40}.
3. The heat of the universe.
4. The weight mass of neutrinos.
5. The mass of the universe.
6. The neutron mass.
7. The relative weight of neutrons, protons, and electrons.
8. The balance between the forces of gravity and electromagnetism.
9. The magnitude of the strong nuclear force.
10. The magnitude of the weak nuclear interaction.
11. Conditions for the production of carbon dioxide.

Without the coincidence of all these features there would have been no universe and no life in it. Does the convergence of all these very remarkable properties make the case for God overwhelmingly probable?

According to the argument in Chapter 2 we need to consider the chance of what has occurred on each of the possible hypotheses on offer. In the simplest formulation there are just two: God exists or he does not. If an all-powerful God exists who intended to create a world such as this he would have been able to 'fix' all these properties 'as a package'. We can then reasonably conclude that the probability that he would be successful would be virtually one. Next we have to consider what that probability would be if there is no God. This is much more difficult. If there was no directing hand it seems incredible that even one of these coincidences would have occurred. The chance that eleven would have all occurred simultaneously is then beyond belief. Even if some are linked so that they are not completely independent the position is not significantly altered—the probability of things being what they are is negligible. If we were to stop here and were to compare the likelihoods the chance of the universe as we know it is immeasurably more plausible on the theistic hypothesis than on the random-happening scenario. We know that if we turn this likelihood ratio into a posterior probability ratio we have to introduce the prior probabilities. We return to this in a moment but here note that the prior presumption of atheism would have to be extremely strong to counterbalance the overwhelming evidence the other way provided by the likelihoods.

However, this argument will not do because there is one atheistic hypothesis which, it is claimed, does render these remarkable coincidences virtually certain. This is the hypothesis that one of the 'infinitely many universes' theories is true. According to these, many universes, either in series or in parallel, potentially existed and hence sooner or later one with exactly the right conditions would emerge. Note that this requires that the mode of generation of each universe would have to be such as to allow a wide range of possible constants to occur and that range would have to include those values which would allow a life-containing universe. Further, if the universes were produced serially, the basic constants of one would have to be sufficiently independent of its predecessors to allow the full gamut of possibilities to be covered. It is not clear to me whether any of the existing 'many universes' theories contains the necessary ingredients to make any of this plausible. Discussions of the matter usually seem to proceed on the assumption that if there is no creator then anything is possible but this may not be so. Nevertheless, we will leave such difficulties on one side and give the chance hypothesis the benefit of the doubt.

We thus have an alternative hypothesis which says that what we observe is also probable if that hypothesis is true. Comparing the likelihoods we then find that they are of the same order and hence that the evidence does not point clearly in either direction. However, both of these hypotheses implicitly require that the basic constants of the universe could have been other than they are. One says that the particular values were fixed by God and the other that they were arrived at by trial and error. A third possibility is that they could not be other than they are and hence that there is nothing remarkable at finding them thus. In that case we would have to ask about the probability of the universe spontaneously coming into existence given that this is the only way that anything at all could exist. There seems no reason whatsoever for supposing this to be high. At best, therefore, this third hypothesis could only compete on equal terms with the other two hypotheses and given that it lacks any generating 'mechanisms' one might justifiably argue that the probability must be small.

The probability of God thus turns on the prior credibility we give to the hypotheses. This appears to be recognized by Montefiore when he comments with regard to the judgement of probabilities that 'each of us is influenced by his presumptions and presuppositions' (p. 175). But he is here talking about the probabilities of the coincidences and these are actually not crucial. What matters is the prior probabilities which no doubt *are* influenced by presumptions and prejudices.

It therefore seems that all the evidence is of little value to us and that we are thrown back on personal judgement on which we know there is no consensus. This is true but it need not have been. Without a 'many universes' hypothesis it would not have been easy to find an alternative hypothesis which could compete on anything like equal terms with theism.

The effect of the argument is thus to throw the spotlight on 'many universes' theories since they seem to offer the best hope for the atheist. Is there any rational way in which we can compare this probability with that of God's existence? We must note first of all that, in the nature of the case, there cannot be any empirical evidence on the matter—we are in this universe and that is that. As we shall see below an attempt has been made to argue that the God hypothesis has a certain logical character which justifies assigning a prior probability but this is highly questionable. Without some such extraneous consideration the dilemma can only be resolved by subjective judgement uninformed by empirical evidence of any kind—otherwise it would not be prior. In my judgement, therefore, the probability of God is left undetermined by the cosmological evidence. To offer the possibility of a high probability of God on this evidence we would have to show that the many universe hypotheses were logically incoherent in some way thus rendering their prior probability zero.

There are two more parts to Montefiore's argument. The second of these concerns the stability of conditions on earth which have enabled evolution to take its course over millions of years. The degree of salinity of the oceans, for example, is crucial for the well-being of cellular organisms. This, and other similar environmental characteristics are indeed remarkable. The naïve argument, which Montefiore does not use, would be that such a state is so wildly improbable that there must have been a presiding divinity watching over the system and making adjustments as necessary. A more sophisticated version would recognize that complex systems have a remarkable capacity for self-regulation. To take an over-simplified example consider the balance in a prey–predator situation. Imagine a world of rabbits and foxes in which rabbits feed on vegetation and foxes feed on rabbits. It is interesting to enquire whether such a population will show any kind of stability or whether one or both types of animal will die out. We can argue as follows. If the rabbit population falls, food for foxes will be reduced so fewer will survive and fox numbers will thus fall. A reduction in foxes will reduce the risk to life for rabbits who will therefore tend to grow in numbers thus allowing the fox population to rise also as more food becomes available. Under appropriate conditions, including the assumption that both populations are initially large, it can be shown that there is an equilibrium state in which both populations can coexist at constant size. Unless those particular conditions are attained the two population numbers will perform complementary oscillations about that equilibrium. That state of affairs will continue indefinitely without need for any external control. The biosphere is vastly more complicated than this but it involves that same kind of interdependence which makes one element respond to changes in all others. Such complex dynamic systems are typically self-regulating in this fashion or they change catastrophically in which case a new regime applies with similar potentialities. It is therefore entirely plausible that near-constant conditions should have been maintained in some parts of the biosphere throughout evolutionary history.

This being so Montefiore would argue that matter must have been endowed with the properties which made it possible. It is, in his judgement, the extreme improbability of this happening by chance that adds weight to the alternative that God acted to make things this way. This conclusion is problematical. It depends on the assumption that, of the many equilibria which might have emerged, only one (or very few, perhaps) would have been favourable to life. This is a technical question of extreme difficulty and it is far from clear where the balance of probability lies. What is clear is that such a steady state is possible—because it has actually occurred. That being so it could be subsumed under the earlier part of the argument as just one more coincidence which was bound to occur sooner or later on a 'many universes' hypothesis.

This leaves us with the final set of evidences which have to do with facts of human experience. These seem to be of a different kind from the others in that they are directly experienced and are not amenable to public examination in the same way. The moral and religious senses, conscience, and the apprehension of truth, goodness, and beauty and, above all perhaps, the experience of love are all things which seem remarkable to us and to call for an explanation beyond the laws of science. It has been argued nevertheless by sociobiologists, for example, that some such things might arise as a natural outcome of the evolutionary process. The human sciences are much less well developed than are the natural sciences and it is premature to say how surprised we should be at their occurrence. They do not in my view contribute very much to the thrust of this particular probability argument for God's existence.

Montefiore's argument thus turns almost entirely on whether there are good reasons of a non-empirical kind for thinking that the existence of God is a priori much more probable than that there are (or have been) sufficiently many universes with enough randomness in their set-ups to have made the highly special nature of our universe probable.

It seems to me that there are two other matters which are not included in Montefiore's case but which bear on this question and which are treated elsewhere. If there is a God one might expect him to have communicated his existence in a recognizable fashion. We have already raised this question in relation to miracles and other supposedly extra-scientific happenings but have yet to consider the more direct claims made for the Bible as a medium of revelation and of the meaning of its central event. This we do in Chapter 7. Secondly there is the question of the nature of the selves which are doing the reasoning and whether they are wholly part of the physical universe. This was discussed in Chapter 3.

Before we leave Montefiore's argument we note one further point which clearly demonstrates that the logic of the case is more subtle than our presentation suggests. We have argued that there are only two hypotheses about the origin of the world which it is reasonable to entertain: either that God does exist or that the world was the result of a stupendous process of trial and error. These hypotheses are not, of course, mutually exclusive. The trial-and-error method could have been the very method chosen by God to produce a universe. It may seem wasteful to us but it might have been the only feasible way. Opting for trial and error, on whatever basis, is thus not necessarily a rejection of God. Ultimately therefore there is no way in which we can absolutely reject theism nor, more importantly, ever mount a serious case against it using scientific evidence. What we can do is to seriously question whether, if God exists, he has any interest in or control over what is going on. Some of the most damaging attacks on religious belief have been of this kind and it is to them that we turn in a later section. First we look at Swinburne's attempt to arrive at the probability of God.

It follows from our discussion of the matter in Chapter 2 that Bayes' rule is the appropriate inferential tool to use if we wish to arrive at the probability of a proposition such as that God exists. The chief exponent of its use to elucidate this question is Swinburne (1979) whose book *The Existence of God* treats the matter in great detail. A simpler and more limited account was given in Bartholomew (1984) but there is no need to go into the details here. The essential thing to know is that Bayes' rule tells us how beliefs should be changed by evidence.

The possibility of using Bayes' rule as a means of arriving at a probability for God's existence has to contend with two fundamental difficulties, namely the choice of prior probability and quantification of the other probabilities involved. Swinburne circumvents the problem of quantification by abandoning the attempt to get a numerical probability at the end of the exercise. Instead he adopts the weaker strategy of assessing whether a new piece of evidence increases or decreases the probability and then aims to see whether the final probability is near to zero or one. For this purpose he introduces the notion of what he calls correct C-type and P-type induction arguments. Roughly speaking the first says that an argument from evidence *e* to the truth of the hypothesis *h* is valid if the probability of *h* when *e* is included in what we take account of is greater than if we left it out. The second type of inductive argument which justifies such an inference says that the inclusion of *e* makes *h* more likely than not. By assembling a variety of such valid arguments and determining their cumulative effect by Bayes' theorem, Swinburne arrives at the conclusion that, before personal experience is taken into account, the probability of God's existence is not close to either zero (impossibility) or one (certainty). It is the additional evidence from personal experience, which he discusses in some detail, that leads to the final conclusion that God's existence is more probable than not. Swinburne's reason for considering personal experience separately is that he treats it somewhat differently. The essence of his argument is that unless the evidence for God's existence from all other sources is very weak indeed (i.e. has very low probability) then the cumulative weight of evidence from personal experience, which he judges to be very high, cannot be seriously diminished. Put the other way round, the evidence from personal experience is so great that it could only be outweighed if it was radically at variance with the evidence from all other sources. For this to be so the probability of God as judged on this evidence would have to be extremely small and this, he claims, is not the case. The part of the argument which depends on personal experience cannot be summarized adequately in a brief space but two things are central.

One is what Swinburne calls the Principle of Credulity which says that 'perceptions ought to be taken at their face value in the absence of positive reasons for challenge' (p. 275). This he asserts is fundamental and simple and it enables him to do without Bayes' rule. The second feature is the cumulative effect of very many pieces of evidence derived from individual personal experience. Although the evidence of one's own personal experience might be unconvincing, when it is backed up by that of many others it becomes overwhelming. Swinburne does not directly address the probabilistic analysis of how the combined testimony of many individual experiences accumulates. This is surprising in view of his use of the sophisticated technical apparatus of Bayes' theorem in the earlier stages. There is no discussion of the combination of probabilities for the conjunction of many testimonies nor of the question of the degree of independence which may be supposed to exist between them. It is probably the case that reading of other's experiences, for example, may induce similar experiences in oneself and mass hallucinations are not unknown. Nevertheless the sheer volume of such testimony throughout human history, much of which is unquestionably independent, would almost certainly substantiate Swinburne's claim and very possibly add strength to it.

The very detailed analyses which Swinburne makes of the other evidence involve two very questionable steps. The seriousness of these should not be overstated since their whole purpose is to establish the weak conclusion that the probability of God is not negligible. One of the difficulties is rather technical and was touched on in Bartholomew (1984) and expanded somewhat in Bartholomew (1988). It hinges on the possibility of using Bayes' theorem at all where one cannot enumerate all the possible alternative hypotheses to that of the existence of God. (It would be too simplistic to suppose that there is only *one* alternative.)

The second difficulty is more accessible. It concerns the possibility of assigning the prior probability to God's existence which the application of the theorem requires. We have to be in a position to say something about this in the absence of any evidence at all except for what Swinburne calls the 'background' knowledge which lies behind all our reasoning. Swinburne contends that this can be done by reference to the 'simplicity' of the God-hypothesis. The idea is that the simpler a hypothesis the more likely it is to be true. As a glance at the discussion following Bartholomew (1988) will show it is not universally accepted that the hypothesis is simple or that, if it is, that fact alone justifies giving it a high prior probability. The central question is whether the character of the hypothesis itself can tell us anything about its truth. It is not at all obvious that it can. For this is itself a hypothesis about the character of the world which must also be the subject of uncertainty and to which one would have to assign a prior probability. The crux of the matter is whether one can assign a prior probability to any hypothesis prior to having any knowledge whatsoever. If one does claim to be able to do this it must surely be based on one's general knowledge of the way things are and this is posterior to the originating event and not prior. We are trying to do the impossible by asking what degree of belief would be justified in the hypothesis that God exists prior to anything existing at all including the human mind which is being asked to make the assessment. This seems quite impossible if not absurd.

There are other ways of introducing prior probabilities but these involve the importation of equally arbitrary principles. For example, the Principle of Insufficient Reason which says that in the absence of any information as to which of a set of possible alternatives is true we should regard them as equally probable. Like Matson (1965), I regard this as unacceptable, not least because of the difficulty of saying how many alternatives there are.

It appears then that the use of formal probability methods by Swinburne is questionable at a number of points and it is far from clear whether the deficiencies can be remedied even in principle. Even if this is true it does not mean that the argument is without value and it certainly does not mean that its conclusion is false. An important element in Swinburne's reasoning concerns various probabilities of the world being the way it is *given* that God created it. Though these may not be particularly large Swinburne contends that on all other conceivable hypotheses they are much more unlikely. In that sense the hypothesis of theism is better supported. (This is an example of 'likelihood' inference.) At an informal level the fact that theism is well supported by our experience of the world in general combined with the cumulative testimony of many people's experience provides a good rational basis for belief. It may fall well short of a precise numerical calculation but is a considerable advance on Gaskin's much less structured approach to striking the balance of probabilities. It may, indeed, be about as far as one can go in harnessing probability theory in the attempt to answer one of life's more fundamental questions.

PROZESKY: THE BALANCE OF PROBABILITY

A fascinating and judicious account of where the debate about God now stands is given by Prozesky (1992). His treatment is in much the same spirit as that of Gaskin and we might well have considered them together since they come to much the same conclusion. However, Prozesky is more explicit about his use of probability and his treatment owes something to that of Swinburne which we have just examined. Prozesky's admirable summing-up of the position provides a good point at which to leave the more general arguments and move on, in the next section, to some scientific issues.

Prozesky conducts his analysis in the form of a debate, first taking one side and then the other. As the debate proceeds the balance of probability between the two contending hypotheses moves up and down before finally coming to rest. Like Stannard he makes much use of the comparative method of forming probability judgements by asking, 'Is A more likely than B given all the evidence?' He clearly recognizes the argument must be cumulative and hence that there is need to judge by how much the next piece of evidence should change the current balance. This is done subjectively but we are given a clear statement at each stage of what judgement has been made. Prozesky does not use Bayes' rule though he is aware of Swinburne's approach and, in particular, he sets great store by the argument of simplicity in establishing the prior probability of God.

Prozesky's declared aim is to see each side of the argument from the inside and to treat both fairly and honestly. He fully recognizes the complexity of the task and has no illusions about his own powers of effecting a synthesis. 'I am of course acutely aware of how vast is the ocean I have tried to chart and how small my ship and her instruments' (p. 173). In the face of such honesty it may seem churlish to criticize but it is entirely within the spirit of his treatment that others should test his judgements. It seems to me that there are questions to be raised and perhaps unintended implications in the logic of the probability arguments.

Prozesky is quite explicit about the hypotheses that are being entertained. He is not concerned simply with the proposition 'God exists' but with the question, 'Are there rational grounds for believing that an eternal, infinite and perfectly loving God exists or not, a God whom Christians say is Trinitarian in nature, who has revealed himself in the great events and scriptures of the Judeo-Christian traditions and who entered history as Jesus Christ, the world's only saviour?' (p. 171). The alternative is described as secularism, or naturalism which sees no place for God. The very preciseness of the theistic alternative is, as we shall see, a cause of stumbling.

We have already noted, and challenged, Swinburne's postulate that the simpler an explanation the greater its prior probability. Prozesky accepts this and since he regards the notion of God as a very simple idea the debate begins with a clear advantage to theism. The pendulum swings the other way when we come to natural evil which argues against an all-good and loving God. Prozesky recognizes that it may have been essential to leave a degree of flexibility in the created order as the price worth paying for the freedom and autonomy of individuals. However, this does not help orthodoxy because, in his judgement, such a view demands total control over and hence direct responsibility for everything that happens. Here and subsequently we may note a Calvinistic undercurrent in Prozesky's view of orthodoxy. But even within the boundaries of main-line Christianity he gives much attention to the fact of evil but hardly any recognition of the interpretation to be placed upon it in the light of God's intimate involvement with evil in the crucifixion. One would have thought that the centrality of eucharistic worship in so much of Christianity would have indicated something relevant to the evidence being weighed. Even more surprising is the unwarranted exclusiveness attributed to orthodoxy. Why, if God did reveal himself at all, Prozesky wonders, should he have restricted it to so few? If there are such benefits to be obtained from the knowledge of God why be so parsimonious in their distribution? It is perfectly clear from the New Testament that the revelation was not intended to be limited to any group but was to be proclaimed to the whole world. The initial differences between Peter and Paul show that some found it hard to come to terms with that fact but the whole missionary enterprise is predicated on the belief that the church is a channel of revelation and not a container of it.

Prozesky also argues that 'If there really is a perfectly good God who is present everywhere in the way that Christians say he is, and if a relationship with him is the only way to undergo moral upliftment then his presence can hardly fail to improve all those who welcome him into their lives' (p. 152). Here, surely, is an undeniable consequence of the theistic hypothesis which can be tested empirically and in Prozesky's judgement it fails the test. There are, he claims, very many good people who owe nothing to a trust in God. This, of course, is true but irrelevant to the point in question. The proposition claims that 'his presence can hardly fail to *improve* all . . .' The fallacy is a common one much publicized in rela-tion to so-called league tables for schools, hospitals, and uni-versities. The quality of a school is to be judged by how much it improves the level of educational attainment rather than by the final level reached. Prozesky offers no evidence on this point and it would be extraordinarily difficult to come by. But even if we deal with the matter on Prozesky's own terms the case is far from proven. We all know that some women are as tall as some men but that alone does not tell us whether they are taller, or shorter, *on average*. If we had evidence, for example, that atheists were disproportionately represented among aid workers and blood donors or that they gave more generously to charity we would have the beginnings of a case. Even then it would be fraught with problems of definition and interpretation but in the absence of anything beyond vague generalities Prozesky's evaluation counts for little.

We have used these examples to show that the final conclusion at which Prozesky arrives is open to serious question but the most interesting point arises directly out of that conclusion. Before stating this it is important to notice that the theistic hypothesis bifurcates along the way into a traditional branch and what Prozesky calls alternative Christian theism. This latter arises by jettisoning some less well-supported tenets of traditional belief. The conclusion is then expressed as follows: 'what I have been calling alternative Christian theism is significantly more probable than its mainline, orthodox cousin, and about as probable as secularism' (p. 173).

This seemingly bland statement implies more than it may seem to say. Suppose first, as Prozesky seems to suppose, that these three are the only possibilities. Then whatever numerical probabilities we might choose to assign to them they must add up to one. Since Prozesky gives secularism and alternative Christian theism about equal probability and says that both are significantly more probable than main-line theism then both must be in excess of $1/3$. Let the amount by which they exceed $1/3$ be d. Then it follows that the probability of main-line theism must be $1/3 - 2d$. The probability of theism of one or other kind (assuming them to be mutually exclusive) is then the sum of the probabilities of the two taken separately, namely $2/3 - d$. We can certainly say that d must be greater than zero and that it cannot exceed $1/6$ because if it did the probability of main-line theism would become negative. Thus the probability of theism of some kind must, on this reckoning, be between $1/2$ and $2/3$ so God's existence is more probable than not. It is not clear whether Prozesky's alternative Christian theism would embrace all other kinds of theism. If not we should admit other theisms of the Jewish, Islamic, or Hindu variety, for example. Readers with a modest algebraic competence can explore the consequences of so doing. If these were supposed to have probabilities equal to that of main-line Christian theism, for example, our conclusion would not be essentially changed. However, the multiplication of hypotheses would have implications for how the evidence is to be weighed and, especially, for the assumption of mutual exclusiveness of the various theisms.

Without necessarily endorsing all his probability judgements it is clear that Prozesky's analysis does not lead to the conclusion that the probability of God's existence is close to either zero or one. This places him with Gaskin and Stannard rather than with Montefiore or Dawkins.

DENTON, DAWKINS, AND GOULD: CHANCE IN NATURE

We now move on to arguments where the rules of probability are invoked to infer something about the truth of propositions relevant to the existence or nature of God. In a few cases actual numbers have been used but for the most part it is sufficient to establish that some probability is either very large or very small. This type of argument has a long history going back at least to Arbuthnot (1710) who used it to establish, as he thought, the existence of divine providence from the evidence of the preponderance of male births in London parishes. The logic of his argument and some examples of more recent efforts along the same lines were discussed in Chapter 3 of Bartholomew (1984) and will not be repeated here except where it is necessary as a first step to taking the analysis further.

We shall take three examples. The first is an argument against evolution by natural selection where Denton (1985) has used probability arguments in an effort to show that the production of molecules of evolutionary value is beyond the reach of chance. This may be regarded as a development of the claims of le Comte de Noüy and Hoyle and Wickramasinghe, discussed in Bartholomew (1984). The implication, if his conclusion is true, is that if chance cannot explain life then we must look to some purposeful activity on the part of a Creator. Secondly we shall return to the work of Richard Dawkins according to whom the random character of the evolutionary process counts strongly against the idea of any directing purpose. This leads on to the claim of Gould (1991), in his book *Wonderful Life*, that major catastrophes in the early stages of life on earth effectively rule out any idea that we were an intended product of the universe.

The problem of the origin of life has to do with how complex molecules can arise from simple molecules. And not only do the molecules have to be large, but they also have to have the sort of physical structure which makes self-replication possible. The argument of those such as Hoyle and Wickramasinghe is that if simple molecules were linked up in a random fashion the chance of getting anything biologically useful is remote. So remote, in fact, that the age and size of the universe is not great enough for there to have been time and space for it to happen. But the assumptions which this calculation makes about how these molecules are formed are such as to destroy all confidence in the answer. Denton (1985) has recycled the argument in a form which makes the fallacy easier to see and also to suggest a way of making it more realistic. He uses, by way of analogy, the example of forming words from the letters of the alphabet. He imagines that letters are strung together at random in an attempt to make meaningful words. He calculates, for example, that if one draws three letters at random the chance of getting a meaningful English word is about 1 in 30. When the word length is seven letters the probability falls to 0.00001 and when it is twelve the probability drops to 10^{-14} which is virtually zero. In the molecular situation the letters represent the molecular building bricks and the words are the complex molecules with biological usefulness corresponding to 'meaningfulness'. In practice the complex molecules are much longer than the words considered here but the calculations are intended to show that the chance of getting a meaningful word or molecule falls very rapidly indeed as the number of elements increases. It is this very rapid decline in probability with the length which leads Denton to regard the claim that life could have arisen by chance as impossible.

The fallacy in this line of reasoning is that there is not one 'chance' hypothesis but many. We shall use the same analogy to show how another random model of molecule formation could give rise to useful large molecules with much higher probability. But first we note that even if Denton's argument were correct it is not sufficient to show that life could not arise in this way. Any event, however improbable, will certainly happen sooner or later, somewhere or other, given enough time and space. If there can be one earth why not many others and if one universe why not an unlimited number as envisaged in some understandings of quantum theory? May we not actually be the result of the trillions-to-one chance? Admittedly this strains credulity almost to breaking point but it cannot be refuted on logical grounds alone.

However, there is a better way of countering Denton's argument which opens the way for an altogether more plausible account of life's origins. This regards the formation of ever more complex molecules as a *process* taking place over time. How things become linked together will then depend not only on the ingredients available but on the current state of the 'soup'. Developments will depend on the total environment which, itself, is the product of earlier stages of the same random process. In Bartholomew (1988) I gave an extension of Denton's argument about word formation to show how, by viewing the development of the process over time, what was virtually impossible from his viewpoint becomes distinctly possible. The idea was that 'words' would be formed by random linkages of existing partly formed words. Those that were meaningful (i.e. biologically useful) at any stage would persist whereas others would be prone to disintegration. Since many long words are compound words one would expect the proportion of meaningful long words to be greatly enhanced by some such process. This argument, of course, comes nowhere near establishing a high probability for the appearance of life but it does make two important points. First that it is not enough to speak loosely about life arising 'by chance'; we must be more specific about the framework in which it operates. Secondly the evidence provided by Denton is not sufficient to show that the evolution of life is 'beyond the reach of chance'.

This view of evolution as a random process rather than a once-for-all randomization of the raw materials adds a new depth to the question and raises many technical questions about such things as the viability of intermediate forms and so on. The crucial question for our purposes is whether viewing the process from this more realistic perspective strengthens or weakens the case for theism. We defer a full discussion until we have considered other examples but we note now that the argument can be taken either way. The traditional line, which I have refuted in Bartholomew (1984), is that a very small probability associated with a chance hypothesis counts in favour of theism on the grounds that one can then ignore the possibility of such a rare event having happened and hence accept the theistic alternative. Looking at it another way, if chance is part of God's strategy for creation then theism would require a high probability of life emerging. On that view Denton's argument, if correct, would tell against theism.

All that we have shown so far is that some rather impressive-looking calculations purporting to show that the creation of life is beyond the reach of chance are flawed and that one can conceive of a process which suggests that it is otherwise. Before worrying too much about what conclusions might be drawn we must ask whether there are any stochastic (i.e. chance or random)[2] models of the evolutionary process which point to a high probability of life emerging on earth. Eigen (1971), whose work on the subject I discussed in *God of Chance*, thought there were on the basis of his work

---

[2] In speaking to audiences from different specialisms I have found that terms such as 'stochastic' and 'random' have particular connotations in some fields. No such distinctions are made in this book.

on molecular evolution. Gould, to whose contribution we shall shortly come, also thinks that life in some form was probably inevitable even though we were by no means a likely consequence of its appearance. But, to my mind, the most convincing demonstration that the complexity needed for rudimentary life forms could be achieved without external intervention is to be found in the writings of Richard Dawkins. He is concerned not with the origins of life at the molecular level but with its evolutionary development to give life as we know it today. It is in that context that we shall discuss it but here we note that the underlying idea about complexity arising from simplicity has wider applications.

By the use of what he calls 'cumulative chance' Dawkins seeks to show that the quite rapid appearance of highly structured forms can, in fact, occur without the need to invoke a designer. In Dawkins (1986) and elsewhere he describes a computer program which allows one to 'breed' many generations of what he calls 'biomorphs'. These are patterns displayed on a monitor. The offspring of any generation are subject to random mutations and the operator selects that member among the offspring which is most like some predetermined target shape and this is then used to breed the next generation and so on. By this means highly structured forms arise many orders of magnitude more rapidly than would be the case if one had to assemble all the pieces at random each time. This process does not, of course, exactly mimic evolution and one might be misled into arguing that the human operator at the computer must be replaced by the divine operator of the universe if the process is to work. In reality it is the environment which does the selecting and this itself is partly the product of earlier stages of the same process. Failure adequately to incorporate this aspect severely limits Dawkins's model as a complete explanation of evolutionary development and it remains to be seen whether its promise can be fulfilled. Nevertheless, Dawkins's argument succeeds in its primary purpose which is to show that chance acting cumulatively can bring about apparently purposeful change very much more rapidly than the crude all-at-once notions of how chance operates that we encountered earlier.

A more serious challenge to traditional belief comes from the world of palaeontology where, according to Stephen Jay Gould, the fossil record suggests disasters on a scale which would have wreaked havoc with any divine plan to produce human life. His account of the new understanding of the course of early life on this planet as deduced from the Burgess Shales in British Columbia is lucidly set out in Gould (1991). His central conclusion, for our purposes, is summed up in the following sentence from the preface which runs like a refrain through the whole book. 'Wind back the tape of life to the early days of the Burgess Shale; let it play again from an identical starting point and the chance becomes vanishingly small that anything like human intelligence would grace the replay' (p. 14). Later he speaks of the awesome improbability of evolution. To set this conclusion in context and to evaluate its strength we must look, however briefly, at the fascinating story which Gould tells. The Burgess Shales contain the fossil survivals of a veritable explosion of life forms at the end of the Cambrian period about 530 million years ago. Ancestors of all the four main anthropoids on earth today are present in the shales but so are fifteen to twenty other species which appear to have no descendants. For whatever reason there seems to have been a drastic pruning which Gould attributes largely to natural disasters. Accidents in the past are therefore responsible for the body forms which survived and on which subsequent evolution has been based.

At first sight this seems like a variation on Dawkins's theme of natural selection operating on the great variety of life which nature offers. But, according to Gould, it was not fitness for the environment which determined which species were to survive but 'the luck of the draw'. He infers that major catastrophes eliminated fit and unfit alike without regard to their suitability for subsequent evolution into beings such as ourselves. Gould believes that the evidence of the shales means that we must abandon the traditional idea of a 'cone of evolution' and replace it by something else. The cone takes its name from the shape of the family tree of organisms as they are supposed to have evolved over time. At the root are one or more basic types of organism. As evolution proceeds the tree branches outwards and upwards in the form of an inverted cone giving a growing variety of organisms of ever-increasing complexity. Such a view supports the traditional picture of the 'ascent of man' traced back through the primates to the earliest forms of life. Gould wishes to replace the cone with a rather different kind of tree which produces many branches near its root most of which are then eliminated before they can develop any farther. The few that survived have given rise to all the life forms present today. If the tape of evolution were to be replayed, to use Gould's favourite metaphor again, it is inconceivable that the same branches would have survived and so the world would have been populated by very different creatures and nothing resembling human intelligence is likely to have arisen.

Gould does not labour the atheistic tendency of the picture which he presents and he often uses biblical metaphors. But this should not disguise the fact that his conclusions are much more damaging to the notion of a providential God than is Dawkins's cumulative chance. We can, of course, always fall back on the argument noted earlier that, however unlikely was our appearance on this planet, given enough time and space something like us would have arisen somewhere in this or another universe. But we can do better than that because although Gould is strong on description and detail, in which he clearly revels, he is much weaker on inference. We must first ask whether the evidence which Gould presents does in fact support his conclusion. There are several weak links in the argument and one serious fault of logic.

What we know or can know about happenings as far back as the Cambrian period is of course strictly limited. The Burgess Shales are a tiny fraction of the whole globe and it would be a remarkable feat of detection if we could, with any confidence, reconstruct the events which lay behind the fragmentary record available to us. It is nevertheless perfectly clear that a great variety of body forms, which might possibly have formed the basis of evolution, once existed. Gould can see no reason why some should have survived rather than others and since there is evidence of mass extinctions in such early times it seems plausible to him that survival was a matter of chance rather than some intrinsic superiority of design. But this raises two questions. Is it plausible that whole species should have been eliminated at one fell swoop? If the varieties found in the Burgess Shales were distributed over the whole globe this seems very unlikely. If, on the other hand, those species which died out were local to north-west Canada maybe they never were major species on a worldwide scale at any time. The relative abundance of the species at this particular locality may or may not be a good guide to the global situation. The more successful and numerous species would be those most likely to survive a physical upheaval and its climatic aftermath.

Gould does not appear to take into account the relative frequencies of the body types and the effect which they would have on chances of survival. Information of this kind, which seems to be lacking, is essential for forming a realistic judgement about what might have happened if the tape of history were to be rerun.

Gould also leans heavily on negative evidence which, when it concerns the work of others, he justly points out is the most treacherous kind of argument that a scientist can ever use. He cannot see any reason why some body structures present in early organisms were better fitted for life than others. To conclude that there were no such reasons and to then deduce with such confidence that the probability of the appearance of intelligent life is extremely small involves an extrapolation of heroic proportions.

Indeed, as I now intend to argue, there is further evidence which points in the other direction. That evidence is the undisputed fact of our own existence. This is part of the data on which inferences about origins, purpose, and so forth must be based. The present state of the world is just as much a part of that evidence as are the fossils of British Columbia. Gould's logical flaw is in making no use of this. One might well challenge his conclusion by saying that if his hypothesis about human origins makes our existence so improbable then maybe he should look for an alternative which renders it rather more probable! The likelihood method set out in Chapter 2 and used several times since requires us to compare the plausibilities of competing hypotheses by computing their likelihoods—that is, the probabilities which they assign to what has actually occurred. It is not the actual probability that matters but its size relative to those relating to other competing hypotheses. Clearly there is no possibility of being able to enumerate such hypotheses and compute their associated probabilities in any precise sense but it is surely not difficult to imagine other scenarios which would render our appearance rather more likely. For example, that certain early life-forms were more successful and sufficiently numerous to give them a head start in the race for survival, making them capable of withstanding the shocks of a hostile environment. If anything like that were true successive runs of the tape of evolution might very well have turned out much more alike than Gould is willing to grant.

Before leaving *Wonderful Life* we might pause to look at another of Gould's arguments against the notion of purpose. He notes that on a cosmic time-scale it took about half the time available (about 10 billion years in all) for self-consciousness to emerge. Given the uncertainties and errors in the evolutionary path, especially the fact that there were extremely long periods with nothing much happening, this seems to be leaving it very late. It might just as easily have taken 20 billion years to reach self-consciousness and by then the earth would have been incinerated! Is it credible that a God whose main purpose was to produce beings such as us would have run such a risk of failure? Should he not have either given himself much more time or hurried things along? It is, in fact, possible to make calculations about the time when self-conscious life might have been expected to appear on various assumptions about the varying lengths of the preliminary stages. These show that the chance of it happening well within the sun's life-span need not be small at all but since they are entirely speculative they need not detain us except to note that any such calculations are much to be preferred to mere assertions.

At this point it may be helpful to take stock of where we stand. All three examples are concerned with the role of chance in some form or other and with what can be inferred from the fact that some occurrences relevant to the existence of a purposeful God appear to have very small probabilities.

The first thing to notice is that none of these arguments, however interpreted, constitute a disproof of God's existence. To begin with they are about the process leading to life and not about the origins of the raw materials. The question of how there came to be anything in the first place is still left open. A god who merely got things started and thereafter lost interest would be far removed from the God of the major religions but it should nevertheless be made clear that even when science has done its worst this is as far as it can go. Secondly, there is the argument we have noticed several times already which may be stated as follows. No matter how improbable the evolution of self-conscious beings may have been the chance was certainly not zero, otherwise we should not be here. That being so, the appearance of beings comparable with ourselves could have been made as near certain as desired if enough attempts were made. Given a God of unlimited resources, unrestrained by human notions of economy, such a seemingly profligate creative strategy might have been the best option. Again this establishes a minimalist position which I, personally, do not find very appealing, but in logic it is irrefutable.

Beyond this point the argument turns on what kind of God one is thinking of, and, especially, what sort of involvement is required of him in the creative process. If one believes that the doctrine of creation requires a constant active participation of the creator in the sense that if he were not continually interfering then evolution would not have taken its appointed path then the current scientific under-standing poses profound problems. It is, of course, impossible to refute the claim that what appears random to us is, when seen in the perspective of eternity, the purposeful act of God. However, as I argued in Bartholomew (1984) the abandon-ment of this position does not impoverish or diminish our doctrine of creation but enriches it. We have to think of a much more sophisticated creative process than the simple mechanical model which owed so much to Newton. It calls, perhaps, for a more intimate relationship between God and the creation in which the very nature of the stuff of the physical universe is designed to produce creatures (among other things, perhaps) such as ourselves, capable of sharing with him in the enjoyment of creation. His greatness and power is to be seen not so much in the individual direc-tion of the courses of trillions of fundamental particles but in the original creative act and in the 'higher' activities of bring-ing to fulfilment what traditional doctrine calls the 'commu-nion of saints'.

Are the exceedingly small probabilities which have arisen in our examples consistent with the existence of such a God? If Denton's calculations were correct they might suggest that unaided natural selection was not enough and hence that an active God was necessary to help things along. But we have argued that the probabilities may not be so small which suggests that there is something in the nature of the material universe which makes the appearance of life likely if not inevitable. But this too points in the direction of a designer because it is rather remarkable that this should be so. The role of chance in Dawkins's view of evolution would only count against God's existence if it implied that almost every other course that evolution might have taken would have failed to produce self-conscious beings. This would be extremely difficult to do but two things argue against it. Brains are inevitably highly complex structures. Since in the evolutionary struggle complex entities have had, and would be expected to have, an advantage over their simpler competitors, we might expect that increasing complexity would be a characteristic of any evolutionary path. This makes it very plausible that the complexity necessary to support intelligent life would be a likely outcome. Secondly, the environment places severe constraints on the size and shape of viable organisms. For example, in order to work successfully the various organs of a body have to be mutually compatible. The weight of a body goes up in proportion to the cube of its linear measure whereas the strength of its bones is proportional to the square. This places fundamental limits on size. Further, the environment consists, in part, of other creatures competing for food and other resources. It may well be that the combined influences of all these factors effectively determine the main form which any intelligent life can take. We do not know whether this is so and may never be able to find out. But in order to read atheism in biological history one must assume that randomness at the micro-level is reflected in an equal degree of indeterminacy at the macro-level of living organisms. This is known not to be the case in general and the phenomenon known to evolutionists as convergence (see e.g. Dawkins, 1986: 94) provides an illustration of the point from within evolution itself. The evidence produced by Dawkins, and Monod before him, is thus entirely consistent with belief in God.

The possible consequences of major catastrophes in the early history of the earth which might have radically altered the course of evolution have to be reckoned with in any theistic interpretation. According to our view any Creator would know that such hazards existed and would need to prepare for them by ensuring that life would emerge with sufficient potential both in quantity and variety to survive onslaughts from the environment in sufficiently good order to continue along the path of ever-increasing complexity. The condition described by Gould (1991) in which there was sufficient 'space' for a great diversification (he calls it an explosion) of life-forms to develop is just what one might have expected to find. But whatever may be the truth about what happened in those early days the fact that we did emerge strongly favours those hypotheses which make self-conscious life a very likely outcome and that is what theism requires.

Perhaps the only thing that can be asserted with confidence is that since a cosmos such as ours is certainly possible then a God could certainly bring it about whether by a one-off act or by repeated trials. If there is no God one is ultimately left with having to assert that at some point something of enormous potential happened, or existed, for no reason whatsoever—which brings us back, full circle, to something very like the traditional argument from design.

It seems to me that probability arguments of this kind can say nothing directly about the existence of a prime mover, first cause, or whatever name one chooses to use. We can and have used them to argue that there is no inconsistency with theism and that any fully worked-out alternative with a serious claim to belief is a long way off. The arguments also throw some light on the question of what kind of being God must be by giving some insight into how he has chosen to work.

Since we have claimed that even the strongest anti-theistic arguments cannot resolve the question of where the substance of the universe came from in the first place it is appropriate to notice that some would dispute this. Among cosmologists there have been attempts to get behind the 'big bang' to obtain some understanding of how something could come out of nothing. If it could be established that matter and energy could have arisen from nothing then the difficulty of explaining the origin of the cosmos would be removed. Atkins (1981), for example, has explained how the quantum theory does allow such a possibility. By means of a 'random' quantum fluctuation there could come into being an equal quantity of matter and antimatter which, if put together, would 'cancel' out and leave the 'nothing' from which it all arose. It is known that matter and antimatter both exist in the universe and it seems distinctly likely that the amounts are equal. One may therefore be led to conclude that the 'big bang' need not have been engineered by the divine originator but would necessarily occur sooner or later from the inherent properties of the 'nothingness' which existed before.

Like all attempts at explaining origins this merely puts the question one stage further back. It requires the existence, in a certain sense, of the quantum laws which make the whole thing possible. And where did these come from we may well ask? We have reached a point where our ability to conceptualize what is meant by absolute nothingness is strained to the limit. Nevertheless if the thrust of Atkins's argument is to show that the existence of a material universe may be highly probable even if there is no God, the theist will reply that the quantum fluctuation is a way of describing how God creates something out of nothing. Again the alleged probability, or improbability, of some event—in this case the most fundamental event of all—takes us no nearer to resolving the choice between theism and atheism.

THE ANSWER

Returning to the question of our chapter title our answer must be that, in the strict sense, it is impossible to say. This is because the only way we could arrive at a probability would be first to assign to the proposition a prior probability. In every other case, except the question of God's existence, we have background knowledge on which we can make some judgement about the prior probability but in the case of God, who is prior to everything, there can be no such background evidence. The only other possibility seems to be to find something in the structure of the proposition itself, such as simplicity, which implies such a probability. I am uncon vinced that this can be done. Claims to have arrived at a probability of God cannot, therefore, be justified.

The same argument applies to any version of the atheistic hypothesis whether it be that the laws of physics could not be other than they are or that our universe is the outcome of a vast number of trials.

In the absence of prior probabilities the best we can do is to use the likelihood approach. Following this route we favour those hypotheses which give higher probabilities to what we observe. We are not then permitted to go as far as assigning posterior probabilities to hypotheses but we can regard likelihoods as telling us about their relative plausibilities. If we consider first the remarkable cosmic coincidences, the theistic hypothesis (and at least one of the atheistic hypotheses mentioned earlier) gives them a high probability.

When we cast the net more widely to include the full range of evidence subsequent to the creation we have the various attempts of Swinburne, Gaskin, Stannard, and Prozesky to weigh the likelihoods. Although they do not express their methodology in these terms I think their results are best interpreted in this way. They all come to much the same conclusion: that on the objective evidence there is no clear advantage to any of the hypotheses. (In Swinburne's case, this is before personal experience is taken into account.)

My own personal judgement is that the scale is tipped substantially in favour of theism, chiefly because I see chance as playing an essential and constructive part in the scheme of things. Since this necessarily entails a degree of natural 'evil' its presence does not count so heavily against theism as in some assessments of the evidence.

Turning finally to those such as Gould and Dawkins who think that chance in evolution virtually rules out theism and to Denton who argues, contrarily, that chance cannot explain it, we have found fault with the inferential logic in both cases. If the plausibility of a hypothesis is properly judged by the probability of what has actually happened then that of a purposive creator stands up well against its rivals.

If all of this is counted as natural theology it is abundantly clear that it cannot deliver the certainties which many might hope for. In one sense the results are extremely modest but in another they are far-reaching. The most substantial achievement is the demolition of some widely canvassed but superficial arguments for atheism. At the same time, we have demonstrated the intrinsic difficulties facing anyone who sets out to establish the probability of God.

7
The Bible

If there is a God who interacts with the world and if that interaction takes place primarily at the level of the human mind then one would expect the divine voice to be heard here and there, at least, in human utterances and writing. One might then look for evidence of the supernatural in the sacred writings of religious communities who claim to hear the voice of God through this medium. Such writings are venerated by their custodians as vehicles of divine truth and are seen as prime evidence of an unseen world—some would say the sole and sufficient evidence. If they are right, most of the other evidences considered in this book are of a secondary nature and though they may be valued as a useful corroboration of belief, the real foundation lies elsewhere.

The question for the present chapter is, therefore, whether a scientific approach to the text of the Bible can throw any light on the claim that it is a vehicle of divine revelation. To some extent the answer to that question depends on what kind of literature we take it to be. Much of the text, the Gospels in particular, appear to be straightforward accounts of things which were said and done. Do we take them at face value and investigate their reliability as history or do we allow for the possibility that, for example, they are documents of the Early Church cast in narrative form? This too is a matter of some uncertainty which might benefit from an analysis of the probabilities involved. However, the issues discussed here can, to some extent, be analysed from a position of agnosticism on such questions, as they are principally concerned with the meaning of sayings and the structure of documents. However, broadly speaking, we have started from the position that Swinburne's principle of credulity applies here also so that documents should be taken for what they seem to be until evidence is found to the contrary. That some testing of historical claims is called for follows from the fact that Christianity and Judaism are historical religions which depend on certain things having happened and having been reliably reported in documents handed down to us. If these records can be shown to be reliable then some of the extraordinary events reported may be taken as evidence of a reality beyond the physical world.

The literature of biblical criticism is enormous and varied. It makes claims, many of which are now widely accepted, about the dates, structure, and origins of biblical books which are sometimes at variance with the claims made by the books themselves and with traditional interpretations of them. Even if accepted, such claims do not dispose of the hypothesis that, in some sense, they contain the word of God, but they do tend to muffle the clarity with which that voice can be heard.

Our first step will be to raise the question of whether modern methods of biblical criticism can be said to be scientific in any sense and hence of whether the conclusions can be accepted with the same kind of confidence as the results of ordinary scientific research. In particular, we shall enquire whether the very considerable uncertainties which necessarily attend such studies are handled according to the logic of probability. To attempt to answer that question as baldly stated would require a range of expertise which probably does not exist in any one individual and certainly not in the present author. Nevertheless the question of how the inferences are drawn is as important as the raw material on which they are based. The former is commonly disregarded and merits more attention than it usually gets. Here we shall look only at two or three aspects of the general question which lend themselves to scientific treatment. Lest there should be any misunderstanding let me repeat that by focusing on matters which lend themselves to quantification I do not intend to imply that other approaches lack validity.

We begin with the way in which biblical scholars handle notions of uncertainty. Many recognize that their conclusions cannot be established with certainty and they often express them in probabilistic language with a good deal of subtlety as we shall shortly see. There are two sides to this practice which might be usefully probed. First there are the processes by which the evidence is weighed, and secondly the language in which the conclusions are expressed. The latter is as important as the former since, without a common currency of language in matters of uncertainty, knowledge cannot become public property. As we noted in Chapter 2, doctors, lawyers, and managers face similar problems and their experience is relevant here also.

A more recent and, so far, very modest approach is explicitly scientific in that it works on the quantifiable characteristics of biblical texts and subjects them to statistical analysis. The term 'stylometrics' has been coined to describe this method of analysing literary works. The increasing availability of computer databases containing the whole text of the Bible and related literature have opened up immense opportunities for analyses of this kind which have, as yet, hardly been touched. Can such unquestionably scientific methods provide any support for supernatural claims on behalf of the biblical documents? An interim answer is offered in the second section.

The final sections of the chapter are concerned, more briefly, with three quite unconnected matters which bear upon the general question of the character of biblical texts. One concerns the discovery of significant words embedded in the text of parts of the Old Testament which purport to point to their divine origin. Although this verges on the bizarre and might be dismissed along with numerology as something for cranks only, it at least offers the prospect of a fairly precise testing. Awkward facts which do not fit in with our preconceptions should not be dismissed on that ground alone. The second topic has to do with what can be inferred about the parentage of the extant documents on which our present study has to be based. The final section introduces the argument that the true character of a literary text is not to be detected by a minute examination of its structure and origins but by the effect which it has on behaviour. If a text has a profound effect on how individuals act it must have a quality beyond the mere aggregation of words in interesting patterns. The Bible undoubtedly has changed people's lives and since this is objectively verifiable it is therefore pertinent to ask whether this means that it has a revelatory character.

BIBLICAL CRITICISM AND UNCERTAINTY

Nearly thirty years ago I attended a lecture in the Harvard Divinity School on the authorship of St Luke's Gospel. I cannot now remember the various theories which were advanced but I clearly recall that the main protagonists in the discussion which followed were very confident that their view was the correct one. It was obvious, even to a novice in those matters, that they could not all be right and that some, at least, had completely misjudged the strength of the evidence. The same situation could be found in most branches of knowledge and is common enough in everyday affairs. Our culture regards reluctance to come to a firm view as a sign of weakness and encourages us to pretend to certainties when the evidence does not justify them. In biblical studies, where much of the evidence is fragmentary and unquantifiable, this temptation is particularly strong. Although the focus of our discussion will be on biblical scholarship the arguments are equally relevant to many of the other areas covered in this book.

Our earlier discussion of the hazards of forming subjective probability judgements should have inculcated a degree of scepticism in the reader who, in consequence, may be tempted not to take probability judgements in the biblical literature too seriously. We shall now look at some examples of the use of probability language in the writings of biblical scholars from this critical standpoint but with the aim of being as constructive as possible.

If the Bible is of central importance in the Christian faith it is obviously essential to get as close as possible to the truth of the events and utterances which it records. This is especially true of its key figure, Jesus. Yet the nature of the manuscript evidence gives rise to much uncertainty about what was said and meant. The earliest manuscripts do not give identical accounts. They differ in what they include and often in the order and language of the material which they present. It therefore seems obvious that there must be a degree of uncertainty about the meaning to be attached to what the Bible says. To what extent this touches on essentials may be debatable. Proponents of theories of verbal inspiration bypass many of the difficulties though even they have to explain how the authentic word is to be distinguished.

Some biblical scholars, it is true, assume an air of confidence, even dogmatism, about their interpretations which seems undented by the equally confident advocacy of diametrically opposed positions by others of their colleagues. However, many more recognize the uncertainties which beset their conclusions and give these full weight in their expositions. Speaking of the historical aspects, Hooker (1991*a*) remarks, 'The historian always deals with probabilities, never with certainties. In one case the balance of probabilities may seem overwhelming, in another case 50 : 50, but always judgement and interpretation are involved' (p. 23). She goes on to remark that those who seek to avoid the uncertainties of historical research by arguing that history is irrelevant can only do so by adopting a prior belief about the nature of faith itself.

Hooker (1991*b*), herself, certainly adheres to her principles in her commentary on Mark's Gospel. Expressions of uncertainty with the liberal use of words such as *probably* and *likely* abound, occurring at a rate of about two every three pages.

Among them are, perhaps, rather more expressions of certainty than a strict interpretation of her precept might allow, but the overriding impression is one of a carefully balanced judgement giving full weight to all the evidence.

The question for us is whether the historian and biblical scholar use probability judgements in a way which is consistent with the principles for uncertain reasoning laid down in Chapter 2, and further, whether those same principles can be used to refine and sharpen the conclusions which they reach.

To begin with we must look at some examples of how probability language is actually used by biblical scholars, how they make their probability judgements, and how they combine them to build up a case. The following examples drawn from three writers list a number of conclusions they have reached with the degree of uncertainty they attach to them. In Barrett's (1962) discussion of the original order of the material in St John's Gospel we find (p. 845):

> *Certain*: that 7: 53–8 (the story of the adulteress) is an addition to the original text.
> *Very probable*: that 5: 31–4 is an addition.
> *Good reason to doubt*: whether ch. 21 forms part of the Gospel as originally planned.
> *Probable*: that the redactional glosses are few in number and small in extent.
> *Unlikely*: that many additions have been made.
> *Less to be said*: for the theory of textual dislocations.

Or again, in the late G. W. H. Lampe's note on the authorship of St Luke in the same commentary (Lampe, 1962: 820):

> *Quite uncertain*: how far specified traditions depend on the 'we' sections of Acts and how far on genuinely independent records or reminiscences.
> *Probably*: some independent tradition about authorship had come down to second-century writers.
> *Unlikely*: that without such traditions Luke would have been identified as author on internal grounds.
> *Certainly*: Gospel was written in and for Gentile Church.

Very Uncertain: the date of the Gospel.

Probably: the idea that it must have been written before AD 64 rests on a misunderstanding of the purpose and plan of the work.

By no means certain: that the apparent chronological inaccuracies . . . are to be explained in a particular way.

Very probable: that Luke was known to the fourth evangelist.

On the whole it seems probable: that Luke handles Mark freely; that Luke's passion story is taken from Mark.

Thirdly, after rehearsing the arguments about the dating of the Last Supper, Hooker (1991*b*), in her commentary on Mark's Gospel, concludes: 'The weight of the evidence therefore seems to be in favour of the Johanine dating: in other words it is *likely* that the Last Supper took place before the Feast of the Passover (John 13: 1) and that the identification with the passover meal was made after the event' (p. 334). The question then arises as to why Mark believed the Last Supper was a passover meal and Hooker provides an explanation based on confusion over the first day of unleavened bread and the day on which the passover lambs were slaughtered. This she concludes '*probably* explains Mark's dating'. But where do *likely* and *probably* stand on the scale of uncertainty: are they more or less than 50 : 50?

These examples certainly exhibit a commendable degree of restraint on the part of their authors but do they do more than signal the incompleteness of the evidence? There is first of all the question of calibration. Do the authors mean the same thing by the use of phrases such as 'likely' or 'very probable'? If the empirical evidence reported in Chapter 2 from other fields is any guide this must be very doubtful. It is not even always clear how the various expressions are to be ranked. Is Lampe's 'quite uncertain' more or less probable than his 'unlikely' or are both so imprecise that it is pointless to try to distinguish them? If that is the case, are they intended to convey more than a blanket statement printed on the title page to the effect that all conclusions which follow are uncertain?

This somewhat dismissive judgement of carefully balanced conclusions may seem to do scant justice to the subtleties of the process and the complexities of the evidence. Experts, quite properly, pride themselves on the quality of their judgements and it may well be that some people, who are thoroughly immersed in the subject-matter do have the ability to assess accurately degrees of uncertainty. It may even be that any attempt on their part to analyse their thinking and display it for others to see would be self-defeating. After all, most of us can run downstairs but we would be likely to stumble if we paused to analyse how we do it! Nevertheless a greater awareness of the hazards of subjective reasoning about uncertainty might profitably lead to more concern with the structure of the argument and with the logic of uncertainty which must govern the weighing of evidence no matter what its provenance. It is therefore pertinent to examine the mode of reasoning employed by those who work in this field in the light of the principles laid down earlier.

The simplest and most easily defensible type of subjective probability judgement is of the comparative kind. To assert that A is more probable than B or that A is the most probable out of a set of alternatives requires no absolute assessment of a probability. It merely points us towards the option which is most favoured by the evidence. Barrett (1971), for example, comes to a conclusion about the structure of the First Letter to the Corinthians in the words: 'I record the view that no partition theory in regard to 1 Corinthians seems more probable than that Paul simply wrote the letter through beginning with chapter i and finishing with chapter xvi . . .' (p. 15).

Hooker provides many such examples. For instance, when discussing the reported saying of Jesus, 'let the reader understand' (Mark 13: 14), in the passage about signs of the end, the comparison is two-edged. After dismissing the interpretation that it means 'the reader of Daniel' as *very unlikely* and mentioning the possibility that Mark was just copying a written source, she offers a third explanation that Mark is alerting his readers to the need to decode the language. This explanation itself is susceptible of several possible interpretations. Hooker thinks it *more probable* that the straightforward historical prediction given in Luke (21: 20) is an explanation on Luke's part based on his own knowledge of historical events rather than a deliberate obfuscation by Mark because of the dangerous political situation in which he wrote. She judges, however, that the *most likely* explanation is none of these, but is that Mark intends us to understand what Jesus says is 'to take place in the temple is both the fulfilment of Daniel's prophecy and also the sign of the arrival of the last things'. This example well illustrates the intricate way in which judgements can be interlocked yet without conveying the basis on which they are made. Much simpler is the question of why the comment, 'She had done what she could', has been included in the story of the woman who anointed Jesus' feet (Mark 14: 8). This has been interpreted as an anointing of his body for burial seen in retrospect as making up for the omission of that act at the time; Hooker thinks that it is *more likely* to be a symbolic act foreshadowing his death. The reason for this preference is that the resurrection showed such an anointing to be unnecessary and hence there would be no need to rectify it. Like so many similar cases the judgement is affected by the background beliefs which are taken for granted. A non-believer in the resurrection, for example, would see the odds rather differently.

This brings us to a fundamental difficulty with all such subjective estimates of probability. Bayes' rule tells us that the probability of any proposition is compounded of two parts: the prior probability and the likelihood. The former is based on the knowledge which we bring to the problem before we examine the particular data and the latter comes from the data themselves. Whether or not we explicitly recognize it, this dichotomy is embedded in any rational assessment of uncertainty. This often exhibits itself in the appearance of circularity in the argument. Hooker (1991*b*) is quite explicit in the matter when she comments (p. 13):

> The problem of separating tradition from redaction had thus proved as complex in its way as that of separating history from interpretation; in each case, the results depend very largely on a prior decision about the creativity of the evangelist or the community . . . for the answers one gives to questions about Mark's purpose and theology depended to a large extent on how much one attributed to Mark, and how much to his sources. Since we do not have his sources, to act as a 'control', we cannot say how much the material is directly attributable to Mark himself.

The prior belief we adopt on the one plays a major part in what we believe about the other.

One of the best examples is provided by the interpretation to be put upon the saying, 'There are some standing here who will not taste death before they see the Kingdom of God come with power' (Mark 9: 1, tr. Hooker). We now know that no consummation of cataclysmic proportions took place within the lifetime of those who heard the saying. Three hypotheses seem therefore to be possible.

1. Jesus did not actually say these words.
2. He said them but they have been misinterpreted to mean an event of such proportions.
3. He said them, as reported, and he was wrong.

If we were to reject (3) on the a priori grounds that Jesus could not be wrong, the choice between (1) and (2) would depend to some extent on the degree to which plausible alternative scenarios under (2) could be found. If, additionally, we take the prior view that words attributed to Jesus in the Gospels must have actually been uttered by him (2) is the only hypothesis to be entertained and the only task is then to decide which of the interpretations offered is the more plausible. But where does the evidence for ruling out (1) and/or (3) a priori come from if not from the accumulated weight of many pieces of evidence of the same general kind found elsewhere in the same Scriptures? Each decision depends on others which are no better based. Unless we can claim to have some external and independent authentication of a particular view of Scripture there is no escape from this circularity.

It is perfectly possible for rational thinkers to assign very different probabilities to the same event or proposition but only if they start out with very different prior beliefs. There is no neutral ground on which to anchor the chain of reasoning.

One might seem to get around the problem by appealing to what might be called the intrinsic probability of something. By this we mean that there is something about the structure or nature of the belief itself which implies something about its probability. This is much the same as Swinburne's claim that the 'simpler' a hypothesis the more intrinsically probable it is. Hooker has two examples which she refers to in these terms—one questionable and one defensible. The first concerns the story of the stilling of the storm (Mark 4: 35 ff.). Hooker thinks the story is intrinsically improbable on the grounds that it was the seasoned fishermen who were afraid and Jesus, the landlubber, who slept calmly. But there are intrinsic prior beliefs here rather than an intrinsic probability. Equally one might argue that if the storm was of sufficient severity even the experts would be alarmed whereas the inexperienced Jesus, believing himself to be in safe hands, would be undisturbed. It all depends on your prior beliefs about the nature of the storm and the threat which it represented. The second example is of a different kind. In Mark 14: 36 the use of the word *Abba* by Jesus of his Father is recorded. Is this genuine? Hooker's argument is that it is because of its rarity in this context. This is attested by the use of the Aramaic word here as well as in Romans and Galatians. The intrinsic probability of its genuineness rests on the fact that unusual things are likely to be remembered. Hence the fact that they are reported strongly suggests that they are genuine because people do not usually invent things which are improbable.[1] This is a psychological matter capable of empirical testing and provided that the extrapolation in time and culture can be justified does seem a legitimate way of imputing a modest probability.

Sometimes the link with a parallel case is made explicitly as in one discussion of the authorship of the Epistle to the Hebrews. One tradition assigns it to St Paul, but this is widely rejected. Another ascribes it to Barnabas, but Luther proposed Paul's colleague Apollos. This case has been argued by Montefiore and summarized by Barrett (1971: 8). The method is to establish a series of links between Hebrews and the First Letter to the Corinthians (generally agreed to be by Paul) which make it seem plausible that 1 Corinthians was written as a follow-up to a letter from Apollos (the present Hebrews), to put right a situation which, in part, that earlier letter had helped to create. There are over a dozen such points all of which 'fit' the hypothesis. On this ground one might allow a high probability to the Apollos theory though Barrett himself declines to do so. In essence the argument is that *if* Paul wrote 1 Corinthians then a good case can be made out for Apollos's authorship of Hebrews. This is another example where one probability depends on what we believe about another event of the same kind.

In the commentaries we have referred to there are a few attempts at the use of informal methods of combining probabilities and, sometimes, the recognition of the pitfalls in doing so. An example of a conjunction arises in Barrett's discussion of whether many additions have been made in St John's Gospel, although it is only implicit. Presumably one might allow that it was quite probable that one out of a number of disputed passages might be an addition, whereas the probability of ten disputed passages all being additions would

---

[1] A similar principle was proposed by Perrin (1967) for judging the authenticity of the sayings of Jesus. They are to be judged as authentic if they differ from the trend of the Gospel tradition. The trouble with all principles of this kind is that, aside from the practical difficulties of applying them, they take no account of gradations of probability.

be much diminished. Given the known propensity to over-estimate the probability of a conjunction we might well judge that the probability that all or most were additions to be very small.

When discussing the authorship of Mark's Gospel, Hooker (1991*b*) recognizes that the weight of the combined testimony to the link of Mark and Peter of Justin Martyr, Irenaeus, Clement of Alexandria, Origen, and the Anti-Marcionite Prologue is severely weakened if they all depend on Papias for that information. However, she does not go on to say anything about the probability of such dependence which would be necessary if the weight of the evidence is to be properly assessed.

A crude quantitative approach to assessing probabilities is sometimes adopted which involves counting arguments on each side of a case. For example, the claim that Luke was known to the fourth evangelist rests on a number of links between the two writings. The greater the number of links the more likely the proposition seems and the greater weight these carry against alternative arguments. Taking the approach a step further some arguments will seem stronger than others and so will be given more weight. These 'weights' are then combined in some way and 'balanced'. The extent to which these mental processes conform to the logic of uncertainty is certainly something which bears close examination. Hooker, on several occasions, refers to the number of scholars who have taken a given view implying that there is strength in numbers, but again there is the danger of circularity in which one probability is floated on a raft of no better-founded beliefs. The difficulties are compounded if there is dependence between the scholars.

There is one isolated but interesting example in Hooker (1991*b*) concerning the ending of Mark's Gospel. The Gospel appears to end abruptly at verse 8 in chapter 16 but most versions then go on to give another, longer ending; was this first ending intentional or accidental? Has the original ending been lost by, for example, the 'last page' wearing out through

much use? One way to try to answer this question is to compare probabilities. If there are good arguments, as there
appear to be, for Mark ending at the point he did it would be
a rather remarkable coincidence if an accidental break were
to occur at just that point. Much depends in this case on the
arguments for a natural ending at verse 8 but *if* that is
accepted *then* the accidental loss theory has little probability.

This varied collection of examples vividly illustrates the
uncertain nature of the biblical material. Whether we are
concerned with historicity or interpretation it seems that
there are few certainties to be had. Although some biblical
scholars seek to give full weight to the uncertainties their
efforts appear to have been no more successful than those of
their colleagues in other disciplines. There are, however, a
number of encouraging signs. One is an attempt to measure
the degree of consensus among the members of the US-based
Jesus Seminar. This has about one hundred members drawn
from a variety of denominational traditions. They meet to
debate and vote on the authenticity of the sayings attributed
to Jesus. The intention is to produce 'red-letter' editions of
the Gospel material of which Funk *et al.* (1989) is the first.
Each member classified a passage as red (3), pink (2), grey (1),
or black (0). An average of the individual scores (given in
brackets) was then calculated and this serves as a measure of
the group's view of its authenticity. The authors emphasize
that this is a measure of consensus rather than truth. One can
easily point to the weaknesses of such an approach but it represents a bold attempt to express explicitly the degree of
belief among a considerable group of scholars.

A very good appreciation of the inevitable uncertainties in
weighing the words of Jesus can be obtained from chapter 13
of Peacocke (1993). Included in this chapter is E. P.
Saunders's probabilistic classification of the substance of
Jesus' teaching. Thus, for example, he regards it as 'certain or
virtually certain' that Jesus preached the kingdom of God but
only 'probable' that he did not emphasize the national character of that kingdom. Likewise it is 'highly probable' that

Jesus' disciples thought of him as 'king' and he accepted that role.

These attempts to be more precise and consistent about probability judgements point the way forward. Whether or not our appeal for better calibrated probability judgements falls on deaf ears one thing is certain and that is that without some move in that direction the uncertain conclusions of biblical scholars can have little objective value.

One point which constantly recurs and bears repetition before we move on is the often crucial role of prior probability. We have seen that what it is reasonable to believe about A depends upon our presuppositions. A belief, for example, in the verbal inspiration of Scripture radically affects the answers we give to all questions of its interpretation. Eventually, of course, that trail of presuppositions leads back to the ultimate question of the previous chapter and that, we have argued, is the great imponderable. A more explicit recognition of this simple fact would, at least, curb the wilder excesses of biblical interpretation and contribute to the cause of tolerance if not of truth.

STYLOMETRICS

The attempt to discover the origin and, especially, the authorship of biblical documents by statistical analysis is a relatively recent activity though its origins can be traced back to Augustus de Morgan. In 1851 he suggested that disputes about the authenticity of certain epistles attributed to St Paul might be settled by comparing the average word lengths in the various documents. Word length is only one among many characteristics which might betray the hand of the true author. In actual fact sentence length proved to be a better discriminator though no modern investigator would consider it sufficient to look at only one such characteristic. Much more is likely to be revealed by studying a whole cluster of such characteristics.

There is now a substantial stylometrical literature covering many parts of the Bible. From this there may be selected the names of three people who have pioneered the subject but with somewhat different emphases. A. Q. Morton (see e.g. Morton, 1965, 1978, 1980, and Morton and McLeman, 1966) has produced a number of studies mainly on the epistles attributed to Paul but he has also worked on St John's Gospel. His principal method has been the study of sentence length distributions but he has also used other indicators such as common words, the parts of speech of the last words of sentences, and such like. In the case of St John's Gospel he has also looked at whether the book can be regarded as made up of sections whose length is determined by the size of codex available to the writer. A team of Hebrew scholars including Y. T. Radday (see e.g. Radday, 1973, and Radday *et al.*, 1985) has examined many books of the Old Testament including Isaiah and Genesis. They have deployed multivariate methods which are capable of looking simultaneously at many variables and this has been greatly facilitated by use of computers. Finally, Kenny (1986) has returned to the New Testament and carried out an examination of many of the traditional questions from a statistical point of view. His analyses are elementary, being based on one variable at a time, but covering a much wider range of characteristics (99 in all) than his predecessors, a feat which was made possible by having the text available in a computer file. Kenny's book contains a useful and not uncritical review of earlier work and he notes that its lukewarm reception among traditional biblical scholars owes a good deal to the exaggerated and unjustified claims for stylometry made by some protagonists.

Before looking more closely at the methods and conclusions reached by stylometric analysis it is important to be clear about how it all bears upon the central question of whether the Bible provides evidence for the existence of a world beyond this. What form might such evidence take? If, for example, it could be established that some or all of the Gospels were eye-witness accounts which had been handed down with no substantial changes then the remarkable happenings which they recount, such as the resurrection of Jesus, would have to be taken very seriously. If the whole Pauline corpus could be shown to be the work of a single hand then it would make more sense to look for a coherent Pauline theology than if it is the work of several authors. Documents which can be given an early date are, one supposes, more likely to be historically accurate than those compiled many years afterwards. Documents which have been compiled from many sources and heavily edited are more suspect than those which have come down in pristine condition. Can stylometric analysis help us to arrive at the date, authorship, and origin of ancient documents?

The short answer is 'yes but not much'. A longer answer requires us to look in some detail at the analysis itself. An illustration of many of the basic ideas is provided by Morton's early study of the Pauline epistles though, as we shall see, this is not beyond criticism. Sentence lengths vary within a single piece of writing but some authors tend to use longer sentences than others. If we look at the epistles which bear Paul's name it turns out that the average length of sentences is much longer in some than in others (leaving aside the question of what constitutes a sentence). The average sentence length in Ephesians and Colossians is roughly twice that in Galatians and 1 Corinthians. The latter are generally thought to have a stronger case for Pauline authorship and thus sentence length evidence might be held to count against Pauline authorship of Ephesians and Colossians. But since sentence lengths for a single author vary a good deal we must first satisfy ourselves that the difference of a factor of two is much greater than could be reasonably expected between two works of the same author. To provide some yardstick for such differences, Morton (1965) looked at the variation in average sentence length between works in Greek prose which were known (with reasonable certainty) to be by the same author. He took, for example, the histories of Herodotus and Thucydides and speeches of Lysias, Demosthenes, and Isocrates. To simplify somewhat, he showed that the variation of average sentence length between parts of a work by the same author was no more than would be the case if the samples of text studied had been selected at random from a common population. When this test was applied to the Pauline epistles some significant differences were found which led Morton to conclude that Romans, 1 and 2 Corinthians, and Galatians formed a group. A second group consisted of Philippians, Colossians, and 1 and 2 Thessalonians, together with the so-called pastoral epistles. Ephesians and Hebrews appeared to stand apart as single groups. A group here means a set of epistles having mean sentence lengths showing no more variation among themselves than could be expected between different works by the same author. If the first group is by St Paul (and Morton took it as axiomatic that Paul was the author of Galatians) then it begins to seem unlikely that the epistles of group 2 and the isolated epistles were by Paul. In so far as these conclusions were broadly in line with the results of traditional methods they could have been regarded as reinforcing conclusions arrived at by other methods.

Morton (1991) has developed this work to take account of the possibility that the typical sentence length might vary according to where it comes in the work. To look merely at the frequency distribution of sentence length is to disregard information about position. To put the matter in an extreme form it would be possible to have two authors who were indistinguishable as far as their sentence length distribution was concerned but who differed in that one maintained the same average length throughout a work whereas the other tended to have the short sentences towards the beginning and end, with the longer ones in the middle. Variations of this kind can be detected by plotting what is known as a 'cusum' chart. The cumulative sentence length up to any point in the text is compared with what it would have been had average sentence length not varied through the text. Morton claims that this method is a good discriminator, that it is effective with quite short texts, such as some of the New Testament epistles, and is particularly useful for detecting interpolations in the text.

Let us pause at this point to consider what has been learnt about the possibilities and potential of stylometric methods. To begin with it is clearly impossible to say whether any of the epistles were written by Saul of Tarsus who became Paul and apostle. To be able to begin to do that we should require a reasonable corpus of Pauline literature whose authorship was certain. We could then ask whether the disputed material had the same statistical characteristics as the genuine material. Even if it did, we could not logically conclude that Paul was the author because there might be other possible authors with the same characteristics. If we looked at sentence length alone it would be surprising if there were not many authors with much the same sentence length characteristics as Paul. However, if we were to look at many more characteristics we might think it rather more of a coincidence if the disputed epistles agree with Paul in all of them. This kind of consideration leads to the notion of a 'stylistic fingerprint' which might uniquely distinguish one author from another. Whether or not such a fingerprint exists is an empirical question on which a final answer could, perhaps, never be given. Even if it did exist it is unlikely that we would ever have enough material for any given author to determine what it was. Nevertheless, like most idealizations, the concept of a stylistic fingerprint points us in the direction we should move in order to achieve greater precision. Style is a complex phenomenon and it clearly cannot be encompassed by a single indicator such as sentence length. First, there are a whole series of variables relating to the author's vocabulary, for example its size and composition. Then there are questions of grammar and syntax. Even within the rules of a given language there are many permissible variations in usage. All of these things, and many more, can be quantified to some extent and be made ingredients of the analysis. Certain words, for example, occur frequently in some biblical books and rarely in others. Nouns, adjectives, verbs, and so forth may be used with different relative frequencies by different authors. Different constructions and tenses may be used more commonly by some authors than others.

Variations will occur for reasons other than changes in author. A single author's style may vary according to the subject-matter, the intended audience or with time as the author acquires a richer vocabulary and wider experience. In principle all of these things can be allowed for but as variables are multiplied so does the volume of material needed to disentangle their effects have to be increased.

Without going further it is clear that certainty is unattainable. This is not simply a matter of shortage of data—though that is important—it is also that certain necessary information, such as what St Paul's style actually was, is lacking. Such conclusions as can be drawn will usually be of a negative kind. That is, we may identify an important difference which calls for an explanation such as the difference in average sentence length between Galatians and Colossians. What we cannot do is be sure that any such difference is due to a difference in authorship rather than something else. The force of this remark has been nicely illustrated by Kenny (1986: 110 f.) who points out that there is another hypothesis which explains the sentence length differences in the Pauline corpus equally well. It is not implausible to suppose that Paul became fonder of longer sentences as he became older, a not unknown phenomenon, Plato apparently being another possible example. If that were so the observed differences might reveal more about the chronology than about the authorship. In fact Kenny shows that if the epistles were written at equally spaced intervals of time in the order Galatians, 1 Corinthians, Romans, 2 Corinthians, Philippians, 1 Thessalonians, 2 Thessalonians, Ephesians, and Colossians, then the logarithms of their mean sentence lengths would increase roughly linearly with date of authorship. Whether or not this is a more plausible hypothesis than that of different authorship is not something which can be decided on statistical grounds alone.

Kenny's own work on the Pauline corpus excludes sentence length which he regards as poorly defined in Greek prose. He remarks, for example, that the variation in length between modern editions can be large enough to indicate different authorship! Instead he concentrates on frequencies of key words and parts of speech using, in all, 96 of the 99 indicators. His analysis shows very considerable variations between the epistles but not in a manner which would allow one to allocate them to homogeneous groups. For example, the percentage of text composed of articles has the second highest value in the whole New Testament for Colossians and the lowest for 1 Timothy. Prepositions are much commoner in the Pauline corpus than in the rest of the New Testament, but 1 Corinthians is the exception with the lowest rate in the New Testament as a whole. If one were to attempt to classify the epistles on the basis of a single indicator there would be almost as many classifications as indicators. Instead Kenny asks whether there are any epistles or groups of epistles which stand out from those traditionally attributed to Paul when all the indicators are taken into account. To do this he measures the 'distance' apart of any pair of epistles by the correlation coefficient between their scores on the 96 indicators. Two epistles which have a similar profile in the indicators will thus be counted as close together and the less similar the profiles the farther apart will they appear to be. On this basis the only thing which clearly emerges is that there appears to be no clear grouping of the kind which would identify a subset as having special claims to Pauline authorship. The best that seems possible is to list the epistles according to how close to the centre of the cluster they are. If the centre is regarded as typically Pauline then when ranked according to conformity with the 'ideal' the epistles come out in the following order: Romans, Philippians, 2 Timothy, 2 Corinthians, Galatians, 2 Thessalonians, 1 Thessalonians, Colossians, Ephesians, 1 Timothy, Philemon, 1 Corinthians, and Titus. Kenny (1986: 100) finally concludes that on the statistical evidence alone he sees 'no reason to reject the hypothesis that the twelve Pauline epistles are the work of a single unusually versatile author'.

This brief summary does not do justice to Kenny's analysis and nor to his reasons for rejecting Morton's case for regarding Romans, 1 and 2 Corinthians, and Galatians as the 'true' Pauline epistles. In spite of its comprehensiveness Kenny's analysis lacks sophistication, as he readily allows, and it is possible that something more could be said about the significance of the differences which he has found. Nevertheless it seems clear that the statistical evidence for assigning different authorship to members of the Pauline corpus is likely to be weak.

Kenny also uses the same type of analysis to examine two other New Testament questions of authorship: whether Luke and Acts were written by the same person and whether St John's Gospel and the Apocalypse have a common author. He measures the distance apart in the same way as for the epistles of eight major works of the New Testament. On that reckoning Acts is closer to Luke than any other work. Luke is closer to the other Gospels than to Acts, which may be accounted for by their common subject–matter, but is closer to Acts than to any other work outside the Gospels. This seems to provide support for the traditional assumption of common authorship for Luke and Acts. In the case of John and the Apocalypse the case for different authorship is strong. They are farther apart than any other pair except for Mark and Paul.

The fact that the stylometric analysis supports the consensus among biblical scholars on these two matters is reassuring and suggests that it should be taken seriously in matters where the position is less clear. In particular it suggests a cautious approach to the Pauline corpus.

The work of Radday and his colleagues on some of the Old Testament books also uses a multivariate approach. Their work on Genesis, for example, is concerned with the hypothesis that the material is derived from three sources usually known as J, E, and P. The question, therefore, is whether the variation between the parts is greater than that within. The matter is complicated by the fact that the book contains three types of discourse: human speech, divine speech, and narrative which one might expect to have different stylistic characteristics. The material can also be divided into prehistory, patriarchal, and Joseph stories. Radday contends that such stylistic differences as exist between the J, E, and P sections can be adequately accounted for by the different types of material which they contain. Although Radday's analysis is more sophisticated than his predecessors in that he used modern multivariate methods his conclusion of single authorship has been challenged by Portnoy and Peterson (1984) among others on the grounds that the analysis depends on unjustified assumptions. Radday also used exploratory techniques which make no prior judgements about which parts of the book might be attributed to J, E, and P. The question is then simply whether the 96 segments into which the authors divided the book fall naturally into groups which might then be subsequently identified with those traditionally assigned to J, E, and P. This too led to no clear case for multiple authorship.

The essential strategy followed by both Kenny and Radday was to construct a large number of different measures of style and then to try to classify the material—books or sections of text—into relatively homogeneous groups. One can then make a case for the separate authorship or origin of two items on the ground that they are far apart. If they are close together there is no need to invoke the hypothesis of separate authorship. The real difficulty is in knowing whether such differences as may be found are real and, if so, whether they should be attributed to authorship or to a difference in audience, subject, or whatever. Some of Kenny's measures, for example, do reflect the subject-matter. The relative frequency with which an author uses the past, present, or future tense would obviously be different in works of history and prophesy. Proper names will obviously occur more frequently in genealogies than elsewhere. What is needed are measures which are independent of topic, type of literature, length of passage, and so on, and which can therefore be taken as indicative of authorship. One set of possibilities which figure prominently in Kenny's work (as also in Morton's) are the very commonly used words such as prepositions and conjunctions. These are bound to occur in virtually any kind of writing. A second approach is to look at words which occur very rarely since they tell us something about the richness of an author's vocabulary. The name *hapax legomena* is given to words which occur only once in a given text and these have long been recognized as important indicators of vocabulary. *Hapax dislegomena*—words which occur only twice—have also been found to be useful in this connection. There is a growing body of empirical evidence that useful indices can be based on such measures. They have been used in this way by Holmes (1992) in a study of the Mormon scriptures. He combined them with three other measures derived from distributions of vocabulary based on probability models of text formation. Radday *et al.* (1985) have used two of these in the study of Genesis and used it to show that there are clear differences between the three types of speech which occur in that book.

Holmes himself is able to provide convincing evidence that the Book of Mormon was the work of Joseph Smith himself and not a collection derived from much older sources as Mormon tradition supposes. The issue is complex but here at least we have strong scientific evidence against a traditional claim. It is always possible, of course, to argue that Joseph Smith was retelling in his own words what had been revealed to him.

This somewhat brief and selective tour of the stylometric analysis of sacred texts should have been sufficient to disabuse the reader of the notion that they provide a new key to the Scriptures which will provide a definitive account of origins and authorship. However, the results, though meagre so far, are based upon publicly verifiable information processed by methods of analysis which are open to professional scrutiny and correction. At the very least they serve to limit the range of hypotheses which can be plausibly entertained and so focus attention on the more viable options. To that extent they help us in making judgements about the primary question of whether the Scriptures provide evidence of supernatural reality. It would be a mistake to suppose that just because the weakness of the stylometric approach is so transparent that its conclusions are any less secure than those reached by the more informal ways in which traditional biblical scholars draw their own conclusions. The present state of play is, perhaps, best summed up in Kenny's (1986: 122) closing words: 'it suggests to me that as the stylometrist's work progresses it will illumine a familiar landscape, rather than overturn beloved landmarks'.

THE DIVINE SIGNATURE

Even if the stylometrist's goal of finding some textual fingerprint which uniquely characterizes an author were to be achieved that would not, of itself, tell us anything about whether the author was 'inspired' in any sense and hence of whether the text could be considered the vehicle of divine communication. However, studies have been carried out, especially on the Hebrew of the Pentateuch (the first five books of the Old Testament), which purport to show that those books contain information in coded form which is extremely unlikely to have arisen if the authorship were purely human. Extensive searches have been made by scholars in Israel using a computer for such hidden 'messages' of which the following is a typical example. It concerns the occurrence of the letters AHRN which is the Hebrew spelling of Aaron. In the first thirteen verses of Leviticus, which deal with the priestly duties of the sons of Aaron, there are among the seven hundred or so letters no less than thirteen examples where the four letters AHRN occur equally spaced and twelve where they occur in the reverse order. The spacing varies from four to one hundred and eighty. This sounds remarkable but the sceptic would need to be convinced that this was not a chance occurrence. One approach to answering this question is to see how often the other eleven meaningless permutations of the four letters occur. If they occur as often as those that have meaning then one would not be inclined to attach any particular importance to the observation. In this case, however, if we count the permutations in pairs each number being the reverse of the other the occurrences vary between five and eleven compared with twenty-five for the meaningful permutations. It is difficult to imagine how a human writer could have consciously inserted such patterns into a text or to know how otherwise they might have come there.

This sort of occurrence, like some claims for extrasensory powers, is likely to be dismissed by many people with scientific training as too preposterous to be worth looking in to. Such dismissal may also be influenced by the fact that investigating such matters does nothing to enhance one's scientific reputation. Three Israeli scholars, Witzum, Rips, and Rosenberg (see their contribution to the discussion of Bartholomew, 1988) have, however, developed the necessary mathematical theory to enable the significance of such curious coincidences to be tested. They extend the idea to include word pairs which have an obvious connection, such as hammer and anvil, and quote an example where the odds against a particular configuration appearing in Genesis by chance are overwhelming. If, as appears to be the case, 'significant' words are embedded in the text of the Pentateuch on a scale which is highly unlikely to have occurred in normal human writing what are we to make of it? At least three responses are possible.

1. We can insist that in spite of the improbability they must be purely accidental and hence they tell us nothing about the character of the text. This would be justified on the grounds that all other explanations are simply impossible. Like the link between birth date and zodiac sign, it is just one of those curious quirks of nature that we have to accept. Or

one can argue that the results are significant of no more than the researcher's adaptability—or selectivity. Weitzman,[2] for example, points out that if we take the forty-sixth psalm in the Authorized Version, the forty-sixth word from the beginning is *shake* while the forty-sixth from the end is *spear*. Are we then to infer that Shakespeare wrote the psalm or had some special interest in it?[3]

2. The 'signature' could have been placed in the text deliberately by human agents. It is difficult to imagine what the motive might have been unless the scribes thought that God or Aaron could be honoured by including their names as often as possible in the biblical text. In that case they would have been consciously engaged in a complex acrostic game. Whether or not this is more plausible than the chance hypothesis is difficult to judge. In any case this would not rule out divine inspiration because the incorporation of marks of authenticity could itself have been divinely directed.

3. It could be the authenticating mark of the divine origin of the text. The possibility of communications with beings on other planets has led to consideration of what characteristics a message should have in order to be identified as the work of intelligent beings. One could imagine a divine author posing a similar question and then ensuring that the hidden code, once discovered, would be recognized for what it was. That such a strategy would not be fool-proof is clear from the existence of the two other interpretations noted above.

As so often in our exploration of the borderlands of the seen and unseen we reach a point where the relative plausibilities of the alternative explanations on offer depend not only on the data to hand but upon our prior beliefs about the existence of a divine being and of his willingness to act in specified ways. To a degree the answer to the question we

[2] In his contribution to the discussion of Bartholomew (1988) he inadvertently referred to 48 words and the 48th Psalm instead of the 46th.

[3] If Shakespeare himself had had anything to do with the production of the King James Version this would not be quite so surprising!

put can only be obtained if we assume most of what we desire to prove!

The credibility of reports of historical events contained in books such as the Bible depends on more than date and authorship. In general we are likely to give more credence to reports which are corroborated by independent witnesses. Reports which have been first written down at some distance in time or space from the actual happening are more likely to have become corrupted especially if they concern unusual happenings or people. In the case of oral testimony the number of intermediate retellings allows ample opportunity for errors to accumulate. Although written records are less susceptible to error, repeated copying by scribes who may introduce their own clarification or 'corrections' also leads to a deterioration in the quality of records as time passes. Any evaluation of the biblical record as a testimony to the manifestation of the divine must therefore reckon with the fallibility of those who have handed the record down.

A substantial part of biblical research is concerned with precisely these issues and the factors we have mentioned figure prominently in attempts to reconstruct the original text from the variants available. Most of the discussion, however, is necessarily qualitative and the judgements to which scholars come result from a subjective weighing of many fragmentary pieces of evidence. The question to be raised here is whether it is possible to quantify any aspects of the problem and so provide a degree of objectivity in the assessment of the evidence. This problem arose in an acute form in our consideration of the miracles reported in the Bible. Here we shall indicate a few tentative first steps which have been taken in this direction.

In the case of the biblical records the text has been carefully preserved for many centuries. The basic written sources date back to the fourth century (though there are earlier fragments) so the main issue concerns the relationship between the events reported in the manuscripts and what actually happened three hundred years, or thereabouts, earlier. In the early decades this will have been largely a matter of oral transmission followed by a period of crystallization in written forms with subsequent copying as the records were disseminated throughout a growing community. That variations in the record did occur is evident from different versions which have come down to us. This disposes of the claim sometimes made that a text which was so important in the purposes of God would have been divinely preserved from corruption.

John Craig, a mathematician, Scotsman, and contemporary of Isaac Newton made a pioneering attempt to quantify the reliability of historical records especially in relation to the Gospels (see Stigler, 1986). In his book *Theologiae Christianae Principia Mathematica*, published in 1699, he actually gave a formula which purported to show how the probability of the truth of an assertion would depend on the number of witnesses at a given distance and time from the event in question. He even used his formula to refute those who believed that the second coming of Christ was imminent. He did this by calculating how long it would take for the record to become worthless and then appealing to the question of Jesus in Luke 18: 8, 'But when the Son of Man comes, will he find faith on the earth?' His argument, apparently, was that the second coming would occur when the Gospel records ceased to have any evidential value. According to him this would occur in the year 3150! In the intervening years his reasoning has been dismissed with varying degrees of disdain by those who have noticed it and today it would be consigned, along with numerology and other such absurdities, to the intellectual dustbin.

Such a conclusion would, in Stigler's judgement, be premature. He has shown that Craig had insights far ahead of his time to which he was unable to give adequate expression because the modern theory of probability was not available to him. What Craig was really after, according to Stigler, was a way of describing how the odds on a particular happening were affected by distance, in the various senses, from the event. By translating Craig's ideas into modern notation and by discarding some of the less satisfactory parts, Stigler produces a testable hypothesis and demonstrates empirically that it fits the facts in one case at least.

Too few data are available to provide a proper test of events in the life of Christ so Stigler took the more recent example of Pierre Simon Laplace (who, ironically, had been a severe critic of Craig). It is virtually certain that Laplace was born on 23 March 1749 and that he died on 5 March 1827. There are sixty-five biographical accounts spanning the period 1799 to 1881 which give either a birth or a death date. Of the fifty which gave a birth date twenty-six were correct. Stigler was able to test whether the chance of reporting the birth or death date correctly depended on the time that had elapsed or the distance, measured crudely by whether or not the obituary was in French or another language. The broad answer is that they do and in the way that Stigler's reconstruction of Craig's model implies. Stigler's detailed analysis shows the position to be a little more complicated and he is well aware that it needs refinement. Nevertheless his example shows that there is a prospect of quantifying the extent to which accuracy declines. Whether or not these preliminary results can be generalized to an extent which would warrant their extrapolation to the time of Christ remains to be seen. What is abundantly clear is that only by extensive and painstaking empirical work can one begin to build up the kind of foundation which would permit an objective evaluation of the likely reliability of ancient texts as far as historical accuracy is concerned. It is not obvious that subjective assessments, however well informed, can be treated with greater confidence.

Craig and Stigler were concerned with the possibility of finding an empirical relationship which would describe how the reliability of documentary or oral evidence declines as it becomes more remote from its source. A different kind of approach has been pioneered by Weitzman (1987). His work relates to the evolution of manuscript traditions in general and not, specifically, to the Bible, but his analysis is very pertinent to biblical criticism.

The extant manuscripts of any ancient work will be the survivors of a process of copying and loss extending over many centuries. The general problem to be tackled by scholars is that of determining what can be inferred from the manuscripts available about the originals from which they are derived. By studying similarities and differences it may be possible to identify manuscripts with a common ancestor and so begin to construct the 'family tree' from which they are descended. Once such relationships have been established it may be possible to make a choice between rival readings. Weitzman notes that traditional scholarship has thrown up some interesting questions which it is not able to answer. His aim was to construct a probability model describing the development of family trees of documents in an attempt to throw light on such questions.

It is common to find that all extant manuscripts share some errors and this fact is most naturally explained by supposing that they have a common ancestor—known as an archetype. Oddly, it appears that family trees (known as stemmata) often have just two main branches stemming from the archetype. Various explanations have been proposed for this phenomenon, an obvious one being that it is an artefact arising from some flaw in the method of constructing stemmata. The history of a manuscript tradition will be a very uncertain affair; over many centuries there will have been wide fluctuations in the chances of birth or death for ancient manuscripts. The sackings of Constantinople by the Crusaders and then the Turks will have led to many 'deaths' while the foundation of the monasteries and the invention of printing will have had the reverse effect. What Weitzman did was to model these effects from 450 BC to AD 1950 in the case of Greek manuscripts and from 50 BC in the case of Latin. He was then able to ask whether one should be surprised or not, for example, at the preponderance of pairs of stemmata arising from a single archetype. On this particular question it appears that it is not surprising and hence that the traditional method of constructing the trees is not called into question on this ground, at least. The reason has to do with the likely form of the frequency distribution of the number of 'offspring' of an archetype. It turns out that, given at least two offspring, it is very likely that there will be exactly two.

For our purposes this study makes two important points. First, one can only adequately interpret extant manuscripts in the light of an understanding of their history which takes full account of the many accidental happenings to which they have been subject. Secondly, probabilistical analysis can yield important qualitative information about what sort of family trees one might expect to be inferred from the characteristics of the extant manuscripts. Modest though these achievements may seem they provide a measure of scientific underpinning for the critical enterprise and emphasize once again that uncertainty must inevitably remain.

THE INFLUENCE OF THE TEXT

Many would argue that the prime evidence for the unique character of the Bible is to be found not in its style or authorship but in the operational test of its effects. This, furthermore, is something which is open to objective verification. If the Bible could be demonstrated to have an influence for good far beyond that of other literature then that would be a powerful argument for its divine origin. This was what C. H. Spurgeon doubtless had in mind when he said 'Defend the Bible, I would as soon defend a lion.' Literature is a means of communicating the insights and experience of one individual to others. Great literature deepens and enriches the understanding of those who read it. Its effect on the way that people think and act is enormous. Given the power of the written word one would expect it to be used, as we noted at the start of this chapter, as a vehicle of God's interaction with the world if such interaction is to be found anywhere at all. The fact that any such revelation involves human intermediaries muddies the waters and will inevitably raise the matter of ill as well as good effects. But it is still relevant to ask whether the effects of the Bible in history are much greater than can reasonably be attributed either to its literary qualities or to the creativity of its human authors. This is a matter which requires a much fuller treatment but the following should be noted in passing.

There are countless examples of individuals who profess to have been profoundly changed, sometimes by reading the Bible alone or, more often perhaps, by a fragment which 'speaks to their condition'. Those branches of the Christian community which set great store by the value of personal testimony would claim that the Bible is very commonly a powerful agent in bringing about conversion. The 'word', whether read or preached, is seen as having a sacramental character in the sense that through it the Living Word is encountered. The strength of the evidence, viewed scientifically, which this provides would need to take full account, among other things, of psychological knowledge about personality types and so forth. It would be interesting to see a careful study of cases which would be free of partisan interests. My impression is that this is one of the many strands of the intellectual case for belief which, though not overwhelming of itself, is commonly undervalued.

Part III

One may not make a notion appear less
unreasonable by calling it an Idea rather
than a belief.

8
Belief and Behaviour

THE NEED TO CHOOSE

At the core of Christian belief is the ~~idea~~ *belief* of God who is
responsible for all that exists and is active in it. We have
enquired whether this belief is consistent with the world
which science reveals to us and, if so, how likely it seems as
compared with rival explanations. We have taken a variety of
topics which are widely believed to bear upon the question,
and it is now time to see what it all adds up to. Even before
looking at this in detail it is clear that the answer must be
somewhat equivocal. While we have been at pains to
demonstrate the extravagance of some of the more extreme
claims on both sides of the argument we have nowhere
found any piece of overwhelmingly strong evidence either
way. We must accept that our subject does not allow the kind
of objective certainty which some seek. The inconclusive
battles which have been fought over the ground are clear
enough evidence that the data at our disposal are too ambiguous to allow for that. It is true that we have held out the hope
that the cumulative weight of many strands of argument,
none conclusive on its own, may nevertheless be enough to
settle the issue for practical purposes. But before attending to
these matters it is necessary to introduce a new element into
the picture.

The practical question is not simply whether the case for
supernaturalism is established beyond reasonable doubt but
whether the case is strong enough to justify commitment. It

is a question of behaviour as well as belief. If the claims of a religion such as Christianity are true then a response is required. Decisions in all areas of life often have to be made on inadequate evidence and it is relevant to enquire what are the appropriate principles which should govern rational behaviour in such circumstances.

Before embarking on a discussion of these principles we must make a point about the limitations of scientific method which is often overlooked. There is no question that the classical approach of experimental natural science is a well-tried and trustworthy method of acquiring knowledge. But as a way of establishing a basis of knowledge for rational behaviour it is distinctly limited. If we imagine a spectrum extending from pure physics at one end through the biological and social sciences to business and historical sciences at the other it is easy to see that its effectiveness is largely confined to one end. Consider, for example, the movement in the prices of stocks and shares. Vast amounts of data are available on the daily prices of thousands of stocks and shares and great amounts of effort are expended first on trying to understand their movements and then on predicting them. However, in this field, one can hardly expect to uncover simple laws, invariant in time and space, which would bear comparison with Ohm's law, for example. In the nature of the case one can never, in practice, experiment with the stock market, and neither is it possible to replicate observations under properly controlled conditions. It is simply not feasible to turn the clock back and obtain a rerun of history. Nevertheless it is possible to approach such processes scientifically. We can search for patterns in the data which persist long enough to be useful for predictive purposes. We may have modest success in predicting movements, at least in the short term, and estimating the error to which they are subject. We may be able to construct models of price change which incorporate well-tested economic and psychological theory and which give a measure of insight into the underlying nature of the process. Such analyses can be useful but they cannot pretend to establish regularities with the same generality as classical science. This example is fairly typical of a wide range of problems occurring in social science which aims to detect regularities in the ever-changing flux of human affairs. A further trouble with studies which involve human behaviour is that the very act of observation may significantly influence what is observed. The observer is a part of the system and that fact must be allowed for in the interpretation of the results. Even in the best regulated studies there will still be a large amount of unexplained variation with consequent uncertainty in the conclusions which can be drawn. The map of knowledge will not then be divided neatly into the known and the unknown but will rather resemble a bog in which the well-versed may tread reasonably surely between the higher and securer footholds. Any attempt at a synthesis requires a delicate balancing and sifting of evidence but the cumulative effect of many evidences, weak in themselves, may nevertheless sometimes be linked to form a structure capable of bearing considerable weight.

What goes for social science is equally familiar in everyday affairs though we seldom think of it in those terms. We have to make countless daily decisions and if we are rational we aim to do this on the basis of the best evidence available. There is usually little time to collect data and what we have is incomplete and often fallible. Individuals who will only act when they have full information and have carefully weighed it will be paralysed by indecision. The best recipe for living is to balance the gains and losses, trading information for timeliness. In short, we all recognize that we must act on inadequate data. The scientific method in its fulness simply will not work in practical affairs. We retain its spirit and such of its apparatus as circumstances allow but we have to make commitments, sometimes for a lifetime, on evidence with which no reputable scientist would be satisfied. This is not out of laziness or because we have lower standards but because there is no alternative. The number of decisions to be made is just too great and the information too limited to do otherwise.

The matter of religious belief is more like this everyday decision-making than the building up of a picture of the world where we do not take the next step until our present foothold is secure. If belief in God and Christian doctrine were a purely intellectual matter of no practical consequence then a more or less permanent state of agnosticism would be appropriate. This is precisely the point reached by Gaskin (1984) and Prozesky (1992) in their weighing of the evidence about the existence of God. But that is not the case here. It would be a shame to miss the whole point of living because it took a lifetime, and more, to decide what it was!

Those, like Stenger (1990), who demand convincing proof before abandoning their materialism are therefore likely to remain marooned in that position because it is difficult to see how their requirements could ever be met. In reality we have to make decisions in the face of uncertainty and that involves taking risks. Decisions about careers, about choice of spouse, about investing spare cash, are obvious examples. Business decisions like whether to open a new factory or publish a book are fraught with uncertainty but to delay may be to risk losing all. Risk-taking is integral to life and growth and there can be no decision which is ultimately more significant than the one we make about the nature and purpose of our own existence.

Belief and behaviour are linked. What we believe influences, but does not completely determine, how we act. How we act reveals in part what we believe and, by the experience which it yields, will modify our beliefs. We must therefore adopt a strategy which allows for frequent and fruitful interaction between belief and behaviour since the one will help to develop the other. The timid seeker who dabbles a toe in the water may avoid the risks of plunging in but will never experience the delights either. When making decisions probabilities are not enough. Gains and losses must also be weighed in the balance and the key question for the present chapter is how this should be done. Just as in Chapter

2 we made a digression into the technicalities of measuring and combining probabilities so now we must look at how probabilities must be weighed against the costs and benefits which follow from actions we might take. Again, the spectator can skim this section but will then have to take the results on trust.

DECISION-MAKING IN THE FACE OF UNCERTAINTY

The question of what it is best to do is not the same as what ought to be believed. The choice of action depends, in general, both on the probabilities of what may happen and on the rewards or penalties associated with the outcomes. For example, the decision whether or not to take an umbrella depends not only on what we judge to be the probability of rain but on how we regard the inconvenience of carrying the umbrella and the effects of a soaking. The decision whether to invest in a new supersonic airliner requires not only a calculation of the probability of success but also an assessment of the financial and other gains and losses involved in the outcome.

The question of how one ought to make choices in the face of uncertainty in the light of the consequent gains and losses is the subject of a vast technical literature which goes under the name of decision theory. Decisions in business, government, and medicine as well as the multitude of everyday personal choices that we all make partake of the same general form. In each case there are a number of things which could happen but we do not know which will occur and there are penalties or rewards associated with the outcomes. The question for us here is whether this body of knowledge has any relevance to the choice we all have to make about the nature and purpose (if any) of the world in which we find ourselves.[1]

---

[1] It may be noted that belief and action are brought together in the pragmatist philosophy associated with William James according to which a belief or theory is judged to be true in so far as it 'works'. Belief is not then simply a matter of

We have to weigh both the uncertainties and the gains or losses, not separately, but in combination. In some cases, as we shall see, there is not much room for argument about what constitutes a best choice. This is the case with the version of Pascal's celebrated wager to which we shall shortly come. But in other situations things are less straightforward.

Before proceeding we need some terminology. The formal representation of a decision problem has three elements. First, a set of choices or actions. Secondly, a set of what are usually called 'states of nature'. We may think of these set out as a list of all the things that could happen. In the umbrella example, those might be simply 'rain' or 'no rain', or we might think it appropriate to distinguish a finer division of possibilities such as 'heavy rain', 'light rain', 'sleet', and so on. This would be a relevant thing to do if the consequences would be different for each of those outcomes. The third element in a decision problem is the set of 'pay-offs' associated with each combination of choice and state of nature. Pay-off is a convenient self-explanatory term to cover both gains and losses.

In making investment decisions these pay-offs may be directly measurable in terms of money but more often they will be less tangible and we may be able to do no more than rank them.

It helps to set out these elements in a table of the following kind. The rows represent the choices open to us, the columns the possible states of nature and the entries in the body of the table the pay-offs. We might set out the umbrella problem in this fashion as follows.

evidence but of the will to believe, in James's words. See also Cohen (1992) in this connection. This approach is quite distinct from that followed in this chapter which starts from the theory of rational decision-making. In that case the benefits are evaluated before any action is taken.

	Rain	No rain
Take umbrella	Keep dry	Have to carry umbrella and risk losing it
Do not take umbrella	Get wet	Keep dry

This table merely lays out the position and as we shall shortly see there may be room for argument about whether the problem has been correctly specified. Nevertheless it is often a great aid to clarity of thought. In the present example it is obvious that there is no clear-cut solution to the problem of which is the best choice. If it rains, taking an umbrella will yield the best outcome but if it does not, leaving it at home will be better. We shall incline to one choice or the other according to whether we judge the likelihood of rain to be high or low so the probability of rain is obviously relevant. But how do we balance the relative probabilities against the corresponding pay-offs?

In some cases we may not have to bother about the probabilities. This is the case in the simplified version of Pascal's wager to which we now turn.[2] In this formulation of the problem the choice is between believing or not believing. The states of nature are that God exists or that he does not. In that case the decision table might be as follows.

	God	No God
Believe	Eternal bliss	Nothing lost
Disbelieve	Eternal separation from God	Nothing lost

If there is no God it is a matter of indifference whether we believe or not whereas if he does exist then belief is clearly

---

[2] According to Flew (1976) this is much older than Pascal, its origin having been traced back to the Islamic Al-Ghazdi. The choices *belief* and *unbelief* might, for our purposes, be more accurately rendered *make a commitment* or *not*. For recent statistical discussions see Daston (1988: 60–3) and Hald (1990: 64).

the better option. In this case the decision to believe is said to 'dominate' unbelief because it leads to an outcome which is at least as good as the decision to disbelieve no matter what happens. This conclusion does not depend on the probability of God's existence which can therefore be disregarded. Everything depends on the valuation we place on the outcomes.

This version of the wager is not precisely as Pascal stated it. He did not rate the outcomes under the 'no God' hypothesis in exactly the way that we have. If there is no God, for example, he said that if we believe, we lose the life spent in the service of an illusion. More important, he supposed that the two states of nature were equally likely but this does not play an essential part in his argument. It is the infinitely greater benefit of eternal bliss when set against the everlasting separation to be expected in the event of God's existence which carries the day with him.

This formulation of the problem can be, and has been, criticized on various grounds, notably by Flew (1976). Different theologies would put different valuations on the outcomes and not all of these would lead to the same conclusion. For example, believing might be judged to be rather burdensome if there was no God because it would involve pleasures forgone as well as duties to be performed. These things depend on our personal evaluations of outcomes and, of course, on what kind of being we suppose God to be. The latter could be accommodated within the general framework by enlarging the set of states of nature. We could, for example, distinguish between a God who punished unbelievers eternally, one who merely denied immortality to unbelievers, and so on. Equally, the number of possible decisions could be increased by adding, for example, an option to disbelieve for ten years and then, if still living, switch to belief. A more bizarre option would be to toss a coin to decide what to do.

It is worth pursuing Flew's criticisms in more detail. He first deals with secondary matters having to do with the valuations of the outcomes but his main thrust is against the restriction to only two states of nature. The kind of God envisaged by Pascal, he argues, is one who acts in line with Roman Catholic doctrine. We can easily imagine other kinds of God whose actions in response to our belief or disbelief might be very different. In particular, he says, there might be a God who treats believers of the Roman Catholic persuasion in exactly the same way as they believe he treats the unbeliever! Our formulation should therefore include other possible states of nature one of which would have a reversal of the pay-offs for this case. Further, since there is no limit to the number of states of nature that we can imagine, we ought to allow for infinitely many. That being so and given the absence of a dominant strategy, we can only make a choice if probabilities can be assigned to the states. But if, as Pascal supposed, 'there is a God, [and] He is infinitely incomprehensible' (Flew, 1976: 62), there is no way we can make such an assessment. In any event, according to Flew, we can only assign probabilities if we have a finite set of options. Far from us being forced to make a reasoned bet, as Pascal claimed, the situation does not allow us to make any reasoned bet at all.

On the technical point of whether it is possible to assign probabilities to an infinite set of states of nature, Flew is wrong, though there are deeper issues here beyond our scope. It is perfectly possible to have an infinite set of probabilities summing to one (as they must) though it is less easy to see on what basis they might be assigned in a case like this.

The most dubious aspect of Flew's argument is the freedom it gives us to invent states of nature with whatever pay-offs we please. If it were indeed true that God was 'infinitely transcendent' so that we could know nothing of him, all imaginable hypotheses would have to be entertained and we should, indeed, be at an impasse. But if it is possible to enumerate those hypotheses worthy of serious consideration then progress can be made. States of nature specially contrived for the sole purpose of providing a counterweight to others which seem to favour belief do not gain credibility on that score alone. It is certainly true that a realistic treatment requires more states of nature but it is not obvious that more than a small number are credible. This makes the issue less clear-cut but it does not make it hopeless.

However, it is not the purpose of our discussion to pursue the ramifications of this particular example. It is used simply to show how the decision problem may be set out and how it may be soluble without reference to the probabilities. The more usual situation is that there is no clear choice in that the choice to be preferred depends on which state of nature turns out to be the case. This is the point at which probabilities must to be brought into play.

A somewhat similar discussion about the relationship between belief and action appears at the end of Gaskin's book, to which we referred earlier. At the end of the book he has come to the conclusion that belief is 'weakly reasonable' or has 'weak probability' and he then raises the question of how the choice should be made. To help in this he lists some of the consequences (p. 176). He asks 'if we cannot decide that theism is probably true, would it nevertheless be reasonable to believe it because it is of practical value to us?' Gaskin's own view is that if the question is only 'Does it work?' then it becomes, for many people, interesting at a much less serious level of commitment. 'That is why' he says 'it is so important for Christianity that theism should be in some measure reasonable and probable, and most certainly not incoherent' (p. 171). I agree and in the final chapter we must see whether that claim can be made. Gaskin's own final judgement is so finely balanced that he inclines to a kind of benign agnosticism with a wistful look over his shoulder at what might lie beyond. The one judgement he does allow himself, one of value rather than probability, albeit suitably hedged about with qualifications, is that 'for the generality of the world most of the surviving influences of theism are better than most of the present consequences of atheism' (p. 179).

Before we continue this line of thought it may help to

anticipate a difficulty which believers might well have about the direction which the argument is taking. It seems to assume that belief is a matter of cold calculation having more regard to self-interest than a concern for truth. Some forms of 'hell-fire' preaching have, indeed, seemed to come close to just such a position but most believers would regard belief as much more than a decision to act as though certain propositions were true. Furthermore, a period of 'trial commitment' would seem as much a contradiction in terms as a 'trial marriage'. In both cases the essence eludes us if total commitment is lacking.

All of this is true and would be fatal if used as an argument to persuade people into belief. The value of the approach is to be found in its negative rather than its positive aspects. It is no more than an analysis of the rationality of the choices we make. If such an analysis shows a particular choice to be irrational according to the principles embodied in the rule we apply to our decision-making then we have to explain to ourselves how we can defend it. We may, for example, question the principles, the structure of the problem, or the evaluations we make of the outcomes. But, whatever conclusion we come to, we have to be explicit about the basis of our reasoning. It would be perfectly possible to choose the action which led to the worst outcome if we could convince ourselves that there was some higher consideration which demands that we do this. In either case some such analysis as we have given is a prerequisite for making even that choice. Pascal's motivation for introducing the wager was, however, rather different. According to him the question of God's nature and existence are beyond the reach of reason and so efforts to make a case for belief are futile. All that is left to us is to consider how best to act. This is a defensible view but it seems to rule out any possibility of revelation or of relevant knowledge gained from experience.

We now return to the question of what to do if there is no dominating choice. One possibility, which we can quickly lay aside, is to take a pessimistic view and look only at the worst that can happen under each choice. Such a jaundiced view of the world would then require us to choose the actions with the 'least bad' outcome. As we shall see below this may be justified if the state of nature is determined by an opponent out to better us, but in the present case this is not so. We must therefore consider whether there is any other rule for combining the probabilities and pay-offs which embodies what we would recognize as compelling principles of rationality. There is such a rule and it requires us to make that choice which gives us the greatest *expectation*. Expectation is used here in a technical sense though one which is closely related to its everyday meaning. To get an idea of what is involved let us take a simple example. Suppose whether or not we win a pound depends on the toss of a coin. On a single trial we either get £1 or nothing. If we have many trials, and if the coin is fair, we shall win on about half the occasions and lose on the rest. In a thousand trials we would therefore expect to win about £500 or, on average, 50p per trial. This is our 'expectation'. It can be thought of as the 'certainty equivalent' of the gamble in the sense that in the long run we should gain as much by taking the gamble as by settling for 50p each time without any risk. The idea easily extends to the case where we have unequal probabilities for outcomes and to where there are more than two outcomes. Formally, the rule is to multiply each pay-off by its associated probability and to add up the results.

The most obvious deficiency of this approach is that there is no 'long run' in most of the important decision-making situations that we face. In a 'one-off' situation we either win or lose and the long run seems irrelevant.

It can, nevertheless, be shown that the expectation rule does also apply in the single case in the sense that it can be shown to be the consequence of certain rather innocuous postulates about rational choice. For example, if A is preferred to B and B to C then A should be preferred to C. Failure to use the expectation rule would then lead us into inconsistencies in which such unexceptional axioms were violated. This is the typical form of an axiom-based logic which takes rules which are 'obvious' when applied in trivial circumstances and generalizes them to more complicated situations.

A second deficiency is the more practical one which arises from the difficulty of quantifying the probabilities and pay-offs. This may be easy enough in gambling situations but in matters of belief the possibility of doing so seems remote. We have seen how difficult it is to get anywhere near quantifying probabilities of God's existence or the emergence of life on earth, for example. The most we seem able to do is to get some idea of whether or not they are close to one or zero. The case is no better when we turn to the pay-offs. This is certainly a drawback but it need not be crippling. Just as it is sometimes clear that one action is to be preferred no matter what the probabilities (for example, when there is a dominant choice) so it may be clear that one choice is best unless the probabilities (or the pay-offs) take on very extreme values. Thus it may only be necessary to decide on the probabilities to a very rough degree of approximation.

To go back to the umbrella example, we might judge the misery of a soaking as compared with keeping dry to be many times more unpleasant than the inconvenience of carrying the umbrella unnecessarily. In that case the probability of no rain would have to be very much more likely to make it worth leaving the umbrella at home. Although we might find it difficult to put numbers to these various quantities the attempt to do so in an exploratory fashion can be illuminating. Thus suppose that we rate getting wet as ten times more unpleasant than carrying the umbrella. It can then easily be shown by making trial calculations that taking the umbrella is to be preferred unless the probability of rain is less than $1/11$. The only judgement we have to make about the probability is thus whether it is smaller than $1/11$. Given that weather forecasts often give the chances of rain this might be relatively easy to do.

Going back to Pascal's wager we can now look at it in the

light of our earlier conclusion that the best arguments available do not get much beyond asserting that the probability of God is not close to either one or zero. This implies that the differences in the pay-offs under either state of nature are of comparable importance in arriving at a decision. Thus even if we were to replace the pay-offs in the 'no God' situation by different valuations which favoured disbelief, the relative advantage of disbelief in this case would have to be comparable with the advantage which belief has over unbelief if God exists. It is difficult to see how this could be so. Even if we reject this formulation of the problem the same logic must apply to whatever alternative version we propose. It is clear that the wager cannot easily be dismissed and certainly cannot be used to argue that belief is irrational.

The whole analysis can be looked at the other way round. If a person opts for belief *and* is rational in the sense required by the theory *then* we can infer that their implied subjective pay-offs and probabilities must be such as to justify that choice. The same applies to those who opt the other way. This might be construed as an argument for following the majority on the somewhat dubious ground that the best estimates of both probabilities and pay-offs would then be the average of those made by rational, well-informed people. Unfortunately, even if we thought this a good way to proceed, there is no way of collecting the data which would be needed to implement it. Again, this reasoning shows us that rational people who come to different decisions may do so either because they differ in their probability judgements or in their valuation of the outcomes or both. We note in particular that the resolute unbeliever only has to declare that the hypothesis of God, or whatever, is totally impossible to be assured that belief will never become the logical option whether the judgement is made on probability grounds alone or on expectation.

One thing which does emerge very clearly from our discussion of decision-making in the face of uncertainty is that a high probability in favour of the supernatural hypothesis is not necessary to justify rational belief. Even a modest probability can be enough if the consequences are appropriately valued.[3]

DECISION-MAKING AGAINST AN OPPONENT

In the language of decision theory we have been dealing so far with games against nature. The states of nature were descriptions of the world as it is, or might be, and were not subject to arbitrary change. We might be ignorant of what the weather would be but in deciding whether to carry an umbrella we assumed that the outcome was not subject to the whim of some god—malevolent or otherwise. This serves well enough when dealing with most natural processes but, to a degree, it prejudges the outcome. For if God really exists and is active in the world then the way the world is depends in part, at least, on what he chooses to do. And if his choices depend in any way on what we do then our analysis ought to take account of that fact. This is an extremely tall order but Brams (1983) has attempted to make such an analysis. In a pioneering study he has looked at questions of God's existence from the perspective of classical game theory where our quest for God is seen as a game between two players, ourselves and God.

The term 'game' should not be taken to indicate a lack of seriousness. It is used here as a technical term to refer to any conflict situation in which two parties are engaged. The Cuban missile crisis was a game in this sense with the two superpowers having to make decisions in the face of uncertainty about what their opponents would do and with, quite

---

[3] In his *Analogy of Religion* (1858) Joseph Butler made the point very succinctly. He said, 'It ought to be forced upon the reflection of these persons, that our nature and condition necessarily require us, in the daily course of life, to act upon evidence much lower than what is commonly called probable; to guard, not only against what we fully believe will, but also against what we think it supposable may, happen; and to engage in pursuits when the probability is greatly against success, if it be credible, that possibly we may succeed in them.'

literally, earth-shattering consequences hanging on those decisions.

In the matter of belief in God the decision which an individual makes about the ultimate nature and purpose of life is no less serious and it is therefore pertinent to see whether game theory can throw any light on the matter.

There are severe limitations on Brams's treatment of the subject to which we shall return but for the moment we leave those on one side. Brams supposes that we have a two-person game involving a superior being (SB) and a single person (P). A game offers each player a choice of actions and those actions have consequences. The players have preferences which enable them to rank the various outcomes in order of desirability. Each then contemplates the range of outcomes both for themselves and for their opponent and decides what to do.

The matter will become clearer if we take the first game which Brams analyses and which happens to be nearest to the concerns of this book. He calls it the 'Revelation game'. P has two choices: whether to believe or not. SB likewise has two choices: to reveal his existence in a way which convinces P or not. There are thus four ways in which the game can be played since each choice of P can be combined with each choice of SB. How will each player value the outcomes? This depends on what their objectives are. Brams's approach, here and throughout his book, is to suppose that if a superior being exists he will be like God as revealed in the Hebrew Bible (Old Testament). We are then asking how would a rational person behave who wants to know whether a God of the kind portrayed in the Old Testament exists?

In the present case Brams deduces that SB's first aim would be to have P believe in his existence, to obey him, and to worship him. At the same time, if SB exists, he appears reluctant to show himself or give unmistakable signs of his presence. It seems then that SB's favoured option is for P to believe without having convincing evidence of the object of that belief. This would be plausible if SB places value on trust or faith which is only possible in the absence of certainty. P also has preferences. His primary aim is to have evidence for belief whether positive or negative. Beyond that Brams supposes that P has a preference for belief over unbelief. In short P wants to believe, but only on the basis of evidence. P's favoured option would thus be that SB should reveal himself in which case P would believe on the basis of good evidence. However, each player can see the game from the other's point of view and the theory aims to take that into account in identifying rational strategies.

The situation described above is highly simplified though, as we shall see, it is not devoid of subtlety. The analysis depends on whether the players move in turn or simultaneously, whether SB can foresee what P will choose, whether the game can continue indefinitely, and so on. Brams considers these and other such possibilities in the context of this and other games and he spells out some of the theological implications within an Old Testament framework. One of his main concerns is to see how a superior being who possessed one or more of omniscience, omnipotence, immortality, and incomprehensibility might reasonably act and how P might respond. It is important to add, of course, that these theological terms are given technical definitions which do not necessarily correspond exactly with their richer theological meaning. For example, omnipotence (or staying power) is the ability of SB to defer making a decision until P has made his.

In broad terms we might hope to discover whether the 'state of play' in the world as we know it is what we would expect it to be if a superior being of the Old Testament variety existed. This is a formidable task but Brams does arrive at a number of paradoxes and insights which suggest there may be real value in looking at things from the game theory perspective. For example, he is able to identify circumstances under which it would be rational for an SB to act arbitrarily on occasions and this gives a hint as to why there might be evil in a world presided over by a God whose aims were good. As Brams notes this is no easy solution to the problem of evil since it introduces a conflict between morality and rationality but at least it shows that it is not absurd to suppose that long-term good may best be served by a strategy in which individual acts might be harmful in the short term.

It must be emphasized that Brams's analysis is not an empirical study but a mathematical analysis of choice-making situations designed to bring out an inner logic which might not be apparent on the surface.

Before offering some critical remarks on this approach and its conclusions we return to the Revelation game in its simplest form. The situation may be set out in a fourfold table as follows.

		P	
		Believe	Do Not Believe
SB	Reveal	3, 4	1, 1
	Do Not Reveal	4, 2	2, 3

The column headings set out P's two choices and the rows give SB's. The four cells in the body of the table are used to display the preferences. We need one preference rating for SB and one for P. The pairs of numbers given are rankings ranging from 4 = best to 1 = worst; SB's preferences come first and P's second. We argued earlier that SB's preferred outcome was not to reveal himself and yet have P believe, hence the 4 in the first position in the bottom left-hand cell of the table. P's preferred option was to believe on good evidence so his 4 occurs in the second position in the top left-hand cell. The remaining rankings have to be filled in from the known preferences of the two players. For example, SB's second-best outcome is in the top left-hand cell because his supposed reluctance to reveal himself takes second place to his desire to have P believe in him. P's second-best outcome is in the bottom right-hand corner because his desire for evidence is supposed to outweigh his underlying wish to believe. The reader may care to check the remaining rankings. There is nothing sacrosanct about these preferences. Other hypotheses about what SB's and P's aims might be lead to other tables with different analyses. (There are in fact 78 essentially distinct fourfold tables of this kind.)

One can now analyse the game as follows. SB, being rational, should prefer non-revelation because, whatever P chooses to do, the outcome will be better for SB. For if P believes, SB's preference is 4 in the case of non-revelation and 3 otherwise; on the other hand if P does not believe, 2 is better for SB than 1. So SB has a dominant strategy and even if he were omniscient this extra power would not help. P, for his part, can see the game from SB's point of view and so can deduce that a rational SB will choose not to reveal himself. He, therefore, only needs to look at his outcomes in the second row and from them it is obvious that he should choose not to believe. SB then gets his second-worst outcome and P his second-best. In what sense is this a solution? It has the property that if either participant unilaterally departs from these choices they will suffer as a result. If P changes he will get his second-worst outcome instead of his second-best and if SB changes he will move to his worst outcome. Yet the paradox of this 'solution' is that both could do better by changing to their other strategy simultaneously. However, if P were to contemplate moving to 'belief' and SB guesses (or knows) that he was going to do so, SB could do even better for himself by switching to non-revelation. Omniscience would then give SB the advantage of knowing what P was going to do and if P were then foolish enough to depart from his non-believing choice SB could take advantage of the fact. In that event there would be no paradox but the optimal strategies do not change. In this game agnosticism is rational for P.

This brief excursion into the game-theory approach can give no more than a glimpse of what is involved in a full-scale enquiry. It does, nevertheless, serve to show that even in such a highly simplified situation there are surprises.

Two issues remain to be addressed. First, can this way of looking at things throw any light on the possible existence of a choice-making being beyond the reach of our senses? Secondly, is Brams's formulation of the problem adequate? We take the second question first.

We have to ask, not whether Brams had got it exactly right but whether he has abstracted significant elements from an extremely complex situation. The whole art of human enquiry lies in distinguishing what matters from what does not. For a Christian, at least, the main criticism would concern the nature of God and his presumed intentions. If the Old and New Testaments describe a progressive revelation one would not expect to obtain a satisfactory analysis by limiting the study to the earlier parts only. There is very little in Brams about the loving-kindness and patience of God for which ample evidence could be found even within the Old Testament. But for Christians the incarnation would be the principal point of departure especially in relation to the Revelation game and its extensions. While Brams allows for revelation which may fade and be renewed the incarnation speaks of a full and sufficient revelation and once that choice has been made God cannot go back on it. One might then find it more relevant to investigate scenarios in which revelation at some stage in a sequential game was the optimum strategy for SB to pursue.

Another serious limitation of Brams's analysis is the restriction to two-person games; P versus SB. There are actually many Ps; they share their insights and understandings with one another and in some respects, at least, a choice which SB makes in relation to one P is made for all. In so far as the search for God is a co-operative venture it lies outside the scope of this particular theory.

Before offering our final reflections on Brams's approach we look at another aspect of game theory which has interesting implications for our understanding of why God might act in surprising ways. The sort of game we have in mind can be illustrated by the following 'avoiding' game. Each player has to choose one of the two numbers 1 or 2. If they choose the same number, A wins a number of pounds equal to the sum of the numbers chosen. If they choose different numbers, B wins and receives an amount equal to their sum. B's aim is therefore to avoid making the same choice as A. The situation can be set out in the now-familiar pay-off table as follows.

		B's choice	
		1	2
	1	2	−3
A's choice	2	−3	4

The pay-offs are payments to A and, hence, losses to B. Unlike the earlier games we have considered we now suppose that this game is to be played many times.

Clearly there is no dominant strategy for either player and, equally clearly, it will not do for either player to make the same choice every time. For if A were always to choose 2 in the hope of gaining 4, B would soon learn what A was doing and respond by choosing 1 so that A lost £3. It seems then that both will have to vary their choices if they are ever to make a gain. But they will be equally vulnerable if there is any other pattern in their choices because, if there is, then their opponent may be able to detect it and so gain an advantage. Is there anything that the players can do to conceal their intentions? There is only one way in which you can be absolutely certain that your past choices will give no clue as to your future intentions and that is by not knowing, yourself, what you are going to choose. If, for example, you toss a coin to decide, your past choices will be totally uninformative. What then would happen if B adopts this strategy? If A chooses 2 then A's expected gain (calculated as before) will be $\frac{1}{2}(-3) + \frac{1}{2}(4) = \frac{1}{2}$; if A chooses 1 the expectation will be $\frac{1}{2}(2) + \frac{1}{2}(-3) = -\frac{1}{2}$. B's position has improved to the extent that his loss to A need now be no more than $\frac{1}{2}$ per play whereas, in the worst case, it could have been 4. Can B do any better than this? The theory shows that the best possible strategy is to choose 1 with probability 7/12 and 2 with probability 5/12. The reader may easily check that this ensures that A will lose 1/12 per play no matter what number is chosen. B has thus rendered himself immune to the worst that A can do and guaranteed himself a profit into the bargain. (An analysis from A's point of view is instructive and leads to a similar conclusion.) This is an 'unfair' game which A would be ill-advised to play but it was far from obvious at the outset where the advantage lay.

It would be naïve in the extreme to claim that choice situations such as that represented by the avoiding game accurately reflect any aspect of the God/humanity relationship, but that is not its point. Its purpose is to challenge some of our accepted conventions of thought by showing that it may actually be rational to behave in an apparently arbitrary manner. B's choice of a random selection strategy allows A a completely free choice without affecting the long-run outcome of the game. B's long-term objectives are thus ensured at the same time as allowing a good deal of uncertainty about how things develop. The apparent fickleness of B conceals a broader and more flexible notion of what is meant by being in control of the situation. This has obvious implications for how we argue about what it might or might not be reasonable for God to do and hence about whether there is evidence of his presence in what we observe.

Whatever judgements we make about the particular assumptions which Brams made, the more fundamental question is whether or not the avenue opened up by Pascal and developed in game theory by Brams and others is a dead end. It is common for specialists in one field to shout down trespassers from other fields by ridiculing the naïvety of their assumptions or their ignorance of basic facts. The temptation to do this is even greater when the intruder is armed with weapons which make the normal inhabitants uneasy. Such reflex reactions must be avoided. What is being analysed here is the nature of rationality which is something which those with an interest in rational belief cannot lightly dismiss.

It is my view that although the results so far are meagre and, from a Christian point of view, of limited relevance, the game theory approach is worth pursuing. So far it has indicated that a degree of randomness (i.e. arbitrariness) in pursuit of desirable ends may be a perfectly rational strategy. Further, a degree of incomprehensibility may well prove to be a necessary characteristic of what Brams sometimes calls the 'Great Mystery' from whatever point of view we approach it. To recognize even these limited achievements is to undermine some of the more facile attempts to demolish belief by assertions about how God might be expected to behave if, indeed, he exists.

9
Aim and Achievement

We set out with two principal objectives. One was to examine the validity of some of the probabilistic reasoning used in relation to religious belief. This sprang from the recognition that the approach through reason alone could not deliver certainties and was sharpened by the existence of widely differing statements about such things as the probability of God's existence. The second aim was to assess the current strength of the case for belief. It was clear from the outset that such a case would have to rest on the cumulative effect of many fragments of evidence. This meant that care would have to be taken with the logic of uncertain inference and with the extent to which it could be applied in this field. It is now time to see how far these aims have been achieved.

BELIEF IN WHAT?

The central question raised at the beginning was whether reality extends beyond the realm of the material world which science reveals. With due caution about the terminology we agreed to refer to this as the supernatural but we insisted that natural and supernatural be thought of as a single reality, the boundary being determined by the limits of our cognitive processes. It will be clear in retrospect that the focus of our interest has varied considerably. Sometimes our concern has been with the great cosmic questions and sometimes with relatively small and seemingly minor details. The terms *belief* and *believer* have been used deliberately in a very elastic manner. Before we go on to assess the results of our enquiry it is important to be clear about the varying content which we have given to these terms.

The outer circle, as it were, encompasses everything which may lie within the supernatural as we have defined it. It therefore includes not only the territory of the mainstream religions but also the whole gamut of fringe groups who lay claim to tracts of the supernatural. Since much of what happens in these areas is antipathetic or in direct contradiction to traditional religious beliefs it is clear that results favourable to one would be damaging to the other.

Within this outer circle there lies a region which we might call general theism. This says that reality derives from God who is the ultimate explanation for all that is and all that happens. General theism includes all theistic religions and might be loosely defined as consisting of what they hold in common.

Religious systems differ in what they believe about the nature and purposes of God and within that general area we have concentrated on orthodox Christianity and, to the extent that they overlap, Judaism also. The adjective 'orthodox' is necessary to distinguish between supernaturalist and naturalist forms of Christianity. We are concerned here with the central core of doctrine which has emerged from centuries of debate and of which the historic creeds are an authoritative, if inadequate, statement. It will be clear that we have not needed to be concerned with the niceties of doctrine but with the broad world-view that such a belief entails.

The more detailed the specification of a belief system, the more it says about the nature of reality and hence the more opportunities it offers for testing—and falsification. Conversely it is much easier to find support for a vague supernaturalism; just one well-attested fact would be sufficient. If, for example, an out-of-the-body experience could be established as real in one case the boundaries would have been breached but it would say very little relevant to religion in general. The task of establishing theism in the general sense is easier because it only needs to be concerned with the core characteristics. The attributes which do not fit with the world as we find it might count against a particular religious view without detracting from the general case. But, equally, the greater the congruence between the specification and what we find, the greater the credence does the hypothesis have.

It is considerations such as these which have directed the path of our enquiry. The eclectic nature of the course we have taken arose partly from the need for material lending itself to probabilistic treatment but also by the different levels at which useful results might be achievable.

IS BELIEF RATIONAL?

Very few people become Christian believers as a result of carefully weighing all the arguments. Equally, one suspects, very few embrace atheism on the same basis. The actual reasons are often difficult to identify and, when asked, not many acknowledge the influence of rational argument. The language used will vary according to the religious tradition from which the respondent comes but experiential factors will usually rank higher than intellectual considerations. This is hardly surprising when one remembers that belief, in the New Testament, is usually in the person of Jesus and not in propositions. The statement in Hebrews 11: 6, 'whoever comes to God must believe that he exists', is more in the nature of a tautology than an exception. Creeds are better thought of as positions at which one might expect to arrive after admission to the community rather than a requirement for entry.

Why then should it be worthwhile to spend time in arguing the intellectual case for belief when other factors will usually count for more? There are two reasons, one negative and one positive.

On the negative side we start from a contemporary position in which what might be called practical atheism is the norm in intellectual circles. In so far as people with such a world-view have a disproportionate influence in forming the cultural climate, society is increasingly governed by a secular orthodoxy. Ultimately, whether that orthodoxy survives—as in the case of its Christian predecessor—depends on the security of its foundations. Testing the foundations is thus a vital activity whose results are long-term and widely diffused.

On the positive side the ability to demonstrate that belief is rationally defensible is an essential part of the Christian apologetic. While an inner sense of conviction nourished by the mutual support of like-minded individuals may sustain the life of a community it cuts very little ice with those who totally reject its intellectual presuppositions. Furthermore, the availability of an objective yardstick serves as a brake on idiosyncratic developments. Those who insist on great precision in doctrinal definition are prone to end up by diminishing the divinity they profess to serve. For such precision requires one to specify ever more closely God's will and purposes and since this can only be done in human language and images the essential mystery of Being is likely to be lost. The inevitable uncertainty which has permeated our investigation thus has positive value for the believer in that it underlines the folly of attempting to encapsulate the infinite in the finite. That is a positive virtue of the rational approach which is so often lacking in unbridled subjectivism.

AN OVERVIEW

By dividing up the subject into topics we have, in effect, adopted a hierarchical approach to the big question. The paranormal, miracles, and documentary evidence might be thought of as the foothills by which the summit is approached. Had it turned out that the individual topics had yielded near-certainties then their aggregated effect would have been to make a sure foundation on which the more comprehensive treatment of Chapter 6 would have been the crowning achievement. In reality we encountered problems of method and materials which have limited what can be done both in principle and in practice.

On the methodological side we have stumbled on the problem of the prior. In order to assign a probability to a proposition, Bayes' rule tells us that, in addition to the evidence of the data, we need to specify the probability prior to looking at the evidence. In the case of something as fundamental as the origin or the nature of the universe this is impossible because we ourselves are part of the evidence. We have noted that some, scientists especially, do nevertheless regard the theistic hypothesis, at whatever level, as manifestly false and so absolve themselves of the need to consider the evidence further. We have argued that the first step in countering such claims must be to show that key elements of the theistic hypothesis are not inconsistent with the scientific world-view and therefore that it is irrational to assign them zero probability. This allows the argument to proceed but we are still precluded from arriving at a final probability by the indeterminacy of the prior.

What we can do is to judge the relative plausibilities of hypotheses by what we have called the likelihood. That is the probability that each hypothesis assigns to the evidence. On this principle a hypothesis which gives a high probability to what has happened is to be preferred over one which does not. There are two difficulties with this. We can never be sure that our list of competing hypotheses is exhaustive and so there may be some hypothesis that we have not thought of which has greater plausibility. Any conclusion we draw can never, therefore, be a final one. The second is more subtle and appears to give the theist a built-in advantage. We illustrate the point by taking an extreme case. Imagine that we hear of a miracle which is well attested and which appears to serve some unquestionably good purpose.

Let us now consider this alleged happening in relation to

the two following hypotheses: (A) that God exists and has power to act in the world, and (B) that there is no such god. On A the occurrence may be judged to be very probable, even certain, because a god of this kind can presumably do what he pleases. On B it would seem to be very unlikely. In circumstances like this the atheist can never fare better than the theist and will usually do much worse. This makes it all the more necessary for the atheist to insist that the prior is essential for reaching a conclusion since A is so improbable a priori that the higher likelihood is completely swamped. This example shows both the important role of the prior probability and the severe limitations of judgements based only on likelihoods. A corollary of the inability to make full use of Bayes' rule is that there is no calculus by which we can accumulate evidence and so arrive at a final answer. The lesson of all this is that though the use of formal probability arguments cannot deliver all that the theory promises that is no reason for ignoring what it can tell us. In particular it has allowed us to demolish a number of extant probability arguments which purport to establish certain key propositions with near certainty.

Before attempting a final synthesis we now review some of the principle conclusions we have reached in the course of the book.

REVIEW

In the body of the book we have, so to speak, let the world set the agenda by examining a selection of areas where it is claimed that the divine shows through. Many of them turn out to offer very little of substance on which to build a case and some, if established, would actually be unhelpful. Astrology, for example, can be confidently discarded. Its only value, perhaps, is as a salutary reminder that the human race has a deep streak of credulity often only thinly overlaid with a scientific veneer. This should warn us against placing too much faith in what people claim to believe. The fact that millions take their horoscopes seriously certainly does not add up to a case for belief in the occult any more than did the almost universally held opinion that the world was flat prove that it is.

Telepathy and formative causation are things of some scientific interest but are marginal in establishing the case for the supernatural. If they do prove to tell us something new about the world they will lie firmly within the scientific ambit which reveals an ever more intricate and wonderful creation. This would make it all the more remarkable that a universe with such rich possibilities should have come into being. To my mind, at least, such progress makes it increasingly difficult to believe that it all 'just happened'. This is not because it would then become even more necessary to invoke the presence of a divine hand to account for what happens within this enlarged frame of understanding. The lesson of history is that the inherent dynamics of the created order are sufficient to account for what was formerly believed to need the intervention of God and there is no reason to suppose that this will be any less true of new discoveries. The really remarkable thing is that the basic elements of matter and energy (or whatever may ultimately turn out to be the fundamental stuff of the universe) should have the potential to give rise to such enormous variety and complexity culminating, as far as we can see, in the mental worlds of human creation which seem to us so rich in meaning and value. This case for belief is sufficiently grounded in the world as traditional science reveals it. Work on the penumbra, if eventually successful in establishing new dimensions of reality, will merely reinforce it.

There are, however, some topics that we have discussed which do come much nearer to providing decisive evidence for a world unseen. They may, in the nature of the case, never be capable of establishing it with absolute certainty and even if they did they would not give results with a ready-made theology attached.

One of these is the so-called anthropic principle on which Montefiore based his argument. This draws our attention to the remarkable coincidences in the constants of nature which are necessary for beings such as ourselves to exist. This is also interesting from a methodological standpoint because it illustrates with particular clarity the dilemma we face when we reach the limits of knowledge. It is sometimes said that since these coincidences are a necessary condition of our existence, and we could not therefore observe a world in which they were otherwise, their presence should occasion no surprise. I have analysed this argument elsewhere in Bartholomew (1988) and argued that it is not as simple as that. As we noted in Chapter 6 it seems to follow either that there is only one universe (or relatively few universes) in which case these coincidences are truly remarkable or there is, or have been, an exceedingly large number of attempts leading to success with our universe. In the former case there must either be some deeper structure that renders those particular values necessary or some being who chose them to be thus. To me these last alternatives seem to amount to very much the same thing and would, in my view, be powerful evidence for a purposive mind behind the creation. If we reject the postulate that there is only one universe and accept one of the many universe hypotheses then it may be that given a sufficient number of trials the required coincidences would occur by chance and, in that case, our presence would not be so surprising. It is nevertheless still remarkable, even giving full weight to possible lack of independence, that there exists even one combination of the basic parameters capable of giving rise to us. We have also noted that the idea of randomly selected universes is not entirely straightforward. There would have to be some kind of randomization system to assign parameter values at each point of creation and I am not sure that this can be given very much meaning in the absence of any prior agent.

But the real problem for the sceptic lies in the fact that, in the very nature of the case, we can never obtain any empirical evidence for the existence of other universes. By definition the one we inhabit is the only one that we can ever study scientifically. One would therefore suppose that the faithful application of Occam's razor would stop short of multiplying hypotheses by introducing the idea of other universes. If there are no data which could require the rejection of the one universe hypothesis surely we should adhere to it. But if we do we can hardly escape the conclusion that it has been fixed to make life possible. The only rational ground on which we can then avoid this is to argue that these coincidences are themselves evidence for other universes simply because of their extreme improbability. But this extreme improbability requires the prior assumption that there is no one there to fix the initial conditions. Would it not be more rational to prefer the explanation which gives a very much higher probability to what has actually happened? For if there were a creator such a being would, as we noted above, presumably be able to achieve what was desired with something approaching certainty. Our sceptic can therefore only maintain this position by insisting that the prior probability of there being a creator in the absence of any knowledge whatsoever is exceedingly small. This is an entirely arbitrary choice which has no basis in fact.

The situation is not entirely dissimilar to that in another of the key areas in the search of evidence of things unseen. We have drawn attention to out-of-the-body and near-death experiences and we might have added various claims of communication with the dead. Here we have a range of experiences which are unquestionably real and which may have a profound influence on the recipient. Like all experiences there will be concomitant brain activity. The question of what significance should be attributed to these experiences turns on what is cause and what effect. The testimony of those who have experienced these things is that what they encountered was 'real' and this was what gave rise to the observable brain activity. Those who seek to explain the phenomenon in materialistic terms attribute the experience to degenerative changes which are taking place in the brain, implying that the brain state creates the illusion of the experience. If they were then to go further and argue that everything we experience is consequent upon what is happening in the brain they would confront the seemingly insuperable problem of explaining how automatons who are pre-programmed to do and to think can utter truths about their own nature. The introduction of an element of chance into the working of the brain may help to explain something of the variety and unpredictability of behaviour, but it actually explains nothing because 'chance' is not an agent but merely the statement that we cannot identify an agent.

If on the other hand we allow that there is an autonomous self and hence that brain states, in part at least, are the consequence of what that self thinks and experiences then what is reported is just what one would expect. If there actually are other dimensions to reality one would have expected the brain to be more responsive to them when other stimuli from this world are weak or confused. If one assumes that to be the case it certainly does not follow automatically that those experiences are intimations of another order but it does make it entirely plausible that they should be.

If we adopt an intermediate position in which events can cause brain states and brain states can give rise to illusory experiences we have to explain how one could distinguish between those experiences which are self-generated and those which are brain-generated. It is no answer to argue that experiences of a supernatural character can be induced by drugs because they may also be induced by a real external happening. A frightening experience may lead to a rapid pulse, sweating palms, and the like. The same physical symptoms can be produced by a suitable injection of drugs. In the one case the body produces the chemicals itself in response to the external stimulus, in the other the stimulus is missing but the drugs come from outside. The same response can thus be produced in two ways; the fact that the response *may be* artificially stimulated in no way detracts from the reality of

the actual experience. Thus if it were possible to induce a
sense of being detached from the body with a suitable cock-
tail of drugs it would say nothing about the reality of the
experience when it occurs without such a stimulus.

It is the extreme materialistic position which faces the
greatest difficulties in this area. I have argued that the explanations currently on offer do not meet the basic requirement
of coherence. This is aside from the deeper question of
whether a self is capable of providing a coherent account of
itself; if not, the self, like the existence of other possible universes, is beyond the reach of science.

Many of the topics we have discussed have a historical element; that is, they are concerned with whether or not something actually happened. This is particularly the case with
some of the alleged miracles and the interpretation to be put
on biblical records. This brings us up against the simple truth
that science must accommodate the facts whatever they may
be. If, for example, it could be established beyond all doubt
that water had been turned into wine then it would be no use
scientists arguing that this was impossible. The transmutation
would become part of the data of science and theories which
could not assimilate the fact would have to be abandoned or
modified. It is unfortunate that the extensive debates about
historical accuracy have been so little informed by the logic
of uncertainty and hence that there are few 'assured' results
to which we can point. In this field the thrust of our argument has been to emphasize the uncertainties and so to
undermine the presuppositions of much theological argument. Paradoxically this strengthens the case for belief by
making it less dependent on inherently improbable interpretations of Scripture. At the same time it makes it harder to be
dogmatic on particular items of doctrine.

We have left two of the more traditional areas of support
for belief in a supernatural dimension until last because, to
many who are uncommitted, they appear to be both the
most central and the weakest. According to such sceptics, talk
of miracles is simply a hangover from an earlier world which

has now been buried for good. The Bible is just a collection of ancient literature whose claims to a special status have been almost totally eroded by historical and archaeological research. The claim which some of the other side make that it is the word of God because that is how it describes itself is a classic case of first assuming what you desire to prove.

Having said that, I believe that Chapters 4 and 7 do provide grounds for strengthening the role of these topics in the formulations of belief and the two hang closely together. The term 'miracle' has so many connotations that it might be better to abandon it in favour of something like 'sign'. A miracle as we defined it is something which would not have been achieved without God's involvement. In so far as this may be in collaboration with human beings it may be recognizable only through the significance of what is achieved. If it is a major act it may or may not appear 'miraculous' but, I have argued, one would expect it to be within what is possible within the framework of natural law. One would therefore be right to be very doubtful about axeheads floating on water or, even, a person walking on water but, as we noted earlier, what is reported is what the observer perceived to have happened and not necessarily what actually did happen. The same perception can often be generated in a variety of ways but it is not the mode of generation which matters but the message which it is intended to convey. I am aware that this stance may appear to dodge the main question of whether inexplicable events provide evidence for a divine agent since if nothing happens outside natural law we can never use that fact to establish the supernatural. But that is not the main question. Miracles as defined here are God's acts and are recognizable as such only to the extent that they are beyond what natural systems and human agents could achieve. The fact that, on this definition, it is often difficult to know whether or not a miracle has occurred may be inconvenient for apologetics but is in the nature of the case. There certainly are events on record in the Gospels and elsewhere which have all the marks of a miracle and this makes the question of the veracity of the accounts so important.

If there is a God of the kind that Christians believe in, one would expect him to be active and therefore to be able to do things, directly or indirectly, which are observable by us. Given his superior status and power one would expect them to excite surprise and wonder as he draws out potential possibilities of which we are as yet totally unaware. This means that we should not be surprised at remarkable happenings and since, presumably, they are intended as part of God's communication with us we would expect them to occur especially within the realm of human experience. Conversely, when we encounter profound changes in human attitudes, beliefs, and behaviour we can legitimately regard this as evidence pointing to such a divine agent. That such happenings are almost commonplace is a major strand in the intellectual cause for belief.

We noted at the end of Chapter 4 that, for Christians, there are two central events which, if accepted, totally change the way in which all other evidence is regarded. There is one point in history, it is claimed, at which the seen and the unseen merge and at which the true nature of reality is focused. It may seem mildly outrageous to those not conditioned to think in these terms that the particularity and, on the cosmic scale, the insignificance of these events should be so central to the believer's case. They will rightly demand to know what is the evidence that these things happened and whether they can bear the interpretation put upon them.

It is here that the Bible plays its proper and central role. The traditions of the Christian community contained in the books of the Bible is virtually the sole source of what we know about this crucial event in history. It is therefore imperative that we examine it with all the tools at our disposal and with the minutest care. I have argued that there are some tools of a quantitative kind which can contribute to that study and that, so far, at any rate, they tend to put a mark of caution against the more radical and speculative ideas of biblical criticism. When this is coupled with the need to recognize and explicitly allow for the high degree of uncertainty, which the fragmentary nature of the evidence entails, our interpretation is likely to be more cautious and conservative. Indeed, I have maintained that the operational test of the Bible as an instrument of change may be a surer guide to its true nature.

Given the central place, deep roots, and powerful effect of the doctrines of incarnation and resurrection in the Christian tradition one would be well advised to examine very carefully the case that they may be rooted in reality and hence may indeed be the key evidence of the unseen among us. But we cannot expect this to be taken seriously unless we confront the sheer improbability, as most see it, that these things could have actually happened in the world which scientific research has revealed to us. Their very uniqueness means, of course, that we have no well-tried tools to deal with them. The most that we can expect to do by rational argument is to show that the grounds for judging them to be so improbable are not well founded. There seem to me to be three ways in which this must be done, two of which have been the subject of earlier chapters. First it must be shown that the historical evidence is at least as good as that relating to other happenings of the same period and kind. Secondly, that nothing essential to the truth of the matter is inconsistent with the scientific account of the way the world is but can be fitted into the overall picture in a plausible way. Thirdly, that these events have considerable explanatory power in the sense that they show how all things hang together in a coherent, meaningful, and satisfying way which answers, in principle at least, the deepest questions of the human heart.

These are all major undertakings which have been and doubtless will continue to be major preoccupations of those concerned about ultimate questions. Our purpose has been to shift the ground somewhat towards the use of the language and logic which the subject demands. We have moved far enough, I believe, to show that the simple certainties of the atheist are no less vulnerable than is the unthinking dogmatism of the believer.

ATHEISM CONSIDERED

Absolute atheism, that is the categorical assertion with total certainty that there is no God, is extremely rare. Indeed it is difficult to see how one could possibly claim to have proved the *absence* of anything especially in so fundamental a matter. Aggressive atheism of this kind is, one suspects, more readily understood in psychological terms. What we have called practical atheism is a more serious proposition. When it is explicitly justified it usually takes the form of scientism, that is the belief that everything that is can be explained, in principle, in scientific terms without resort to the supernatural. The supernatural, if such exists, can thus be ignored because it has no practical consequences whatsoever.

It is entirely appropriate to speak of practical atheism as a belief because science has not yet explained everything. The venom which Sheldrake's hypothesis of formative causation has attracted was not occasioned by his claim that there were gaps in existing knowledge but by the fact that his critics believed that they could be filled, in due course, within the scientific paradigm. Stenger (1990) is typical in arguing that science has been so successful in closing off one supernatural option after another that we can be confident that everything now lies within its grasp. The only true path to knowledge is by application of the strict canons of scientific method. This requires experimentation under rigorously controlled conditions and the results must be capable of replication anywhere by anyone who has mastered the rules of the game.

In reality, of course, the claim of scientism is strictly tautologous. It implicitly defines the whole of reality as that which can be covered by science. We have followed Pippard and others in arguing that when we come to the human self the inseparability of the objective and subjective makes science impossible. But between the territory of pure science and the self we have identified large tracts of experience where science can never fully reveal the truth. In the social sciences, in particular, it is entirely appropriate to press the scientific *method* to its limits but the essentially transitory nature of much of what is observed means that we can never provide the complete account that science requires. Furthermore it is in precisely this area of experience that the phenomena of most relevance to religious belief occur.

Practical atheism is thus based essentially on an act of faith in the omnicompetence of science and, in that respect, is on a par with theism. Neither can be ruled out on a priori grounds and both must therefore be judged on their degree of congruence with the facts as we know them.

All of this is well-trodden ground but is a necessary prelude to an assessment of the probability arguments. Given that neither atheism nor theism can be disproved, the decision between them must be based on probabilities. We have met probability arguments, notably by Gould, which purport to show that a theism which implies any degree of control over creation is untenable. Such arguments rest on the claim that the way things are can be accounted for by chance. They depend on an inadequate analysis of the evolutionary, or other, processes involved. They fail to recognize that 'chance' and theism are not inconsistent and, indeed, that a degree of chance may actually be conducive to divine purposes. Furthermore, they make no attempt to compare the probabilities of the competing hypotheses which, we have argued, is strictly impossible, nor to compare the likelihoods. To my knowledge there is no valid argument involving the notions of chance and probability which supports atheism rather than theism.

There is a further line of atheistic attack which avoids the difficulties just enumerated. Although it may be held to be impossible, in general, to establish prior probabilities, the atheist may claim that this is not necessary because theism is either incoherent or 'obviously' unsustainable. Whether we regard this as assigning a probability to theism which is strictly zero or merely exceedingly small the practical effect would be the same. The odds would be so loaded against theism at the start that any amount of subsequent evidence to the contrary could not tip the balance. This line of argument is particularly effective when directed against some of the implications of the supernatural outlook such as life beyond death. We have therefore paid particular attention to the credibility of some Christian claims. It emerges that the difficulty often arises because judgements are made on the assumption that there is nothing beyond the natural. Once the possibility of this extra dimension is allowed we have sought to show that a rational account can be given which is consistent with the scientific outlook.

Finally we may note again that the atheist necessarily labours under a methodological disadvantage. For example, the hypothesis that the evolution of human life is the outcome of a random process almost inevitably appears to assign a very small probability to 'life as we know it'. On the other hand theism accords it a much higher probability because a God worthy of the name can, presumably, achieve whatever outcomes he wishes. A comparison of likelihoods then works strongly in favour of theism. The atheist can respond that some of the evidence is worthless because it relates to things which are impossible and that when such evidence is excluded what is left betrays no evidence of purpose and so is much more favourable to atheism. But against this we have maintained that science is incapable of reaching such definitive conclusions on those phenomena which are most relevant. It is difficult to see how a good case can be mounted in the face of these obstacles.

AGNOSTICISM CONSIDERED

If certainty must for ever elude the would-be atheist so it must for the believer and for the same basic reason. The problem with the prior and the difficulty of being sure whether there are other non-theistic hypotheses which might be of comparable plausibility mean that the argument cannot be finally concluded in favour of theism. Even the argument from cosmic coincidences, which Montefiore thought provided overwhelming evidence, failed because of problems with independence and because the 'many universes' hypothesis may be able to account equally well for the way things are. The more-or-less formal uses of probability reasoning used by Swinburne, Gaskin, and Prozesky were all open to serious question but all concluded that, on the objective evidence, the probability of God's existence was neither very high nor very low. The various strands of evidence added to the argument in early chapters tend to support this consensus. Although in my judgement the objective evidence justifies a 'more likely than not' verdict the lack of precision makes it difficult to press that conclusion with conviction.

If probability were to be the sole criterion the rational course would be agnosticism. But we argued in Chapter 8 that probability was not the sole criterion because gains and losses are at stake. Christianity and most other beliefs claim that there are consequences in accepting or not accepting the offer which they make. Decision theory, which aims to embody rationality in decision-making shows us how probabilities and utilities should be combined. It shows that it may be rational, even, to choose something with a low probability if the benefits it confers are sufficiently great. We cannot, therefore, make a final judgement on whether it is rational to believe without also weighing the outcomes.

At this point Christians, especially, find themselves in a difficult position. Not only do they speak with many voices on the matter but most would find it distasteful if not quite improper to allow purer motives to be sullied by considerations of gain or loss. It was in an age when the Church taught that the choice was a stark one between heaven and hell that the author of a Spanish sonnet wrote the following words, translated by Edward Caswell, which appear in many modern hymn books.

> Then why O blessed Jesus Christ
> Should I not love thee well?
> Not for the sake of winning heaven
> Nor of escaping hell.
>
> Not with the hope of gaining ought
> Not seeking a reward . . .

And yet, at the same time, the same Christians find this faith so satisfying and rewarding that it is to be prized above all things. Another hymn, this time by Bernard of Clairvaux, has it thus:

> But what to those who find? Ah this
> Nor tongue nor pen can show:
> The love of Jesus what it is
> None but his loved ones know.

The position is not helped by the perception which many unbelievers have of what is at stake. The mischievous sceptic can have a field day at the expense of the more literal-minded believer. Not only does the mere contemplation of never-ending 'anything' spell unlimited boredom for the sceptic but the prospect of compulsory enjoyment of the rather bland delights of a sanitized heaven, without any scope for the surreptitious enjoyment of a little well-chosen wickedness, is a forbidding prospect. Faced with this the sceptic will profess much to prefer the fleshpots of this world followed by oblivion. The possibility that total oblivion might not be one of the options on offer hardly seems to register.

It is, perhaps, time for Christians to be more ready to spell out, in contemporary terms, in what the new life in Christ, to which all are invited, consists. Deliverance from sin for those who have no sense of sin or everlasting rest for those who see creative activity as of the essence of life are not tempting prospects. The deeply rooted feeling that life is important, that loss of life is a tragedy and the sense that something fundamental is lacking in life all show a vestigial hunger which may indicate a better place to begin.

If we see the utility question not in terms of pleasure or personal gratification but as to do with that which provides fulfilment at the deepest level unbounded by time or space then a passive agnosticism is less tenable.

If there is a reasonable chance that there may be truth in Christianity and if it offers the key to existence then Pascal's wager carries weight and it would be irrational to choose to do nothing.

There is more than this, however, to the weighing of probabilities and utilities. The potential significance of Brams's game theory approach, discussed in the last chapter, is easily overlooked. If there is an active God who makes decisions then his rationality, as well as ours, becomes part of the picture. He, we may suppose, will wish to take account of our interpretation of what he does since this will influence its ultimate effect. The world which we observe and try to understand is therefore the outcome of a subtle interplay of action and expectation. Reflection on the implications of this thought may well temper our over-confident opinions on what kind of world God ought to have made.

A FINAL POINT

The conclusion we have reached might be fairly described by saying that belief is a risk worth taking. But though this might be seen by believers as a legitimate reason for taking the first step they would insist that there is much more to it than that. The evidence that holds them in their belief goes far beyond a collection of disputed arguments. It rests more on C. S. Lewis's 'sense of the fitness of things', which, though it may wax and wane, is ultimately so real that it cannot be denied. Attempts to express it in words fail to do it justice and may by their sheer inadequacy weaken the case which they are intended to support.

At the outset we recognized that subjective evidence existed but declared our intention to see how far we could go without it. Clearly we cannot go all the way nor as far as we might have hoped, but having cleared the approaches to the threshold of belief it would be irrational not to give full weight to what convinces so many.

EPILOGUE

We began by chronicling the crumbling of the certainties which have underpinned the faith of believers in earlier generations. Science, as a way of finding out about the world, has changed that for ever. We have insisted that the rational approach to the existence of supernatural reality necessarily involves uncertainty and must therefore be undertaken using the language and logic of uncertainty. The fact that, in the event, it has proved extraordinarily difficult to reach precise conclusions does not reflect on the method but on the intractable nature of the evidence. It exposes the weakness of all those who pretend to certainties which are unattainable and highlights the incoherence which is liable to accompany the reasonings of those who use the language of uncertainty but ignore its logic. The amount of evidence is enormous but its scattered, fragmentary, and ambiguous nature make it difficult to digest. Although there are some impressive arguments for theism and its associated doctrines, their cumulative effect cannot be demonstrated to have such overwhelming weight as to compel belief. Indeed we have gone further by suggesting that the probability of God, as Montefiore puts it, is strictly indeterminate. This is because it crucially depends on forming a prior probability about his existence before looking at any of the evidence. There are weaker modes of reasoning with probabilities which, in my judgement, point more decisively in the direction of theism. At the very least, atheism is seen to be no less dependent on a leap of faith than theism.

If it were simply a matter of making a judgement on the evidence it would appear that agnosticism was the only reasonable option. But it is not simply a matter of making a judgement but of taking an action. Rationality requires that we make a decision in the light not only of the uncertainties but also of the gains and losses. These show, again in my judgement, that the probability of Christian theism need not be very high to justify commitment. The sceptics had best keep silence until a more coherent case can be mounted for their cause. Believers, assured that their position can withstand the charge of irrationality, can confidently explore the new world in which human reason is not the ultimate arbiter of truth.

References

ARBUTHNOT, J. (1710), 'An argument for divine providence, taken from the constant regularity observed in the births of both sexes', *Philosophical Transactions of the Royal Society*, 328: 186.

ATKINS, P. W. (1981), *The Creation* (Oxford: Freeman).

—— (1992), 'Will Science Ever Fail?', *New Scientist*, 8 August, 32–5.

BADHAM, P. and L. (1982), *Immortality or Extinction?* (London: Macmillan).

BARBOUR, I. G. (1966), *Issues in Science and Religion* (London: SCM Press).

BARRETT, C. K. (1962), 'John', in Black and Rowley (1962: 844–69).

—— (1971), *A Commentary of the First Epistle to the Corinthians*, 2nd edn. (London: A. & C. Black).

BARTHOLOMEW, D. J. (1982), *Stochastic Models for Social Processes*, 3rd edn. (Chichester: Wiley).

—— (1984), *God of Chance* (London: SCM Press).

—— (1988), 'Probability, Statistics and Theology', *Journal of the Royal Statistical Society*, A 151: 137–78.

BLACK, M., and ROWLEY, H. H. (1962), *Peake's Commentary on the Bible* (London: Thomas Nelson).

BLACKMORE, S. J. (1988), 'Visions from the Dying Brain', *New Scientist*, 5 May, 43–6.

—— (1993), *Dying to Live: Science and the Near Death Experience* (London: Grafton).

BRAMS, S. J. (1983), *Superior Beings: If They Exist How Would We Know?* (New York: Springer-Verlag).

BUTLER, J. (1858), *The Analogy of Religion* (London: Bell & Dalby).

CHESTERTON, G. K. (1958), *The Flying Inn* (Harmondsworth: Penguin Books).

COHEN, L. J. (1977), *The Probable and the Provable* (Oxford: Clarendon Press).

—— (1992), *An Essay in Belief and Acceptance* (Oxford: Clarendon Press).

DASTON, L. J. (1988), *Classical Probability in the Enlightenment* (Princeton: Princeton University Press).

DAVIES, P. (1983), *God and the New Physics* (Harmondsworth: Penguin Books).

DAWID, A. P. (1987), 'The Difficulty about Conjunction', *Statistician*, 36: 91–7.

DAWID, A. P., and GILLIES, D. (1989), 'A Bayesian Analysis of Hume's Argument Concerning Miracles', *Philosophical Quarterly*, 39: 57–65.

DAWKINS, R. (1986), *The Blind Watchmaker* (Harlow: Longman Scientific and Technical).

DENNETT, D. C. (1991), *Consciousness Explained* (London: Allen Lane, Penguin Press).

DENTON, M. (1985), *Evolution: A Theory in Crisis* (London: Burnett Books).

DIACONIS, P. (1978), 'Statistical Problems in ESP Research', *Science*, 201: 131–6.

DIACONIS, P., and MOSTELLER, F. (1989), 'Methods for Studying Coincidences', *Journal of the American Statistical Association*, 84: 853–61.

DOWIE, J., and LEFRERE, P. (eds.) (1980), *Risk and Chance* (Milton Keynes: Open University Press).

ECCLES, J. C. (1989), *Evolution of the Brain: Creation of the Self* (London: Routledge).

EIGEN, M. (1971), 'Self-Organization of Matter and the Evolution of Biological Macromolecules', *Naturwissenschaften*, 58: 465–523.

FENWICK, P., and LORIMER, D. (1989), 'Can Brains be Conscious?', *New Scientist*, 5 August, 54–6.

FLEW, A. G. N. (1976), *The Presumption of Atheism and Other Essays* (London: Elek/Pemberton).

FUNK, R. W., SCOTT, B. B., and BUTTS, J. R. (1989), *The Parables of Jesus*, Red Letter Edition (Sonoma, Calif.: Polebridge).

GALTON, F. (1872), 'Statistical Enquiries into the Efficacy of Prayer', *The Fortnightly Review*, NS 12 (Aug.), 125–35.

GASKIN, J. C. A. (1984), *The Quest for Eternity* (Harmondsworth: Penguin Books).

GAUQUELIN, M. (1984), *The Truth about Astrology*, trans. Sarah Matthews (London: Hutchinson).

GOULD, S. J. (1991), *Wonderful Life* (Harmondsworth: Penguin Books).

Groot, M. H. de (1986), 'A Conversation with Persi Diaconis', *Statistical Science*, 1: 319–34.

HALD, A. (1990), *A History of Probability and Statistics and their Application Before 1750* (New York: Wiley).

HARROD, R. (1956), *Foundations of Inductive Logic* (London: Macmillan).

HOFSTADTER, D. R., and DENNETT, D. C. (1982), *The Mind's I* (Harmondsworth: Penguin Books).

HOLMES, D. I. (1992), 'A Stylometric Analysis of Mormon Scripture and Related Texts', *Journal of the Royal Statistical Society*, A 155: 91–120.

HOOKER, M. D. (1991*a*), 'Jesus and History', in A. Linzey and P. Wexler (eds.), *Fundamentalism and Tolerance* (London: Bellew Publishing).

—— (1991*b*), *A Commentary on the Gospel According to St Mark* (London: A. & C. Black).

HOYLE, F., and WICKRAMASINGHE, C. (1981), *Evolution from Space* (London: J. M. Dent).

HUME, D. (1777), *Enquiry Concerning Human Understanding*, ch. 10, 'Of Miracles', Selby-Bigge edn. (Oxford: Clarendon Press, 1902).

HYMAN, R. (1982), 'Does the Ganzfeld Experiment Answer the Critics' Objections?', *Research in Parapsychology*, 11: 21–3.

INGLIS, B. (1990), *Coincidence* (London: Hutchinson).

JOHNSON-LAIRD, P. (1983), *Towards a Cognitive Science of Language, Inference and Consciousness* (Cambridge: Cambridge University Press).

KELLER, E. and M.-L. (1969), *Miracles in Dispute* (London: SCM Press).

KENNY, A. (1986), *A Stylometric Study of the New Testament* (Oxford: Clarendon Press).

KOESTLER, A. (1972), *The Roots of Coincidence* (London: Hutchinson).

KRUSKAL, W. (1988), 'Miracles and Statistics. The Casual Assumption of Independence', *Journal of the American Statistical Association*, 83: 929–40.

KURTZ, P. (1993), *The New Skepticism* (Buffalo: Prometheus Books).

LAMPE, G. W. H. (1962), 'Luke', in Black and Rowley (1962: 820–43).

LEWIS, C. S. (1960), *Miracles* (London: Fontana Books).

LOH, W. (1984), *Social Research in the Judicial Process* (New York: Russell Sage Foundation).

McCRONE, J. (1993), 'Roll Up for the Telepathy Test', *New Scientist*, 15 May, 29–33.

MACQUARRIE, J. (1977), *Principles of Christian Theology* (London: SCM Press).

MATSON, W. I. (1965), *The Existence of God* (Ithaca, NY: Cornell University Press).

MINSKY, M. (1987), *The Society of Mind* (London: Heinemann).

MONOD, J. (1972), *Chance and Necessity* (London: Collins).

MONTEFIORE, H. (1985), *The Probability of God* (London: SCM Press).

—— (1992), *The Womb and the Tomb* (London: Fontana).

MOORE, P. G. (1977), 'The Manager's Struggles with Uncertainty', *Journal of the Royal Statistical Society*, A 140: 129–65.

—— (1983), *The Business of Risk* (Cambridge: Cambridge University Press).

MORTON, A. Q. (1965), 'The Authorship of Greek Prose', *The Journal of the Royal Statistical Society*, A 128: 169–233.

—— (1978), *Literary Detection* (Bath: Bowker).

—— (1980), *The Genesis of John* (Edinburgh: St Andrew's Press).

—— (1991), *Proper Words in Proper Places*, Computing Science Research Report, University of Glasgow.

MORTON, A. Q., and MCLEMAN, J. J. (1966), *Paul, the Man and the Myth: A Study in the Authorship of Greek Prose* (New York: Harper Row).

MOSTELLER, F., and YOUTZ, C. (1990), 'Quantifying Probabilistic Expressions', *Statistical Science*, 5: 1–34.

O'MUIRCHEARTAIGH, C. A., GASKELL, G. D., and WRIGHT, D. B. (1994), 'Intensifiers in Behavioural Frequency Questions', *Public Opinion Quarterly*, 57: 552–65.

OWEN, D. (1987), 'Hume *versus* Price on Miracles and Prior Probabilities: Testimony and the Bayesian Calculation', *The Philosophical Quarterly*, 37: 187–202.

OWENS, D. J. (1992), *Causes and Coincidences* (Cambridge: Cambridge University Press).

PAINE, T. (1795), *The Age of Reason*, D. I. Eaton edn. repr. as no. 69 of The Thinkers Library (1938) (London: Watts).

PEACOCKE, A. R. (1979), *Creation and the World of Science* (Oxford: Clarendon Press).

—— (1993), *Theology for a Scientific Age* (enlarged edn.) (London: SCM Press).

PEAKE, A. S. (1928), 'The Reunion of the Christian Churches', presidential address delivered at the 33rd Annual Assembly of the National Free Church Council. Repr. in Wilkinson (1958).

PENROSE, R. (1989), *The Emperor's New Clothes* (Oxford: Oxford University Press).

PERRIN, N. (1967), *Rediscovering the Teaching of Jesus* (London: SCM Press).

PERRY, M. (1984), *Psychic Studies: A Christian View* (Wellingborough: Aquarian Press).

PIPPARD, A. B. (1988), 'The Invincible Ignorance of Science', *Contemporary Physics*, 29: 393–405.

POPPER, K. R. (1969), *Conjectures and Refutations*, 3rd edn, (London: Routledge & Kegan Paul).

POPPER, K. R., and Eccles, J. C. (1983), *The Self and Its Brain* (London: Routledge & Kegan Paul).

PORTNOY, S., and PETERSON, D. (1984), 'Biblical Texts and Statistical Analysis: Zechariah and Beyond', *Journal of Biblical Literature*, 103: 11–21.

PREVOST, R. (1990), *Probability and Theistic Explanation* (Oxford: Clarendon Press).

PRIESTLAND, G. (1982), *Reasonable Uncertainty* (London: Quaker Home Service).

PROZESKY, M. (1992), *A New Guide to the Debate about God* (London: SCM Press).

RADDAY, Y. T. (1973), *The Unity of Isaiah in the Light of Statistical Linguistics* (Gerstenberg: Hindlesheim).

RADDAY, Y. T., SHORE, H., WICKMAN, D., POLLATSCHEK, C. R., and TALMAN, S. (1985), *Genesis: An Authorship Study in Computer-Assisted Statistical Linguistics* (Rome: Biblical Institute Press).

RAHTZ, P. (1975), 'How Likely is Likely?', *Antiquity*, 47: 59–61.

RICHARDSON, A. (1950), *A Theological Word Book of the Bible* (London: Macmillan).

SAKS, M. J., and KIDD, R. F. (1980–1), 'Human Information Processing and Adjudication: Trial and Heuristics', *Law and Society Review*, 15: 123–60.

SHELDRAKE, R. (1987), *A New Science of Life* (London: Paladin).

SOAL, S. G., and BATEMAN, F. (1954), *Modern Experiments in Telepathy* (London: Faber & Faber).

SOBEL, J. H. (1987), 'On the Evidence of Testimony for Miracles: A Bayesian Interpretation of David Hume's Analysis', *The Philosophical Quarterly*, 37: 166–86.

STANNARD, R. (1989), *Grounds for Reasonable Belief* (Edinburgh: Scottish Academic Press).

STENGER, V. J. (1990), *Physics and Psychics* (Buffalo: Prometheus Books).

STIGLER, S. M. (1986), 'John Craig and the Probability of History: From the Death of Christ to the Birth of Laplace', *Journal of the American Statistical Association*, 81: 879–87.

STRAWSON, P. F. (1959), *Individuals* (London: Methuen).

SWINBURNE, R. (1971), *The Concept of Miracle* (London: Macmillan).

—— (1976), 'What Is a Miracle?', *Epworth Review*, 3: 86–98.

—— (1979), *The Existence of God* (Oxford: Clarendon Press).

TENNANT, F. R. (1930), *Philosophical Theology*, ii (Cambridge: Cambridge University Press).

TVERSKY, A. (1974), 'Assessing Uncertainty', *Journal of the Royal Statistical Society*, B 36: 148–59.

UTTS, J. (1991), 'Replication and Meta-Analysis in Parapsychology', *Statistical Science*, 6: 363–403.

WEAVER, W. (1963), *Lady Luck* (New York: Doubleday).

WEITZMAN, M. P. (1987), 'The Evolution of Manuscript Traditions', *Journal of the Royal Statistical Society*, A 150: 287–308.

WILKINSON, J. T. (ed.) (1958), *Arthur Samuel Peake 1865–1929* (London: Epworth Press).

WILSON, C. (1985), *Afterlife* (London: Harrup).

ZIPF, G. K. (1949), *Human Behaviour and the Principle of Least Effort* (Reading, Mass.: Addison-Wesley).

Index